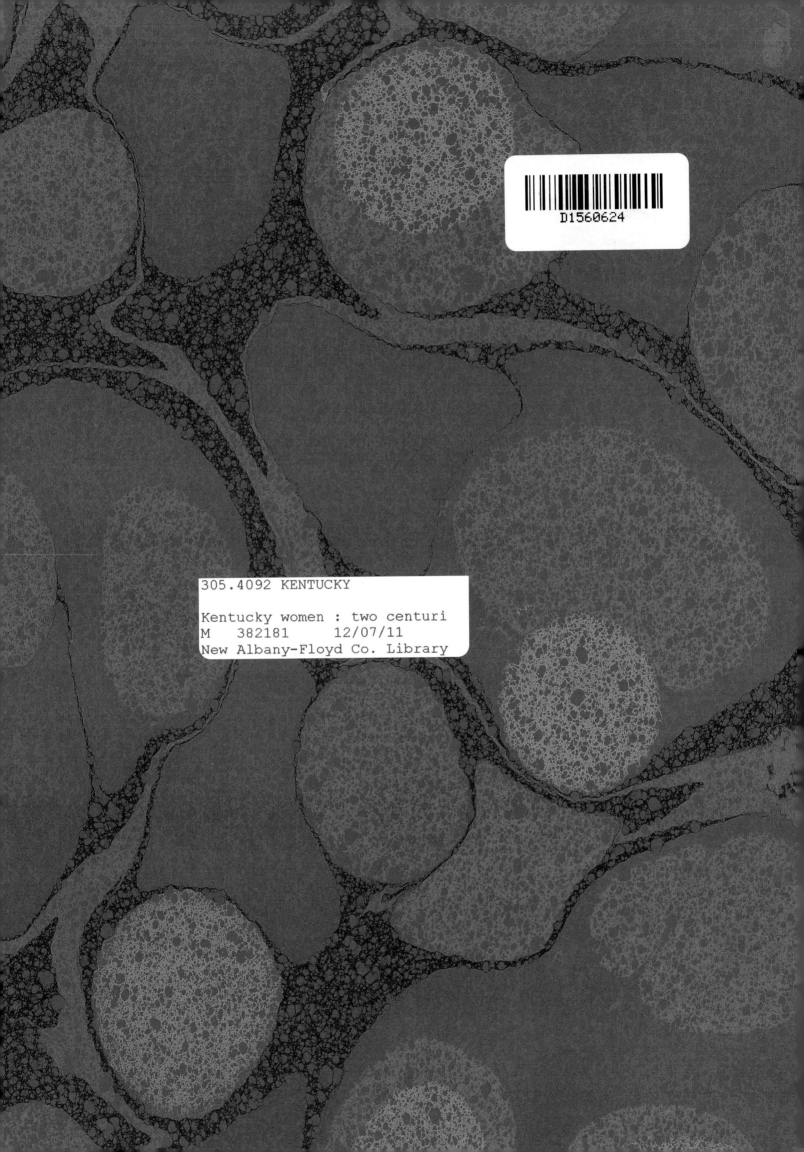

KENTUCKY WOMEN

Two Centuries of Indomitable Spirit and Vision

Genie K. Potter

KENTUCKY WOMEN

*Two Centuries of Indomitable
Spirit and Vision*

Edited by
Eugenia K. Potter

big tree press

Book Design	Crescent Hill Books
Drawings	Eugenia C. Foster
End Papers	Mimi Schleicher
Printing	Printed in Canada by Friesens Printers
	for Four Colour Imports, Louisville, Kentucky

ISBN: 0-9659858-0-6

For my wise and talented mother
Harriet Gill Kelly

She told me to always keep a suitcase packed
and I would discover
the wider the lens, the broader the vision.

and

In memory of my witty friend and mentor
Lucretia Baldwin Ward

She kept a sign over her desk that read
"May the Sweet Baby Jesus
keep your mind open and your mouth shut."

and

In memory of my quotable friend and indomitable mentor
Mavin Brown Martin

She once said,
"Isn't it funny how men always put on dresses when they're doing something
important--like judges, preachers, graduates . . . "

CONTENTS

INTRODUCTION

Before 1900, women in Kentucky were almost invisible. At least that is the impression one gains from reading Kentucky history books. While Laura Clay and Jenny Wiley are rightfully included in many histories, they were not the only significant women of their times. Nor were the suffragists, writers, pioneers and educators who appear now and again in the annals of Kentucky. What saves Kentucky women from extinction is their sense of permanence: eloquent diaries, day-to-day letters, beautiful quilts, humorous stories, and poignant photographs left behind that comprise a scrapbook of women's history in Kentucky.

Scrapbooks are usually very personal, filled with treasured souvenirs and memorabilia which reflect experiences of a particular person, family or event. They may highlight special times and accomplishments, but scrapbooks give only a brief, yet telling, glance. Though largely overlooked by recorders and interpreters of history, the bits and pieces of their lives saved in trunks and boxes and kept under beds and in attics can tell much more about Kentucky women.

Indeed, some women included in this book are known to us chiefly because of the precious fragments left behind which document their lives. But *Kentucky Women* also includes women of recent times. Some women are famous, some are not; some led seemingly ordinary lives, others must be categorized as extraordinary. All of them call Kentucky home at some point.

Though designed like a scrapbook this book is more than a scrapbook. It is a testament to the talent, generosity, skill, patience, endurance, creativity, and diversity of Kentucky women. Those included are a representative sample, not a comprehensive list. Our libraries are woefully lacking in materials about Kentucky women, and the empty bookshelf will still look curiously blank. This publication is neither an encyclopedia nor an academic history, but those volumes need to be written now. I make no claim to be an historian, but readers will grasp historical and cultural themes within these women's lives. More is out there tucked away in dozens of hiding places. It is my hope that some individual or group will undertake a statewide search to unearth and document these treasures of women's history. I am grateful for *Women in Kentucky* by Helen Irvin, published for the state bicentennial and *Women Who Made a Difference*, by Carol Crowe-Carraco, published for beginning adult readers. But young people in particular need to be reminded of the hundreds and hundreds of female role models in Kentucky history. This book is just the beginning and it is intended to encourage many more similar books to be written.

The stories of these women are organized alphabetically. *Kentucky Women* is not meant to be devoured in one sitting, but rather to be savored slowly, flipping back and forth through two hundred years of women's hopes and dreams, anecdotes, accomplishments, and disappointments. These are women who sang and preached, cooked and doctored, farmed and picketed. Some women shot guns, held public office, owned businesses, flew airplanes, crafted furniture. You will discover trailblazers, those who were the first women to accomplish particular deeds, sometimes to little or no acclaim. Some of these women have doctorates and others never finished elementary school. One you might see on national television every night and others are ordinary women standing up for what they believe. Some encounters were sobering and thought-provoking and some were uplifting and enlightening. Regardless of the circumstances, women were willing to share their lives and I thank each one who gave me her time and story.

Readers will be impressed by those who served as volunteers through religious, educational and civic organizations, acting as advocates and humanitarians. Sometimes they started new institutions to fill unmet needs in their communities and sometimes they were outspoken champions for a variety of causes from civil rights to saving forests. Some women worked quietly, achieving goals, setting records, changing lives and communities but rarely expecting anything in return except personal satisfaction.

Kentucky writers, artists, poets, singers and cartoonists wax eloquent about women, but Kentucky historians have rarely done so. No wonder Abigail Adams implored her husband to "remember the ladies." I believe we must not only remember the ladies but shout about them from the rooftops. Praising women in Kentucky is long overdue. When I was an elementary school librarian, fourth graders studied the "Living in Kentucky" unit, and each year teachers and I agonized over the lack of materials about women. *Kentucky Women* is born of that frustration. History is written by people and in Kentucky, like other states, most of those people have been white men. Their view of history is just that: *their* view. That framework reflects their ideas of who is important, what types of events they perceive shape history, and the values and attitudes they espouse. It also decides who should be relegated to a mere footnote or segregated to one chapter and who should be omitted altogether.

History is more than wars, explorations, and politics, as the rise of women's studies departments in universities across the state and nation indicates. I suggest that most women look at history differently. Viewing Kentucky history in the context of its cultural and social fabric (the arts, domesticity, family, religion, work, community institutions) allows readers to see our history through the eyes of many different kinds of people. Until the concept of cultural context, most historians believed that women never had enough power to be influential and make substantive contributions, so they just ignored them.

The research process led me to oral history tapes, boxes of family papers, newspaper accounts, and personal records. Primary source material about women in Kentucky was in short supply, and it was sometimes hidden within the collection of a man or his family. Letters and journals, though written with a reader in mind, were often revealing. I sensed the grief and fears of Catherine Carpenter as she described being left on her own after her husband was killed. I found myself laughing out loud as I read a letter, only recently discovered in an attic, from a persistent beau of Madeline Breckinridge. I was touched by Julia Dinsmore's account of how she, a woman on her own, raised two nieces on a farm, never sure she could provide the next meal.

Equally memorable is my visit with state Representative Eleanor Jordan as she discussed her experiences as a single mother. Or the magic that wallops you the minute you walk into Joan Dance's house and she describes the historical significance rooted in her electrifying art. Or listening to the exuberant surprise of Terri Cecil-Ramsey's voice as she paints her winning picture of the 1996 Paralympics.

I crisscrossed the state, and that story is set in the discount stores, fast food restaurants, libraries, courthouses and other local meeting places which I visited to give me a flavor of regional values and attitudes. A casual observer can learn much by strolling the aisles of a local WAL-MART or sitting down in a Dairy Queen and just listening. What's important in a Kentucky town is discussed at 6:30 a.m. in the local breakfast spot, so that is where I went. But I also found myself at women's kitchen tables from Paducah to Hazard. I ate barbecue from Owensboro to Ashland. It was a privilege to sleep in historical spots, including Mary Breckinridge's bedroom at Wendover. I enjoyed meals with the staff of Pine Mountain Settlement School and breakfast on the porch of Alice Slone's rustic log house near Cordia.

Sometimes my adventures were full of such pure mischief and delight that I'll take those days to the grave. I have laughed at witty observations made by the Mayor of Benham and her Petticoat Mafia City Council before I walked across the street and climbed into bed at the renovated School House Inn. Listening to the Reel World String Band tell war stories of their earliest days of being an all-women's band reminded me that a sense of humor has probably saved women throughout history.

Driving into the hollows and mountains, along rivers and lakes, down city streets and through farmlands I brought home enormous admiration and respect for the women of Kentucky. I delighted in the picture postcard views driving from Midway to Versailles and through Jessamine County in the spring of 1996. One cool fall morning found me driving over the mountain through dense forests and into the driveway of Pine Mountain Settlement School, where I stopped dead in my tracks. The school is situated so that its log buildings and trees toss light and shadows back and forth, creating an ever changing view of great complexity and beauty.

I was compelled to stop for quite another reason while driving between Cordia and Red Fox. In the name of coal and money, gigantic earth movers were literally relocating a mountain and, in the process, fashioning a landscape few people, birds or animals would care to visit. At Calvert City I was taken on a tour of the industrial complex and watched mysterious liquids spew unchecked into the river and cesspools.

Let this book recognize the many and varied contributions of women in our state of many contrasts, a state where differences and county boundaries often divide us. To come together, we must learn more about one another and celebrate our differences but find our common bonds. The stories of these women reflect the breadth and depth of the state's culture, geography and history, and will, I hope, help readers to learn about and appreciate women who are different from themselves.

Scrapbooks offer a window to the past, a chance to live briefly in the world of another person, an opportunity to hear how women in another era and women of today express themselves, to hear what they think is important. Readers will hear women's voices filled with the celebration of winning, tragedy of loss, stark poverty and truth, winsome nostalgia, rare ingenuity, and even some raw bitterness that arises from oppression, abuse and powerlessness. Their commonality is that they are all Kentuckians and for that they are equally proud.

—*Eugenia K. Potter*

KENTUCKY WOMEN

Two Centuries of Indomitable Spirit and Vision

Elmer Lucille Allen

Keith Williams photo courtesy of African American Women's Literary Series.

University would take her a different route. In Indianapolis, she found the only job opening was for a clerk-typist, which led into hospitals as a laboratory technician, and later into a rubber company as an industrial chemist.

"Hospital work is more tedious than industrial work because you deal with people facing life and death. It is very precise work and I couldn't ever let my emotions get in the way. I could sympathize and empathize but I couldn't take it home with me. When children came into the world and didn't survive or were damaged, I had to sit down and really think about that. My job was to help children live and to help adults die with dignity."

As a pioneer African American female chemist, Elmer Lucille Allen worked for almost 31 years at Brown-Forman Distillers in Louisville, "playing with test tubes all day long." She saw a lot of changes in those years. When she arrived, they measured analytical results with a ruler, but today those same results come out on a computer, always compared to the competition.

Was she unusual? A colleague told her she had three strikes against her: African-American, female, and Roman Catholic. "But I told her I was hired to do a job—only I had to do mine better to prove myself." Allen's idea of breaking down racial, religious, and gender barriers is through job performance— "then they trust and respect you. It's the only way and that's why education is *so*

A familiar rite of passage during childhood is playing patty cake in mud puddles and some children might progress to higher levels of production: the proverbial clay snow women that parents rapturously accept but never know quite where to exhibit. Enter Elmer Lucille Allen, whose innate sense of mixing and creating were far more sophisticated than most children. Defying statistical probability, Elmer Lucille Allen grew up and became a chemist *and* a ceramicist. To us mortals, the world of chemists and ceramicists is "magic," but Elmer Lucille Allen is quick to clarify and rebut any such misconception.

Born into a family whose father and brother both were named Elmer, the family chose to call *her* Elmer Lucille. Her mother was a cook for a Louisville household and her father was a Pullman Porter who traveled constantly. They instilled a value of education and Allen "always wanted to succeed so I just worked at it." Sounds like a deceptively simple I-can-do philosophy.

For young African American women in the early 50s "becoming a teacher or a day worker were about the only jobs available in Kentucky." But Allen knew her degree in chemistry from Spalding

Elmer Lucille Allen's ceramics, including the African piece (right).

important." Today, chemistry is still a male-dominated career and work environment, and she wishes more women would enter the field.

Being the oldest in her work group, she assumed the mantle of "wise woman," often reminding younger women that they "shouldn't go to work without stockings or wear short skirts with chubby knees."[1] But Elmer Lucille Allen got away with such hints from heloise because she also brought great humor and genuine people skills to the job site. Therein lies her success: there is not an ounce of scientist peacockery in Allen's blood.

The secret of retirement? "I left with the feeling that they would always be glad to see me." If her retirement celebration were any indication, Elmer Lucille Allen whirled out of Brown-Forman with accolades flying in her wake. CEO and chairman of the board, Owsley Brown, said that he remembers Elmer Lucille Allen "exuding her warmth, making newcomers like myself feel welcome and bringing you right into the Brown-Forman family. She makes everyone feel good about working here."[2]

Not one to sit idle in retirement,

Elmer Lucille Allen continues to work toward a Master's degree in Fine Arts, specializing in ceramics. Clay is a hydrous aluminum silicate. Preparing glazes requires grinding and blending components, weighing and measuring just the right amount of water in test tubes. Allen uses terms like "ingredients and agents and elements," which sound pretty much like a chemist talking. Actually it is the ceramicist side of Allen talking. Retirement and her first one-woman porcelain show arrived simultaneously, and she named the exhibit "Transition." In her artist statement, she writes:

My forms are based on rectangles, squares, polygons and circles. Most of my vessel forms are small boxes or box-like shapes. I research a motif before I make a stamp because I do not want to make a stamp which is offensive to anyone. I love making small hand-built boxes because they give a viewer the opportunity to communicate with the maker. I have not made the perfect box, therefore I continue to make boxes. I am often reminded of what Thomas Marsh (former art professor at the University of Louisville) said: "A potter in Japan can be an apprentice for 20 years or longer." I guess I am still an apprentice because I still have so much to learn.

While many of us may have grown up enthralled with Arthurian legends, there is no Merlin in Elmer Lucille Allen's rational world. There is no mystery, no mischievous magician, no trickster. Instead, what you find is a precise, yet creative and professional, woman who has married chemistry and ceramics with perfection.

3

Ann Stewart Anderson

By Kate Harper

For centuries artists have approached the female form with intrigue, presenting fleshy, full-figured women as embodiments of unattainable sensuality and allure. Edgar Degas' nineteenth century laundry women work with a sultry confidence that at once draws the spectator into the picture's spirit. In the century-long wake of this tradition appears the feminist artist, Ann Stewart Anderson, presenting her audience with unflinching portrayals

now our knees ache from the agony of too many days on the floor.

Hot Flash Fan Journal

of women and womanhood. Like Degas, she uses the atmosphere and spirit of her work to establish her dialogue with viewers.

Born in Frankfort, Ann Stewart Anderson's beginnings as the daughter of a Presbyterian minister kept her from nothing. In fact, it was her father who "let

us do anything we wanted to do," never discouraging his three daughters' aspirations of becoming a doctor, an economist, and an artist. As a child, Anderson painted alongside her mother, herself an art school graduate, but it was her travels that fed her artistic personality, ever cultivating her perception of the world around her. She went to college in Massachusetts, worked and taught art in the Washington, D.C. area, and worked and trained at the Chicago Art Institute. Although she had never liked Egyptian art in school, she spent enough time in Egypt to develop a photographic project, and she continues to use Egyptian symbols in her work. In 1975, she returned to Kentucky, where she moved in with her parents, "believe it or not."

Ann Stewart Anderson's method is largely dependent on the physical nature of her works of art, a sense of familiarity with her subjects, as well as a subtle humor when confronting and presenting visions of womanhood. In her candor about the female "situation"—whether that situation be menopause, gossiping over lunch, or walking down the aisle—Anderson is able to take the orthodox, often voyeuristic, rendering of the sensual female and update it. The raw representations welcome viewers, despite her portrayals of women in their most raw, most bare, and most common existence.

As Ann Stewart Anderson presents shockingly honest visions of womanhood, her lack of modesty may make some viewers blush. In truth, her greatest strength is that she is unhindered by the chains some define as taboo or embarrassing. The essence of her art is that she is so comfortable representing her subjects that the viewer has no choice but to feel comfortable as well. In contrast to more traditional representations of women, Anderson offers sagging breasts and wrinkled skin. Motifs which commonly appear in her work include the solitary seated figure and bottle of Oil of Olay facial cream, an everyday well-advertised object familiar to many

women. While the first calls attention to the single figure, apart from others and alone in her environment, the second represents a light-hearted jab at the cosmetics industry and at many women's preoccupation with trying to appear youthful despite their advancing years.

In a landmark collaborative effort, Ann Stewart Anderson and Judy Chicago created the "Hot Flash Fan," a provoca-

"Hot Flash Fan"

tive piece that not only refers to the trials and tribulations of menopause, but also to the idea that a fan makes fire burn brighter. The idea came from Anderson's immediate reaction to a newspaper column about Geraldine Ferraro, who was the Vice-Presidential candidate, in which she was described as not being qualified for the office because she was in

"The Meeting" 1993

A painting going well is smooth—like a wonderful love affair. Painter and painting are full of mutual affection and admiration. A painting going badly is sheer torment—a sense of panic, despair, bewilderment—a tendency to stay away from it—to avoid the unpleasant task of solution....Dialogue demands sensitive and acute awareness.

Hot Flash Fan Journal,
July 24, 1982

her menopausal years. Since Anderson was the same age and had never thought of herself as menopausal, she suggested that the collaborative pair respond to such outrageous conclusions with a thoughtful, but humorous project. With fifty-two other artists they produced a stunning visual statement of stitched fabric embellished with quilting, trapunto, paint, and pictures, which continues to travel around the country today.

Perhaps it is this humor that is unique to Anderson's work. She believes "humor is very profound" and yet as Anderson is able to tease out the humor, her laughter is touched with tenderness. In the "Ugly Bride" series, the artist remembers:

I was pushing thirty and I wasn't married and everybody else was married and I was having to go to these stupid weddings and showers and I was invited to weddings of people I hardly knew and I got really angry

about it. And so I got angry that the only time a woman is fulfilled is on her wedding day...the ultimate moment...sort of against "all brides are beautiful.."

Anderson's words emphasize the dual approach to her work—humorous though they appear, the "Ugly Bride" series cannot be discounted as comic relief. It houses other issues, namely that sometimes unfulfilled promises are temporarily veiled behind a beautiful wedding gown.

Her paintings are often filled with multi-faceted background designs, just like her life. As art teacher, artist, and now the executive director of the Kentucky Foundation for Women, Anderson enjoys an action-packed arts career. Above everything else, Ann Stewart Anderson is a Kentucky woman, confident in her abilities as an artist, and objective enough to understand the frailties women both experience and perpetuate.

"Mother's Choice, Daughter's Decision" 1994

"Crowning" 1987

Harriette Arnow

By Shirley Williams

The first piece of writing for which Harriette Simpson Arnow was paid was a short story published in the *Southern Review*, and the $25 she received came through the graces of another Kentucky writer, Robert Penn Warren, then an editor of the *Review*. That story marked her entry into the commercial publishing world. Previously she had published short stories in little literary magazines that paid nothing—some of them were mimeographed. Her stints of writing had been interspersed with jobs that paid her keep and enabled her to save a little toward the next period when she could quit working. "Waitressing" came highly recommended to struggling writers, especially if done only in the evenings. That way, Arnow said, you didn't have to get up early, so you could write late into the night.

Harriette Arnow was petite, under five feet tall, or as she explained it, "four feet and eleven and a half inches—with my shoes on!" which made her the antithesis of her best-known character, Gertie Nevels, the large, rawboned, inarticulate mountain heroine of *The Dollmaker*. The author had a way of cocking her head as she talked—and she talked well—and her eyes, intensified by the lenses of her glasses, took on an exceptional luminosity as she spoke. She meant what she said, of that there was no doubt, and conversation with her or even a superficial reading of her books made it clear that she found hypocrisy of any kind unacceptable, even intolerable.

"Writing still requires the things it has always needed," she said. "Experience of life itself, knowledge of the language and background material." When she became a teacher, "much was still intact in speech, customs, farming methods." The remnants of Shakespearean speech were still heard and her accurate ear reproduced it in the conversations of her characters.

Arnow's ancestors for five generations were Kentuckians. Both parents were teachers and both were descended from Kentucky settlers, including Revolutionary soldiers from Virginia and North

Detroit News

Carolina (she was a member of the Daughters of the American Revolution). "I was a great reader as soon as I could read," she said. "And before that I heard many stories from a grandmother and my father, and if they had an unhappy ending—as many did—it didn't worry me. I made them over in my head. So I was imagining stories for almost as far back as I can remember." But imagining was one thing and writing was another.

She attended Berea College but was extremely unhappy there because she found no one who shared her interest in writing. She was to teach in Kentucky for a few years, and that first novel, *The Mountain Path*, is somewhat autobiographical, taking her heroine from Lexington into the Kentucky mountains to teach. But Arnow disclaimed any personal experience in the romance that her heroine had with a

moonshiner, although it annoyed her family. "Annoyed is too mild a word. They said, 'The whole country around will be thinking you fell in love with a moonshiner. Why couldn't you write about good people?' They gave me no credit for imagination."

> "Writing still requires the things it has always needed. Experience of life itself, knowledge of the language and background material."

She was also eloquent about her resentment toward the extent to which woman's work had kept her from her writing—rearing children, household

Arnow makes her point with Albert Stuart at Centre College, 1983.

chores, the costliness of subsistence in time.

Her best-known book is the third novel, *The Dollmaker*, an exploration of the effect of urban life on the uprooted mountaineer. An NBA (National Book Award) fiction winner, Joyce Carol Oates, has called *The Dollmaker* " a legitimate tragedy, our most unpretentious American masterpiece." Regional dialogue is always an "iffy" thing in fiction and easily overdone, but Arnow handled it with panache and accuracy, weaving it in and out of her narrative. Take this passage in which Gertie's domineering mother is trying to convince her she should join her husband, Clovis, in Detroit:

Arnow at James Still's house, Wolfpen Creek, 1974.

She waited, watching. Gertie, watching her, thought there was something like satisfaction in her face as Clytie, still singing, not knowing she was being watched, came in sight, and then began a dance-like skipping on the big flat sandrock at the top of the path. Gertie wanted to cry out to Clytie that her grandmother watched, but could not, not even when she changed again from singing to whistling, and then, no more thinking that anyone watched than a squirrel, flung her arms out wide and did a lively tapping dance that made the ragged coat she wore seem even more ragged...

The only thing that seemed new and clean and shining was a Montgomery Ward catalogue under one arm. Gertie's mother nodded slowly, her eyes on Clytie. There was satisfaction in her voice, and sorrow, deep sorrow when she said, all the anger gone now, 'Look at her, grown up like a heathen, learnen how to dance frum that trashy Mamie, dirty ragged. I'll bet she ain't combed and braided her hair in a week. You know she wouldn't been goen to ruin if'n Clovis was home.'"

The Arnows moved to Ann Arbor, Michigan, where they lived on 40 acres on a dirt road, significant in that roads played an important role in her novels (she wanted to call *Hunter's Horn End of the Gravel*). There they grew a garden and enjoyed their dogs and the leisure to write. Harriette Arnow died in Michigan in 1986.

Bill Atkins

BILL ATKINS
CEO

MELiTA
FARMS
Fruits & Vegetables

Like a wildcat drilling for oil in areas not know to have oil, Bill Atkins is charting an untried course for Kentucky produce farmers. Both ventures can be risky but also lucrative. It takes the tenacity of a woman like Bill Atkins to articulate a vision of how farmers can increase family income by growing produce instead of, or in addition to, tobacco—quite a controversial topic in Kentucky and she is the perfect spokesperson for it.

A geologist by profession, Bill Atkins and her Clark County family have been in the oil and gas exploration business for several generations. Petroleum geology is the science of locating oil and natural gas, and Atkins has moved right into the science of product finding of a different kind. She is accustomed to looking for conditions favorable to *underground* accumulations, but recently she moved *above* ground seeking new farm produce markets. Same science—different product.

Atkins' style is like watching a commodity broker on the floor of the Stock Exchange as she describes all the different entities that must come together to work individually and cooperatively to change the paradigm of raising farm produce: universities and colleges, county horticulturists, farmers, warehouse processors, grocers and customers. Such a paradigm shift means public, private, and academic sectors working together in a collective, cooperative climate to expand Kentucky's production and processing of produce. That's not easy in the best case scenario, but dealing with an old paradigm of tradition and turf protection, coupled with the current national anti-tobacco environment, means that progress might be slow.

Farming in Kentucky means big business, but historically it has been based on an uncomplicated way of doing business. Bill Atkins points out that "cattle farmers take their cows to the stockyards and pick up a check; tobacco farmers take tobacco to a warehouse and pick up a check—no marketing, no public relations to worry about." And no questions about how to raise either one because "granddaddy probably did it, too." But enticing a farmer to supplement, or even replace, the farm's tobacco base to start growing produce involves a whole new way of doing business down on the farm.

Atkins is quick to remind that grocery chains demand a certain standard for their produce, so farmers must meet those standards of quality and acceptability. The Melita Farms warehouse exemplifies the type of facility needed to store a farmer's produce before transporting it to a processing plant, which ultimately trucks it to the grocers. In turn, grocers have to educate the public that Kentucky is growing quality produce that they can accept and buy. Remember the links in the chain: university to horticulturists to farmer to warehouse to grocer to public. There must be no kinks in the chain or the chain breaks.

Technology and communications have made the world smaller, so Kentucky farmers are competing with markets which demand of their workers lower wages, and in some countries, a better education. Kentucky farmers who do not adapt a new business environment will not be able to compete in such a global marketplace. Bill Atkins says that out-of-state markets often identify the state with only whiskey and tobacco, and more investment needs to go into the public relations and marketing of Kentucky's produce. She is saying that growing new products requires

"It's like a miracle to look out the window and see all those cherry tomatoes."

Coming out of the pumpkin patch at Melita Farms.

a business acumen that is not taught in agricultural schools today.

Farmers need field agents who can respond on the spot to the growing pains of new product development. If a farmer has just started growing broccoli and it has spots, she might not know how to treat it. But the disease won't wait — nature has its own little ways of solving problems. Universities need to change their course of agricultural study, and the horticulturists need to learn new ways of solving problems out in the fields. This scenario sounds familiar—like all the changes in school teacher preparation that were needed to make the Kentucky Education Reform Act such a successful venture.

Melita Farms is a good example of a business run by a woman looking for a competitive edge. She appreciated the shifting tobacco environment and did something about it. She walked the talk. Bill Atkins sold the tobacco base and today her family farm in Clark County produces cherry tomatoes and kale as volume crops. The kale that is in the field will be picked in the morning, taken to Louisville to be packaged, and it will be on the Kroger shelves by the next afternoon. Now, that's fresh produce!

All that freshness comes from a woman who reflects an image Kentucky's farm families have always represented—traditional bedrock values that built our country. As she talks, her vocabulary is peppered with words that reinforce those values: self-reliance, responsibility, hard work, discipline. At the same time, she has a yen to partake of nature's gifts, to flee the stifling cities that most urbanites consider stimulating and exciting. "Painters have painted this scene for centuries. You can look up and see a red-tail hawk or a doe licking her fawn. Not as comfortable as sitting in an air conditioned office all day, but it's good for the soul. It's like a miracle to look out in the fields and see all those cherry tomatoes."

With a friendliness born of concern for the community of farmers, Bill Atkins is a visionary who is trying to redefine how family produce farms can be operated and how the soul of farming can intersect profitably with its financial benefits. Some ideas seem uninspired, but Bill Atkins is on to something big.

Both photos: Jeff Kerr for the *Winchester Sun*

b. 1929

Nelda Barton-Collings

When life threw Nelda Barton-Collings a curve ball, she hit a home run. With the untimely death of her first husband, her life went through a deep transformation, and at the age of 48, she had to redefine the way she thought of herself, her children, and her future.

During early retirement necessitated by illness, her husband gave Barton-Collings the training she would need for widowhood. "After the kids got off to school, he was really good to sit down with me at the kitchen table. He'd say, 'I've got my yellow pad here and you read it over by yourself and then if you have any questions you can ask me later' or he'd have me put the sheets into the Standard & Poor notebook and teach me about stocks. He'd write out who to turn to if anything happened. I learned a lot along the way while he was so sick. He did me such a favor because I knew absolutely nothing about our affairs."

She was a quick learner, one who could apply her knowledge and experience to needs and opportunities around her. As a medical technologist and wife of a surgeon, Nelda Barton-Collings knew the meaning of quality health care. A nursing home her husband and a partner bought in 1973 became the cornerstone for a business empire she developed with the same partner. Today as president of a board which manages eight nursing homes, she views them as a growth industry and a service industry.

She didn't become an entrepreneur overnight. After she was widowed, she returned to college to study money, banking and health care. Evidently she learned her lessons well. "I was asked to serve on the local Corbin Deposit Bank board of directors (the first woman). Later my partner said we should organize a bank ourselves, so we did." Tri-County National Bank, home-owned and home-operated, is a closely held operation, and now they have five banks and are planning more.

This woman's ambition and accomplishments follow a pattern begun in childhood. "I played the violin in the orchestra, I was a cheerleader, a drum majorette, valedictorian of my high school, editor of the little school paper—all of those things that you have to compete for. The busier I was the happier I was and I've always been that way. But women aren't used to sitting down. You've got household chores and P.T.A. and all those things which I was very involved in when my children were young. The church youth group, Scouts—anything I could do to help my children."

The family's economic status was an incentive for Barton-Collings, too. "I knew from day one that if I were going to get anywhere in life that it was going to be up to me because my parents didn't have that much money." Her civic-minded father served twenty years as county commissioner. "He had a little grocery store in Providence and when the children were in high school my mother went to work with him." Her parents shaped her character and her husband chiseled her future.

While professional women often network with one another to overcome feelings of isolation or exclusion, Nelda Barton-Collings never felt outside the magic circle. Indeed, she accepted her

The elephant statue was a gift for 28 years of service as Republican National Committee Woman for Kentucky.

father's point of view that "if there were any funds left to send anyone to college it should be the boy (her brother) because they are the head of the household." Nor did she mind when a committee asked "my husband if he would object to them nominating me" to be Kentucky's female representative to the national Republican Party Committee. "I had such great respect for my husband."

Her approach serves her well in the male-dominated environment where she operates. Life in an exclusive all white rural community might be limiting, insular or even give rise to notions of superiority. This woman, however, is modest, traditional, quintessentially feminine rather than feminist, and her success seems to emanate from these characteristics.

What was it like being the first and only woman chairman of the Kentucky

Chamber of Commerce? Barton-Collings downplays the honor. "Well, I am sure it was a big deal for them to ask me. But we had become friends. They showed great respect for me. They didn't change their language for me because I was a woman or anything like that. They knew I wouldn't be offended. They treated me wonderful."

She was equally comfortable during her twenty-eight years of work on the Republican National Committee, which ended in 1997. "I always went by the principles of the Republican Party," she

says, which has long been identified with business and money interests. Ironically, initial progress on a variety of gender issues had already occurred: reproductive rights, support for working mothers, and revaluing single women. Yet Barton-Collings has little interest in what others might call women's issues. "I never really got deeply involved in any one issue because I felt like that if you just take a stand on one issue then you're not looking at the whole picture...I represent women but not their special issues."

Ironies and contradictions abound when one considers Nelda Barton-Collings. She is a woman who might well have been successful in fields normally dominated by men without the women's movement. Though she never exhibited Victorian helplessness or fragility, she willingly deferred to men around her. She carved her own niche, developed her own style and, though feminists might disapprove of her approach, it succeeded. Barton-Collings owns eight nursing homes, five banks, one pharmacy, two newspapers, and various rental property, all of which add up to a considerable sphere of influence for a woman from Corbin who once knew nothing about the affairs of her own household.

(Above) As 1990-1991 Chairman of the Board of Kentucky Chamber of Commerce.

Betty Winston Bayé

"People have to stand for something or fall for anything."

Syndicated newspaper columnist for *The Courier-Journal*, television show hostess, novelist, magazine contributor, a Neiman Fellowship winner, Louisville's community conscience—Betty Winston Bayé *is* the **American Dream**—the dream her parents never had but lived through her. "Baby, you do what we couldn't do," they told her.

As an African American woman, "I understood I had to run and jump faster. Racism never shocked me. I developed tools for survival. But I was taught that I didn't have to give them my gifts." Today she finds a different kind of racism. "People feel freer to explore hatred and viciousness. It seems that the white liberals of the civil rights era who said racism is awful are either silent or have disappeared. Maybe they got tired of the movement. They could always go back to their advantage and privilege, but those weren't options for most black people. Today we need

people of courage because people are scared of 'the Devil' they don't even know."

In 1993, Betty Winston Bayé delivered an address to Leadership Louisville which was printed in her column. This is an excerpt:

What is the American Dream?

....I stand before you today as Betty Winston Bayé talking about her American Dream. In many ways, I'm living out my parents' American Dream. The American Dream is not some static thing. It changes from generation to generation, and from group to group. But before I was born, my parents' American Dream was to get out of the South, quick and in a hurry. Even now, I can't bring myself to sing songs like, "My Old Kentucky Home" because they're reminders of what many of my people ran away from, leaving the South with nothing but a suitcase, a few dollars, and their American dreams.

They were running away from places like My Old Kentucky Home, away from the South, where if they said something someone deemed wrong, they were beaten or killed. My parents' American Dream was up North in New York City. In the 1940s, my parents lived out their version of the American dream in the single rooms they rented in cold water flats in a then-magical place for country folks called Harlem. They worked all week, and sometimes they'd eat on the cheap at Father Divine's restaurants. And come the week-ends, like other Southerners gone North, they'd stomp at the Savoy or cuddle in the darkness of The Apollo Theater as Billy Holiday sang.

But once I came along, and years later, when my two sisters came along, my parents' dreams changed. Sometimes I think their dreams may even have been shattered. Children, for those interested in serious parenting, have a way of reminding people that life isn't just one big party. Indeed, being black in America in the 1940s, 1950s, and before never was much of a party. Those mean hard years had ways of harnessing dreams, of roping folks in with invisible boundaries. But the reality is that my parents' wings couldn't spread as wide as they might have wished. So like many other parents of their times, they poured their dreams into me. They poured their American Dreams, their Southerners gone to the North, dreams into me. "Baby, you do what we couldn't do."

So all my life I've been trying to fly, not just for me, but for all the American dreams that my parents, their parents, and members of our extended family never could realize, not because they weren't smart enough, but because they were born too soon, born at the wrong time in history.

My parents' American Dream, which I realized, was that I would work in an office, and never, no not ever, have to get on my knees to scrub some other woman's dirty floors. Simple dreams really. But not so simple back then, in the 1950s, when as Clifton L. Taulbert, the author says, "back

then, Once upon a Time When We Were Colored." And colored we were. But we sure were proud. And when I was colored, a high school diploma and a job as a typist in an office was the end-all and the be-all.

My dad lived long enough to see that, and he was happy. He lived long enough to see me earn two degrees, and he was happy. And he hung around long enough to see me become a newspaper reporter, and he was happy. And he was there when I received the first $10,000 of the $20,000 advance I received for writing my novel, The Africans. With tear-filled eyes, my father, even though dying of cancer and barely able to talk, let me know he was proud of the things I was doing and that he thought mine was a job well done.

My American dream is deeply rooted in my soul. I urge you to consider how much time we must invest not simply in trying to understand and make sense of ourselves, our own black experiences, but in trying to understand and make sense of the experiences of those of you who have their hands on the levers of power.

Diversity is a challenge. However, it's not nearly as difficult for those of us who all our

lives have had to make peace with diversity, have had to share with others or crash and burn. The challenge of diversity will be hardest, I think, on those not used to sharing, and who see no need to share power or space with others. Diversity is a great challenge for those who are so used to having all the breaks in their life that they really believe that that's the way things are supposed to be.

And so I say to you....I too am America. So black. So blue. So nappy. So happy. I, too, am America.

Each week Kentuckians hear from Betty Winston Bayé as she weaves history and reality into a newspaper column that draws on her perspective as a black female reporter and syndicated writer. Living out her parents' **American Dream** in Louisville, she has come full circle: a northerner gone south. We hope she has come to stay.

(Left) Bayé with media colleagues Ed Bradley and Charlayne Hunter-Gault. (Below) Bayé with 1990-91 Neiman Fellows, Harvard Unviersity.

Mary Caperton Bingham

Pam Spaulding for *The Courier-Journal*

ary Caperton Bingham died the way most of us would plan it. In that inimitable bluestocking, Tidewater accent she was speaking at a Rotary Toast in her honor talking about one of her favorite topics, the library. And with characteristic wit she opened by saying that she was so flattered by this event that "the best thing would be for a pink cloud to come down and take me away." And it did. Just like that.

Trying to understand the public's growing dislike of the media, she railed at the press for unleashing so much unwarranted, uncivil malice toward public figures. With such a lack of trust, the public may be left to do its own research in libraries and come to their own informed decisions about important issues. That was the point of her speech: libraries must make the information highway accessible to all citizens and the Library 2000 fund drive was designed to take care of that.

'Tis no wonder she was the champion of libraries and books—most of her life had been given over to the printed word in one form or another. As a newspaper-woman at the family's newspaper, *The Courier-Journal*, she was the charge d'affaires for her husband's editorial pages during his absence in World War II; she reviewed books for fifty years and spent twenty-five of those years as the book editor. But reading was more than a pastime for Mary Bingham—it was a passion, which she said was "the greatest gift one generation can give the next." With her support of bookmobiles during the 50s she drew readers' attention to the fact that 60% of all Kentuckians (80% in rural areas) had no access to free public libraries. So she did something about it. By 1955, Kentucky had 102 bookmobiles.

Her marriage to Barry Bingham was one of those rare true partnerships, and together they were determined to change Kentucky for the better. They did. In 1928 she had graduated from Radcliffe and he from Harvard. She had been a classics major and won an enviable year's study in Greece. Her abiding interest in the classics and in Shakespeare were evident in her ability to quote both as if they were second languages.

After moving to Louisville, she became as dedicated to fighting strip mining as she was to conserving the rivers. She was an active conservationist and environmentalist all of her life. A devotee of Louisville's waterfront project, the fountain that greets river gazers is a Mary and Barry Bingham gift to the citizens of that city. Of her attitude against coal companies ravaging the hillsides of eastern Kentucky, she once remarked, "I'm not hysterical, but sort of."

To be a Bingham offspring must have been a daunting experience in the face of such enormous intellect and high expectations. But daughter Eleanor gave one of the "toasts" honoring her mother during that fateful pink cloud evening and she said, with grateful heart:

My tiny little giant of a mother has, more than anyone else in my life, been an example of strict and lofty standards. She was always a parent of whom you could truly say you knew where you stood because she always made it crystal clear where she stood—on

any issue from eye makeup to between meal snacks to literacy, civil rights and the value of the 1928 Book of Common Prayer over any mediocre modernized Episcopal texts. But the exacting standards by which my mother raised me have remained the same for her today in completely undiminished power and conviction. Despite the long battle to be so different, I see I have internalized and even come to rely on the same values she once crammed down my throat. No excuses were ever accepted for trying less than one's utmost nor for stopping before reaching the top.

She now struggles to impart to my children those same unwavering standards of fair play, love of learning, informed debate and curiosity about everything in the world. I stand by cheering silently. Nothing shakes her convictions and this very fact makes her a wonderful companion in good times and bad.

Mary Caperton Bingham lived a fascinating, albeit often tragic life, filled with a signature humor and unflinching principles. She was a lively raconteur whose intellect and generosity changed the face of Louisville and the Commonwealth. In a prepared speech the night she died, Bingham would make an uncanny observation, "In the great funeral oration that Pericles gave for the Marathon dead he said that an Athenian who did not acquaint himself with and took no part in public affairs was regarded not as unambitious, but as a man of no consequence whatsoever." Mary Bingham took part in Kentucky's public affairs with *great* consequence before she floated above in the pink cloud which took her away.

> "No excuses were ever accepted for trying less than one's utmost nor for stopping before reaching the top."

(Above) Libraries and bookmobiles are two of Mary Bingham's lasting legacies to Kentucky. (Below) Mary and Barry Bingham announce their gift of a floating fountain in the middle of the Ohio River. Louisville's waterfront was Mary Bingham's lifelong interest.

Sallie Bingham

Julie Dean

By social change I mean, primarily, change in the attitudes toward women that are so familiar to us we may almost not question them: scorn, fear, condescension, trivilization. From these attitudes spring rape, abuse, murder, and all forms of violence, including economic exploitation.

Since the jailer is even more destroyed by his exercise of power than his victim, we can only hope for a change in this country's violent frenzy when men no longer hold power over women. This will not come for a long time. But it will bring, I think, a release for both genders which will allow the creativity so often burdened and belabored now to come into its own.

After a much-publicized gender war that resulted in the sale of her family's media empire, Sallie Bingham set aside $10 million in 1985 and established the Kentucky Foundation for Women. The creation of the Foundation fulfilled her long held dream to invest in women whose "artistic and creative projects are aimed directly toward affecting the lives of women in Kentucky."[1] Her method? To give women the means to use their own creative energies. Her ultimate goal? Nothing less than social change. "Society only changes, and discharges its obligations toward us," she believes, "when we change, and discharge our obligations to ourselves."[2]

Indeed the artistic, social and cultural climate for creative women in Kentucky *has* changed, thanks to more than a decade of grants to writers and artists "whose work embodies a feminist consciousness."[3] As director of the Foundation during its first four years, Bingham oversaw development of policies and a structure that put "money directly into the hands of women," and ensured that "outsiders and rebels" were seen as constituents of the Foundation.[4]

Sallie Bingham began observing and analyzing the role of women, family relationships, society and power as a young girl raised in an elegant mansion overlooking the Ohio River, which she terms the Big House in her 1989 family memoir, *Passion and Prejudice.* She describes how the five children were on stage every evening at the family dinner table, attempting to garner praise from their aristocratic parents by airing clever or witty anecdotes. The experience was painful for Sallie, whose storytelling abilities seemed inadequate at best. She was no happier when famous politicians, diplomats and other dignitaries joined the family for dinner, nor did she find pleasure in the gold plates and utensils which so impressed others.[5] Indeed her wealthy parents' exalted position in society placed her in such an isolated cocoon that she probably never realized other people lived similarly splendid lives.

As a writer of books, short stories and plays, Sallie Bingham reveals clear understanding of class distinctions, social boundaries, patriarchy, political power, prejudice, and Southern aristocracy. She writes about what she has experienced, producing work that is as pungent as incense. In *Matron of Honor*, she draws beautifully crafted pictures of the Ohio River, as seen from the Big House, using visual descriptions that seem to flow from her pen like poetry... "silver as the side of a fish, laid out flat."[6]

Though now living in New Mexico, Sallie Bingham's writing and generosity continue to influence and benefit the women of Kentucky.

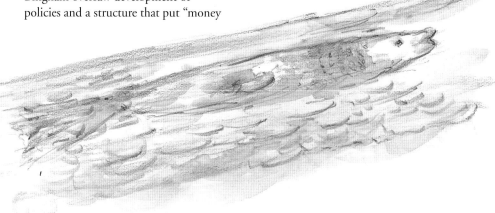

"ON BEING A FEMINIST MOTHER."
by Sallie Bingham
Excerpted from The American Voice
(Summer 1991)

Looking back over nearly thirty years of bearing and raising children, I've been realizing how feminism influenced my whole experience. In those far-off days of the early sixties, before THE FEMININE MYSTIQUE was published, I was a young mother uplifted and overwhelmed by yet another experience no one had explained or defined. There were no words for my terror and triumph when my first son was born: no healing woman's touch; no stories out of a shared past; no legacy from my mother or grandmother, who had borne six and seven children each. To have discussed birth would have meant touching on issues of sexuality, choice and control, which might have set the whole structure of conventional marriage shaking. No one who depended for her financial and emotional survival on the father of her children could afford to do that.

So I was alone in the 'lying-in' hospital in Boston; that phrase bothered me, with its hint of powerlessness, and the fact that I noticed the implication reminds me that I knew, on some level, of my cultural deprivation, of the stealing away of my power as a woman and a mother—or the attempt to steal it away. I knew nothing about taking care of babies, although I had been exposed to some of the mythology of the forties when my younger brother and sister were born: ears taped back with adhesive;

mittens on the tiny hands to prevent thumb sucking, and so forth. I remembered that regimen with horror, but I had nothing with which to replace it, other than the instincts I had preserved because I knew—I had seen—that women understand nurturing.

If war-making is the testing ground for young men, baby-making and raising remains the hardest test for young women, who have far less training for the risks involved. We would hardly send young men into battle with a few words of advice and a lace bed jacket, or its equivalent. But we send women unprepared, unequipped; and yet not only I but many others found the support in our core, the biological message written there in words of fire: this baby is yours to raise. My core was strengthened— by the mountain music I had half-heard growing up, with its tales of strong and relentless women, by the memory of my own nurse's capable freckled hands as she folded a mound of baby diapers or patted a colicky infant's back, by the sense of my own wounded body healed by the weight of a sleeping baby on my breast. My sons restored me even as they destroyed my peace of mind and nearly my sanity; in that act of destruction, I learned everything I know about my helplessness, but also about my ultimate strength.

Call it coping. It is the ability to bring forth life and fit that life for the world. It seems to me now, in 1991, with all my children grown and the world, to some degree, changed by the women's movement, that many young women artists are choosing not to have children. Practically, that decision makes the best sense; as Alice Walker wrote, "a writer who is a woman can perhaps continue her career undisrupted with one child"—but I would even dispute that. The point, though, is that we owe ourselves that disruption, as we owe ourselves the disruption of love.

Without the bearing and raising of children, I wonder by what fearful act we women will strengthen our core. Surely we do not intend to become warriors, hardening into denial. Certainly the choice to remain childless is wiser than my choice, haphazard, dimly lighted, to have three sons; surely these artists' work will benefit from the single mindedness a mother does not recover until middle age—and

by then it may be too late. But how will these women artists learn their own strength? The harsh beauty of determinism, the great wisdom of the body? And to whom, lacking daughters, can I pass my lore?

Or are our mysteries, as women, simply too grand to spread out on the table for discussion? Are we cannily hoarding information about one of the events that makes us, finally, separate and whole? Are our war stories too personal to tell? Perhaps in our silence we are hewing to a shared tradition, as in the despair and strength of child-raising itself. Children bring us to despair, yes. But through it all comes a clarification of ultimate strength and purpose as we find, instinctively, our terrible limits and face our terrible failures. We are alone with our babies, and into that aloneness shines not the light of reason but of a vegetable celebration.

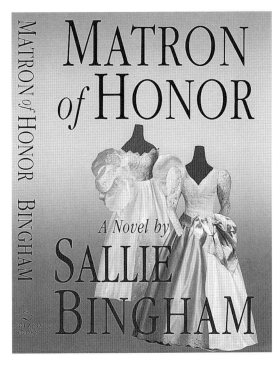

THE Kentucky FOUNDATION FOR Women

GRANTS PROGRAM

THE AMERICAN VOICE

HOPSCOTCH HOUSE

ESTABLISHED 1985

MATRON of HONOR

A Novel by SALLIE BINGHAM

MATRON of HONOR   BINGHAM

Mona Strader Bismarck

Both photos: The Filson Club

By James D. Birchfield

Mona Strader was taught to sew by her grandmother. Her attraction to beautiful, well-made clothes lasted throughout her life. It made her famous in the public eye and also in the fashion industry.

In a succession of marriages, she became Mona Travis Strader Schlesinger Bush Williams von Bismarck de Martini. As Mrs. Harrison Williams, Mona was married to presumably the richest man in America and she enjoyed many luxuries that forged a popular reputation as a dazzling socialite. The Williamses had houses in Manhattan, Long Island, Palm Beach, Paris, and the Isle of Capri. Admired for her beautiful flower gardens, it was on this isolated isle, where water came at a premium, that she imported vast quantities of fresh water to keep her Kentucky bluegrass flagrant green.

Mona represented the model American woman of "the Roaring Twenties," a period of tremendous financial growth and national confidence. There was a carefree outlook on life and a sense of continuing celebration. Even when this period of financial growth was replaced, in 1929, by the stock market crash and the Great Depression, Mona's reputation for beauty and style continued.

Featured in *Vogue* magazine almost fifty times, she modeled clothes by the most noted European designers. One of her favorite couturiers was Cristobal Balenciaga, who one day simply closed his doors. In her book, *D.V.*, Diana Vreeland remembers that day well. "I was staying with Mona Bismarck in Capri when the news came...Mona didn't come out of her room for three days. I mean, she went into a complete...I mean it was the end of a certain part of her *life*." In 1933, Mona was named the Best Dressed Woman in the World, and in 1958, she was elected to the Fashion Hall of Fame.

A favorite subject of many renowned fashion photographers, including her friend Cecil Beaton, Mona was also the

The family home near Lexington, Kentucky.
The Filson Club

cause célèbre of the artist Salvador Dali. A wickedly witty man, Dali painted the Best Dressed Woman in the World wearing rags. In her heyday Mona Bismarck was the inspiration for a song by Cole Porter and a character in novels by Truman Capote and Louis Bromfield.

As a patron of the arts, Mona Bismarck commissioned paintings and donated important works of art to the Metropolitan Museum in New York and the Louvre in Paris. She gave examples of clothing by famous designers to museums in America and Europe. Not one to forget her roots, Mona Bismarck was a generous supporter of Lotts Creek Settlement School in Cordia, Kentucky.

Because Mona Bismarck successfully demonstrated the social impact of clothing design she won widespread recognition in the public and fashion media. Louisville's Cinderella Countess became a symbol of elegance for the very best in high fashion.

Photo by Cecil Beaton; courtesy of The Filson Club

19

Linda Boileau

BOILEAU
by BOILEAU

I always try to speak up for the underdogs: women, kids, animals, the poor, people pushed aside. If you don't do a cartoon about them nobody hears their voices.

I am the only female editorial cartoonist in Kentucky. When I was a student at Kentucky State University, I had a great idea for a comic strip, so I called the editor at the *State Journal* newspaper. "Not interested," he said, "but do you do political cartoons?" I said, "Yes," when in reality I had never even thought about it. But I did one and took it down to him. He handed me the front page article. I did something on that, he ran it, and I kept going back with more. That was in 1984, and I have been there ever since.

I was an only child and grew up on television, so I drew more pictures of prime-time characters like Lucy and Ricky Ricardo and Marshall Dillon and Miss Kitty. Later, I created my own figures and gave them names and developed stories for them. I always drew pictures but never cartoons.

Drawing political cartoons is different. Cartoonists really have to be equally fair to everyone. The wonderful thing about cartooning is that you have the opportunity to make someone think. Even if they disagree, you've opened up their minds to issues. Car-

toons push buttons people don't even know they have.

The reporter's job is to get the facts and report them. My job is to make a statement in pictures about those facts. People say, "I can't figure out who you're for," and that's the way it should be. Everyone has a mask that they put up for protection, for achievement, and cartoonists have to go behind the mask and tell why people are doing certain things.

I try to cut wording because the best cartoons have the least amount of words—sometimes no words at all. Telling the truth in pictures should be very simple and point-blank. But not all cartoons have to be funny because the subject matter may be so dreadfully unfunny. The single mom theme often comes out in my cartoons because the apple never falls too far from the tree. If you don't do a cartoon about them nobody hears their voices.

I am addicted to writing notes. I write down ideas for cartoons and tape them everywhere—on my toothbrush, on the sink—everywhere that it will be on my mind or in my way if I want to turn the water on.

I am working on a book about people behind the scenes in Hollywood. There is tremendous behind-the-scenes preparation that goes into the making of a movie, just as there is in a cartoon. I am the one who sits in the movie theater long after everyone else has gone home, watching to see where it was filmed, who did the make-up. Who makes all those actors and actresses look good? I want to interview all those people and write about them.

I was born and raised in Frankfort and I never left because I had no desire to go anywhere else. The part of me that was shy made me comfortable being here. But today traveling has changed me because it makes me connect with people. I knew that when the opportunity came along to do art work for my hometown newspaper, it was a gift. Where it will take me, nobody knows.

Ruth Hanley Booe

*J*ust about the time Ruth Booe and Rebecca Gooch began looking for a spot to showplace the products from their candy-making business, Prohibition forced the bar at the old Frankfort Hotel to become a dinosaur before its time. The long marble bar was just perfect for candy making and the two ex-schoolmarms always knew a good marketing tool when they saw it.

These two ingenious entrepreneurs operated from one crisis to the next: fire, followed by a local bank which would not lend money to a young widow, interrupted by the stork and near devastation from the Depression, then the death of a spouse. But they were never daunted and instead met each barrier with uncommon pluck, imaginative sales tactics, and $50 from Fanny Rump, a hotel housekeeper. When the Depression hit, Rebecca-Ruth candies were sold by the piece, not the pound. During World War II sugar was rationed and there was no tin available for candy containers, but fortunately customers brought in extra sugar ration stamps and empty coffee tins, with no thought of ever being without their favorite candies.

Mixing business with pleasure came in all flavors. A chance comment by a friend pointed out that the two best tastes in the world were a sip of Kentucky's bourbon and Ruth's mint candy. It took two years to perfect the formula, and it's still a well-kept blending secret today.

Ham actresses for getting their products sold, they often went to the movie theater armed with packages of candy and, with a nudge and a wink, struck up loud conversations that went something like this...

"My, Ruth, this is **WONDERFUL** *candy!*

Booe reads some of her fan mail.

Rebecca Gooch
and Ruth Booe
on horseback.

Where on earth did you get it?"
Only to be followed by similar schemes
reminiscent of an episode from the "I
Love Lucy" television program. Ruth
and Rebecca would stand in front of
their shop extolling the virtues of the
delicious looking candy in the window
until a curious crowd gathered and
bought every single piece. At Kentucky
Derby time, Ruth Booe arrived in
Louisville armed with enough humor
and guile to delight visitors at a local
hotel. She dressed up in antebellum
dress and hawked her confections with a
Southern accent that never hurt sales.

They were able to purchase the apple
marble bar counter for $10 and it still
continues to lower the temperature of
the divine candied delicacies. Each piece
of candy begins as fondant, a creamy
sugary basis of every piece of Rebecca-
Ruth candy. It is made the old-
fashioned way in a gigantic copper kettle
that distributes heat evenly and then is
stirred with wooden candy paddles and
aged in antique crocks. Rebecca-Ruth's
signature mint candy
begins on a marble slab,
then hung on hooks to
be twisted and pulled
first by hand.

Developing a business
ethic that was compatible
with her life ethic led
Ruth Booe to promote
education by subsidizing
tuition payments or
scholarships for students.
She found that the best
ingredients cannot be
separated, even in real
life.

Ruth Booe purchased
the business from
Rebecca Gooch in 1929

and was active in Rebecca-Ruth
Candy until she retired in 1964.
Today, Rebecca-Ruth Candy is
still a family-owned business,
run by Ruth's grandson and
operated out of its landmark
clapboard house with striped
awning in Frankfort. Their
wry marketing testimonials
were actually a true
testament to their trade-
mark *"Now That's Taste"*
on every box of Rebecca-
Ruth Candy today.

MRS. RUTH HANLY BOOE

Mrs. Booe, Developer Of Bourbon Candy, Dies

Mrs. Ruth Hanly Booe, 81, or
112 East Second Street, widow of
Charles Douglas Booe, died in the
Capital Manor Nursing Home at
2:35 a.m. today after a long
illness.
Mrs. Booe, who developed
Kentucky

Delaware and New York,
returned to Kentucky in 1964.
The idea of flavoring candy
with bourbon was suggested by a
chance remark during Frank-
uicentennial
1936. Mrs. Booe
formula for two
fecting the still.
for blending
dy.
dy soon became
omed until

when the New York Times food
editor, Jane Nickerson,
recommended Rebecca-Ruth
candies. Since then the Chicago
Tribune, Los Angeles Times and
Gourmet Magazine have given
recommendations.
However, a setback came on
the heels of the New York Times
boost government regulations
barred the company from sen-
ding its bourbon candy through
the mails

100 Proof Bourbon Whiskey Chocolates

Rebecca-Ruth

net wt. 13

Anne McCarty Braden

The Courier-Journal

Braden interviews Rosa Parks.

By Catherine Fosl

*I*n the summer of 1954, just a few weeks after the U.S. Supreme Court issued its landmark decision in *Brown et al. v. The Board of Education of Topeka, Kansas, et al* against school segregation and as white supremacists scrambled to uphold racist hierarchy at any cost, a charge of dynamite destroyed a house occupied by African-Americans Andrew and Charlotte Wade in a white suburb of Louisville. The blast also turned upside down the life of a young white woman who, with her husband, had recently bought the house on behalf of their black friends, in defiance of racially restricted real estate policies.

Within a few months, Anne Braden, a journalist and local integration activist born into a genteel Kentucky family and reared in the deep south, would find herself in the national spotlight—jailed, charged with sedition against the state of Kentucky, and discredited as a "Red" in newspaper headlines. The Commonwealth Attorney had devised a theory placing Anne and Carl Braden at the head of a communist plot, staging both the purchase and the subsequent destruction to destabilize race relations. The whole notion is hard to believe today, but amid the hysterical fear of communism that punctuated the era, Louisville reacted in much the same way the nation had seized upon similar accusations by Senator Joseph McCarthy and others. A sedition charge, under a law passed in 1919 during an earlier "red scare" and never before tested in court, accused Anne and Carl Braden and five

others (all white) of advocating, suggesting or teaching sedition."[1] No attempt was made during the trial, however, to link either Braden to the bombing. The real charge was communism, and the Bradens' support of communist-led peace and civil rights campaigns made them easy targets.

The underlying violation was their dramatic challenge to the racial status quo. Yet, in the south of those years any such dissent among whites was equated with disloyalty in the region's own peculiar strain of anti-communism that swept the U.S. in the 1950s. Ostracized and even threatened with lynching, Anne Braden became a pariah in Kentucky and later in the region, while the actual bombers were never sought nor brought to trial, and the Wades were never permitted to live in their new house.

Unlike many victims of the anti-communist "witch hunt," however, Anne Braden did not retreat into silence. She was propelled into a lifetime of civil rights activism that now spans half of the twentieth century. While her husband remained jailed, she left their two young

All Counts Dismissed Against Braden And Six Others on Motion by State

Hamilton Hopes U.S. Will Act

The Braden case was officially closed yesterday when Criminal Court Judge L. R. Curtis dismissed the remaining indictments against Carl Braden and other defendants.

The judge's action ended a legal fight that began in June, 1954, after an explosion at the home of Andrew E. Wade, IV, in Rone Court in Shively.

The September, 1954, grand jury investigation of the explosion resulted in indictments against seven persons.

Braden, Miss LaRue Spiker, Miss Louise Gilbert, I. O. Ford, Vernon Bown and Braden's wife, Mrs. Anne Braden, were indicted on charges of teaching and advocating sedition.

Conviction Was Reversed

Bown, Ford, the Bradens, and Lewis Lubka were indicted on charges of conspiring to commit sedition. Bown also was indicted on charges of causing the explosion and contempt of court.

Braden was convicted of sedition and advocating sedition...

go into the alleged political activities of Bown and his relations with the other defendants.

This and the Supreme Court decision in the Nelson case prompted his motion for dismissal, he said.

Little Show of Emotion

All of the defendants except Ford, who is confined to a hospital in California, appeared in court yesterday. There was little show of emotion as Curtis sustained the motion ending their long fight for freedom.

Braden, however, seemed elated a few minutes later when questioned by newspaper and television reporters.

In asking for dismissal, Hamilton read a lengthy statement in court in which he said:

"While my entire staff wholeheartedly disagrees with the opinion of the Supreme Court in the Nelson case, nevertheless, as citizens of this country, and as lawyers, we must accept the proposition that ...cluding...

others. Braden denied being a Communist.)

As to why there has been no federal prosecution, Walker said:

"There are many special problems in such cases, and the Justice Department has a policy that in all such cases express authority for prosecution must be obtained from Washington.

"It is up to the Department of Justice to comment on why such authorization has not been given."

Transferred Home

The Bradens bought the home in Rone Court, an all-white neighborhood, in May, 1954, and transferred title to Wade, a Negro friend, about a month later. Shortly after Wade, his wife, and daughter moved into the stone home it was heavily damaged by an explosion.

The September, 1954, grand jury spent two weeks investigating the explosion and in the ...g to the Com... ...vered evidence ... ...losion was de...

Activist Wins New $25,000 ACLU Award

Journalist at Center Of '50s Housing Case

Reuter

NEW YORK, Jan. 20—Veteran southern activist Anne Braden, a Kentucky journalist embroiled in controversial issues since the McCarthy era, has been named the first winner of a $25,000 prize by

children with her parents and toured the country to raise his bond, using their case as a platform to inform civil liberties supporters nationwide of the links being made in the south between efforts to challenge segregation and charges of communist subversion. Dramatic even by the standards of cold war America, gripped as it was by anti-Communism, the case drew national attention and became something of a cause célebre for the beleaguered American left. Carl Braden's conviction and prison sentence were overturned by a 1956 Supreme Court ruling invalidating state sedition laws, and Anne Braden and other co-defendants were never tried.

Unable to find employment in Louisville, the Bradens refused to be driven out for their beliefs, and in 1957 they became paid field organizers of a small civil rights group, the Southern Conference Educational Fund (SCEF), taking on the lonely task of generating white southern support for black civil rights amid a climate of massive resistance.

When student sit-ins that ultimately broke segregation began in 1960, Anne

Braden was one of the few role models for young white women who rebelled against their culture by joining the civil rights movements, and the Braden house became a gathering spot for student activists. Unlike many women of the era, Braden had never been constrained by post-World War II resurgence of domesticity for women that Betty Friedan labeled the "feminine mystique." For years she and her husband had taken turns with domestic duties and traveling the region. Anne Braden had already gone through the painful process of political transformation many young women of the sixties were experiencing— what she called "turning myself inside out, realizing that the society that had nurtured me and been good to me was just plain wrong."[2]

Anne Braden has devoted her life to the search for racial and economic justice. She spent the decades of the 70s and 80s helping to break what she calls the southwide "police state," which stifled dissent on a range of social issues, including antiwar protest, labor organizing, and the rebirth of feminism. In recent years she has evolved from a pariah

to a heroine, and in 1990, she was selected to receive the first annual American Civil Liberties Union Medal of Liberty.

What made Anne Braden so committed to the life of struggle she chose? Deeply serious and religious as a youth, she embraced the idea of a selfless life well before the transformation of her views on race and class. In *The Wall Between*, her 1958 memoir detailing the Wade case, she likens that transformation to "a picture slowly coming clear in the developing fluid," as she slowly realized that "racial bars build a wall not only around the Negro (sic) people but around the whites as well, cramping the spirits and causing them to grow in distorted shapes." Anne Braden's single-minded pursuit of racial and social justice has been her life's road map.

Madeline McDowell Breckinridge

By Karen W. Tice

Madeline Breckinridge was born into one of Kentucky's most powerful and famous families, and she became one of the most influential women in Kentucky history. Madge, as she was called, was responsible for the founding of many institutions for social justice and reform in Lexington: the Blue Grass Sanatorium, the Lexington Civic League, the Associated Charities, the Lincoln Model School. She was an early advocate of kindergartens and manual education and was responsible for much development in Lexington's parks and recreation department. One of Kentucky's most quotable, ardent suffragists, she was a popular speaker known for electrifying suffrage audiences across the nation. Instead of restricting her life work, recurring tuberculosis and the use of an artificial limb only served as impetus to devote her organizational talents and fiery orations to children, women, and the powerless.

Madeline McDowell Breckinridge, who was elected president of the Lexington Associated Charities in 1903, was heavily involved in the organization's creation and remained a life-long member. The Associated Charities was established in 1900, in response to a call from the mayor to the "Ladies of Lexington" for help in managing the demands for relief that resulted from severe weather that year. Breckinridge, a strong advocate of women's suffrage, wrote a weekly women's page in the *Lexington Herald* that "was not to be given wholly to discussing fashion... instead anything from cabbages to politics will be treated." [1]

As a granddaughter of Henry Clay she had at her command the older class prerogatives of the southern gentry, and in the area of social reform work, Breckinridge was associated with such charity experts as Florence Kelly, Jane Addams, and Sophonisba Breckinridge, her sister-in-law, biographer, and pioneer social work educator at the University of Chicago.

From the standpoint of Associated Charities, effective relief was "scientific charity," engineered by unsentimental experts practicing scientific investigations and treatments. As Breckinridge contended, "Scientific Charity is a term bestowed upon the method of relieving the poor that seeks a basis for its actions not in sentimentality but reason." [2]

Soup lines, bread lines, holiday dinners, and direct handouts were interpreted as "small change charity" by Breckinridge since such efforts did not investigate, the litmus test for worthiness, and thus were "indiscriminate" and promiscuous." As seen by the Lexington Associated Charities, "small change charity" formed the heart of the social works of the Salvation Army, whose

Mr. and Mrs. Henry Clay McDowell
announce the marriage of their daughter
Madeleine
to
Mr. Desha Breckinridge
on Thursday, November the seventeenth
eighteen hundred and ninety-eight, at
Ashland
Lexington, Kentucky

The more predominant theme in Breckinridge's attacks against the Army was their lack of investigation and scrutiny of relief cases. She succeeded in blocking the appropriation, but her victory was short-lived and incomplete. The Associated Charities did not succeed in abolishing the relief work of the Salvation Army in Lexington or anywhere else.

Nonetheless, the legacy of Madeline Breckinridge and the Associated Charities is to be found in the widespread diffusion of the new techniques of professional power it championed. By the mid-1930s, even the Salvation Army had begun to adopt the practices associated with Scientific Charity. And Scientific Charity has contributed to the conservative rhetoric that continues to dominate social welfare reform efforts and practice today.

Photographs from the University of Kentucky Library

The marriage of Miss Madge McDowell and Mr. Desha Breckinridge was quietly celebrated at Ashland, the home of the bride, today at noon, Bishop Dudley, of Louisville, officiating. There were no attendants except Mr. John Payne, who was the groom's best man.

The bride wore a handsome gown of white broad cloth, which was very becoming. She is the youngest daughter of Maj. and Mrs. H. C. McDowell, the great granddaughter of Henry Clay, the most famous of Kentucky statesmen, and a worthy representative of so distinguished a family. She is bright and talented, and already well known in the literary world for clever criticisms and several fine magazine articles.

The groom is a popular and gallant Kentucky gentlemen, the son of Col. Breckinridge and nephew of Gen. Jos. C. Breckinridge, being one of the members of his uncle's staff in his recent command of the First Division of the First Army Corps, and now a lieutenant of the First Engineering Corps. He is also manager of The Morning Herald, which paper he has conducted most successfully for the past year.

After the marriage ceremony a delightful breakfast was served and the bridal couple left for a trip to New York City, where both have numerous friends. Upon their route home they expect to visit Judge and Mrs. Lyman Chalkley at Staunton, Va.

The bride and groom were remembered with quantities of beautiful wedding gifts, telegrams and letters of good wishes, both being widely known and loved.

Only members of the two families were present, among whom were: Dr. and Mrs. Thomas Bullock, of Louisville; Mr. and Mrs. Henry McDowell, of Big Stone Gap; Mr. and Mrs. Will McDowell, Mr. and Mrs. Tom McDowell, Miss Madeline McDowell and Miss Julia McDowell, Col. and Mrs. W. C. P. Breckinridge, the latter's sister, Mrs. D. D. Mitchell, and Miss Curry Breckinridge.

philosophy included a Christian ethic embodied in their motto and materials.

Beginning in 1905, when the Associated Charities and the local unit of the Salvation Army failed to find a means of working together, Madeline Breckinridge initiated a twelve-year struggle against the Salvation Army that culminated in a court action. Her initial target was the Army's intention to establish a soup kitchen. In 1914, she initiated a series of editorials in response to Salvation Army solicitations published in the Lexington *Leader*, the *Herald's* competitor. She reported on battles in other communities, such as Ashland, where the city had been prohibited from granting funds to the Army on the grounds that it was a religious organization.

Breckinridge escalated her battle by seeking court action against the city of Lexington for its allocation of $720 to the Army in order to expand its emergency shelter. Sophonisba Breckinridge described this situation: "And in 1917, the great encounter came! It was one of the most heroic encounters ever engaged in. One knows not where to turn to analogy unless it be to the driving of the money changers from the temple."[3]

Breckinridge

Rest in Peace, oh!
Madge McDowell
She hung herself, with a
Turkish towel,
With a crown upon her
forehead
You can bet

She's making every Angel
a
Suffragette.

Mary Carson Breckinridge

By Carol Crowe-Caracco

*I*n the early years of the 20th century, medical care in rural America was pathetically inadequate. But the prenatal and post-partum treatment of mothers and infants was especially appalling. In the East Kentucky mountains women often had their babies alone or sought the help of "granny midwives" who had no medical training. A strong-willed woman named Mary Carson Breckinridge altered this situation as she worked with community residents to change area lifestyles.

A life of public service was common to her family. Her grandfather became Vice-President of the United States in 1857, and her father served as ambassador to Russia during the 1890s. Her own generation counted a capable newspaper editor and an important pioneer female educator at the University of Chicago.

Born in Memphis and a native of Arkansas, Mary Breckinridge spent the first forty years of her life in aristo-cratic leisure. A series of tragedies—the demise of one husband, divorce from another, and the deaths of her two small children—prompted her to devote the rest of her life to the cause of child welfare. To supplement her unused nursing degree, she trained in a British hospital to become a certified nurse-midwife.

In 1925 she came to Leslie County, Kentucky, and established the Frontier Nursing Service (FNS), a midwifery and child care service which soon expanded into the practice of family medicine. Between 1925 and 1930 the service established an administrative headquarters for Mary Breckinridge at Wendover, six outpost clinics, and a hospital and health center at Hyden. Their infant mortality rate became far better than the national rate and their maternal death rate was far lower. Riding on horseback, Mrs. Breckinridge,

as she was always called, and her staff of nurse-midwives provided nursing care to some 10,000 people.

Not the least of Mrs. Breckinridge's talents was her flair for public relations and fund raising. She began a series of speaking engagements which she continued for almost forty years. On these tours into predominantly northeast and midwest cities this energetic woman with a hypnotic voice never asked directly for money; she

simply told her stories of destitute mothers and sickly babies. In the midst of an account she often paused dramatically and asked, "I wonder who can be taking care of Alabam Sizemore on Camp Creek tonight as she has her baby?" A much impressed youngster later reported to his mother, "Mary Breckinridge said that 10,000 women had babies in the creeks in Kentucky." Other times she passed around a picture of a two-year old toddler and the thirty

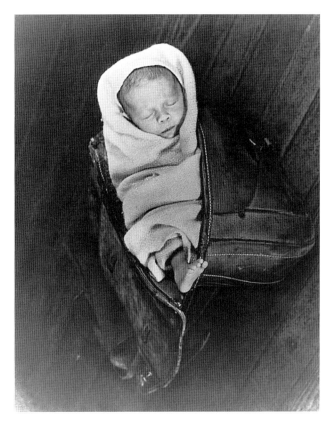

worms, each a foot long, which had come from the child's body. Or she might show the film, "The Forgotten Frontier," which revealed the starkness of the countryside and the work to be done.

From the very start, Mrs. Breckinridge and the FNS caught the imagination of the nation. An aristocratic belle who had danced at the court of the last Russian Czar, she now rode horseback over rough, hazardous trails to deliver babies and provide nursing care in remote cabins. Their mode of travel was a horse; their uniform, a blue-gray riding habit; their satchel, two pairs of saddlebags. Mrs. Breckinridge came to be called "The Angel on Horseback," and the magic of romanticism seemed to permeate their very existence.

But the years during the 1930s and 1940s were not easy years for the FNS. On the heels of the stock market crash came the Great Drought and in 1931, Mrs. Breckinridge broke her back in a fall from her horse. Although she resumed duties, back problems plagued her for the rest of her life.

These difficulties were followed by the distresses of World War II. Rationing horseshoes and diapers seemed inconse-

quential in comparison to the personnel crisis which occurred. The FNS had been staffed with British nurse-midwives or American nurses who had gone to Great Britain for midwifery training. Declaration of war brought the departure of most British staff, and soon wartime conditions prevented travel abroad by American nurses.

Faced with a staffing emergency Breckinridge established a long-time dream, a graduate school of midwifery in Hyden. Thus, Mrs. Breckinridge envisioned and placed into operation the concept of the family nurse practitioner in rural America long before many in the medical profession became aware of the idea. People in other areas saw the success of her ideas and copied them.

Mrs. Breckinridge never stopped caring about the needs of children in the present or in the future. Deep within her was the memory of her own children. Their deaths set in motion her life's work, and her successors at the FNS continue to this day. Perhaps Mary Carson Breckinridge said it best herself, "The glorious thing about the FNS is that it works."

"Baby delivered last week, and the $5 fee was paid with three pounds of beef (local), two bushels of irish potatoes, especially picked out, and one-and-one-half days work on our furnace pipes and water system."

Caroline Williams

'Wendover Big House'
FRONTIER NURSING SERVICE

(Top) Newborn napping in mid-wife's saddlebag. (Middle) Mrs. Breckinridge lived in Wendover. (Left) The women of the Frontier Nursing Service.
All photographs courtesy of Frontier Nursing Service.

Catherine Spears Frye Carpenter

By Lynne Hollingsworth

Catherine Carpenter became one of the uncommon, common people of Kentucky. Born in 1760 in Virginia, she was the third child of ten born to George and Christenah Spears. George Spears was a German immigrant who became a prosperous slave-owning planter. Well educated himself, Spears made sure that all of his children could read and write in English, even his daughters. Catherine was also taught to be a weaver, and eventually she became very skilled in this craft.

Catherine married John Frye, the son of a Shenandoah Valley neighbor. Shortly after, the Fryes migrated with other neighbors across the Appalachian Mountains into the western Virginia county of Kentucky. Unlike some migrations in U.S. history, this movement into the Kentucky wilderness was almost to total isolation. There were no roads, only trails and rivers, and the rivers continued to flow westward. There was little communication back east because travel often took years to complete round-trip. Goods, such as tools, furniture and clothing, had to be manufactured from raw materials found in the environment or from what had been carried over the mountains. Moreover, shelter and food had to be constructed, grown, or foraged off the land. If this were not enough, there was the weather to overcome and Native Americans to defend against.

Although there were few Native American settlements in Kentucky, the land was used as a hunting ground by numerous tribes and as a throughway for travelers. The natives were not pleased that farmers were clearing land and settling in the midst of their territory. This resulted in their allying themselves with the British, one of the most important facets of the American Revolutionary War.

(Left) Last Will and Testament of Catherine Spears Frye Carpenter. (Opposite page) One of Catherine Spears Frye Carpenter's weaving patterns. Photographs courtesy of the Kentucky Historical Society.

Numerous skirmishes between the settlers and the British and natives took place over the land. At the Battle of Blue Licks, the last battle of the war, John Frye was one of the casualties.

Widowed at twenty-two, mother of one daughter and pregnant with a son, Catherine was left on her own. Being a widow on the frontier was far from easy. Catherine married Adam Carpenter, one of the founders of Carpenters Station, and eventually they came to control close to 5,000 acres. While he was busy with family affairs, Catherine was busy bearing ten more children and managing their household. Life went well until 1806, when Adam Carpenter died.

Once again, Catherine found herself a widow, only this time she had nine children under the age of eighteen. Catherine inherited a widow's one-third of the estate, the remainder divided among the children. She also inherited 667 acres of land and she retained possession of a slave boy named Joseph, who became the supervisor of her plantation.

Catherine Carpenter began distilling whiskey as a source of income and raising cattle as another. As her property holdings increased her need for labor also increased and she purchased slaves. She did not sell slaves. At the time of her death, Carpenter owned twenty "Negroes," including Joseph.

Although a slave owner, she was also well-educated, and she seems to have been aware of the social debates raging on the slave issue and was definitely a supporter of the American Colonization Society. In her will, she listed twenty articles of which the first eight dealt not with her children, but with the disposition of her slaves. She freed and provided for her elderly slave, Joseph. She made provisions for her other slaves to earn money for freedom and passage to Liberia. Although she wished to free all of her slaves, she emancipated only the children of freed slaves. For all her good intentions, Catherine seemed to be uneasy with the idea of freedmen. If a slave refused Liberia, she made provisions for the slave to be sold. It seems that Catherine believed that freed slaves should be returned to Africa and those remaining should continue in slavery.

Although Catherine Carpenter was typical of her time, she was also atypical of her gender. Educated to read and write, well propertied, and financially astute, Carpenter exhibited more of the attributes of the males of this era. Catherine helped tame the Kentucky wilderness, saw the territory become a state, lived through four wars to the age of eighty-seven, and was financially successful in spite of giving birth to thirteen children and being widowed twice. Thus, it is fair to say that although Catherine Carpenter was not typical of her gender, she was one of the uncommon, common people of Kentucky.

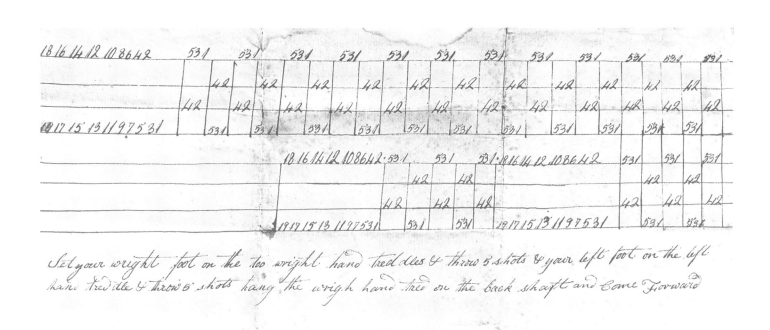

Kathy Cary

Once upon a time Kentuckians ate at home and restaurants were anathema to their sense of family and refinement. Today, we can take a kind of maternal pride in getting some women out of the kitchens and others into the kitchens.

Kathy Cary is a blazing combination of creativity, freshness, and energy who burst upon the Kentucky restaurant scene with the opening of her catering/carryout business, La Pêche, named for nature's perfect peach. Her restaurant, Lilly's, is named for her daughter. She has built a national reputation for her businesses, never losing sight of her Kentucky heritage.

Cary is a conscientious supporter of Kentucky foodstuffs and waxes poetic about organic produce purchased from Hart County. On any given day this restaurateur might offer Kentucky smoked trout, ragout of Kentucky rabbit, or grilled Bluegrass chicken. And with a Kentucky bourbon lineage that stretches all the way back to her great-grandfather's Glenmore Distillery she turns out bourbon-laced sauces that "take practice not to cook off," or she uses bourbon-soaked fruitwood chips to smoke slabs of salmon.

Growing up on an idyllic farm in Oldham County, foxhunting with her father and surrounded by her mother's gift of aesthetic beauty, she remembers being in and out of her grandmother's kitchen and surrounding gardens. "I consider myself a farm girl," she says. "Growing up we had to pick two gallons of strawberries before we could go out on a date, you had to help weed the aspara-gus beds, and when you did something bad you had to weed dandelions for two hours. Good discipline and I got a little sun."

Kathy Cary cut her culinary eyeteeth on a catering business in Washington, D.C., serving the likes of Henry Kissinger and Senator Edward Kennedy. But at the tender age of twenty-one, she was back in Kentucky ready to establish herself.

As Kentucky thoroughbred as they come, perfection rolls out of her kitchens because this chef has a work ethic that makes most people dizzy. Perfection is coupled with inexhaustible energy that she credits "with being a mother—I can't ever put my feet up—I might have to pick up the kids or go to the grocery store." And where did it all come from?

It was probably being a third child where I had to prove myself, but I've always had a very serious work ethic. Maybe it came from the discipline of riding horses–having to do it correctly. Then when I started cooking at 14, I tried to do it right, following the recipes exactly.

But it was probably her grandfather, Colonel Thompson, whose army discipline she inherited.

Riding demands of its horse and rider the same balance, long hours and practice that cooking demands of its cook and food. In both disciplines she's learned to work in harmony as part of a team. "You have to give up some of yourself—this is an opportunity for a woman who is committed and understands all the different facets—not just the kitchen but the financial, managerial and labor, too." What she doesn't add is that running a restaurant is probably the hardest way to make a living in the world. It takes an impresario to cultivate and satisfy customers, to meet multi-deadlines on a daily basis, and to juggle three different businesses plus a family all at the same time.

From her beginnings in Washington, Kathy Cary has gone on to appear on the "Today" show, to present a cooking series on national television, and to cook dinner at the coveted James Beard House in New York City three times. Being featured in *Great Women Chefs*, by Julie Stillman, gave Chef Cary the opportunity to network with other top-notch female restaurateurs. But her culinary concerns extend beyond the restaurant walls to a cooking and gardening program she founded at Louisville's Cabbage Patch Settlement House. Benefitting urban at-risk young people, "From Seed to Table" combines classes in both planting a garden and cooking. Cary nourishes the kids' self-esteem as much as she nourishes their appreciation of fresh vegetables.

She is a prime example of the old adage, hard work pays off. With cool expertise and vigorous style, Kathy Cary has developed a personal cuisine cultivated on a Kentucky farm and matured in Kentucky kitchens that expresses her signatures of place and refined quality.

Tennessee Valley Caviar Tartlettes;
Minted Lamb Kebabs with Aioli;
Kentucky Country Ham with
Blue Cheese and Chives;
Kentucky Trout-Stuffed Endive; Chutney
Bacon Toast; Louisville Benedictine Canapes

**Early Times Mint Juleps,
Sweet Iced Tea, Pink Lemonade**

❖

Capriole Goat Cheese Sausage
with Kentucky Limestone Bibb,
Balsamic Vinaigrette

Yeast Rolls and Country Cornbread

Grilled Kentucky Free-Range
Chicken Breasts with
Mustard-Onion-Tarragon Marmalade,
Fresh Asparagus

Sauteed Shrimp with Peppers
and Onion and Spicy Peach Chutney
Served with Cheese Grits Cakes

Red River Pink Grapefruit
and Vodka Ice

Ragout of Kentucky Rabbit with
Onions, Mushrooms, Eggplant,
Spring Watercress, and Shiitake
Crisps

Shaker Lemon Tart;
Lace Cup of Chocolate Creme Brulee
with Raspberry Sauce; Old-Fashioned
Oatmeal Cake

Early Times Bourbon Balls and
Assorted Chocolates

Louise Caudill

"If you want to do it, you can do it," said Louise Caudill, M.D., and her interesting life clearly demonstrates her words. She always wanted to be a doctor and remembered that in grade school she and a friend decided that "I would be a doctor and he'd be a pharmacist." But it wasn't a straight path from start to finish and her success even now, at age eighty-five, is credited "to a lot of good luck and timing." But her warm wit and sincere bedside manner convinces you otherwise.

When Louise Caudill grew up in Morehead, all the doctors were men, but she does remember her mother speaking fondly of a female doctor in Cincinnati. Nevertheless, Etta Caudill did not approve of her daughter's career choice, which she felt wasn't suitable for a woman. Caudill said her mother was a "hat fiend—she always had a plume or a feather in her head. My father thought she was beautiful so the hats were just fine." Caudill's father, Daniel Boone Caudill, was a lawyer and a banker. "He was the student, interested in our work and our careers," she said. "His philosophy was that girls do everything," and he expected all five children, girls and boys alike, to get as much education as needed.

Caudill graduated from Ohio State University, which she found to be so large that the only thing that "saved my soul was the sorority. I thought I'd go crazy in such a big place." Louise Caudill looked at her first four years "as a way to see what the world was like—not to prepare yourself for life." She majored in playing and physical education.

When she returned to Morehead State Teachers College, she became the first female director of physical education and saved her money to attend medical school. But in the meantime she spent summers at Columbia University in New York City with five other women from Morehead, and she completed a masters program in physical education. In 1946, she received her M.D. degree from the University of Louisville after completing an accelerated program due to wartime. "We went to school year round...no pay and ungodly hours." Nevertheless, Caudill loved family medicine: "Liked toes, eyes—the whole nine yards." She was one of two women in the class. One professor told her that he "didn't care if women went to medical school, but he just didn't think they ought to. And he treated me like that, too." Fortunately he was the only one.

Louise Caudill, M.D. felt she should do something "good" with her medical degree, so she went where she felt she was needed most: to a small rural hospital in Oneida, Kentucky. It was there that she met Susie Halbleib, a registered nurse, who became her medical partner for the next *fifty* years (in January,1998). She convinced her to come to Morehead to help set up her medical practice, and she expected to stay a year. "Nobody in medical school ever talked about the business end of a medical practice, and I had no idea what you needed to open an office." Caudill, Halbleib, and a salesman "bought everything from soup to nuts. We were so inexperienced that we ordered 100,000 diuretic pills that day!"

In the early years these two women would often be gone for days, making house calls, delivering babies in the remote Kentucky hills, only to return to a long line of patients waiting in the stairwell leading to their second floor office. They made thousands of house calls, driving all over the surrounding counties on muddy or snow-covered roads and trudging up the paths with four medical bags in their hands, one a portable examining table.

In 1957, Caudill opened a small clinic, but she knew that the community needed a full-service hospital. She took herself to the leaders of banks, businesses, the university and sold them on the idea. Someone suggested that the Roman Catholic nursing order of Notre Dame would be good hospital managers, and one day Monsignor Towell showed up at the doctor's office. "He took one look at

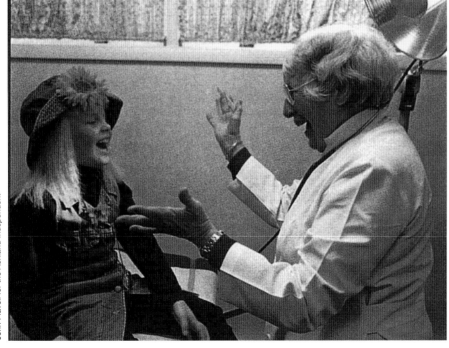

the five newborn babies on the divan and never asked us about *need* again. That was just happenstance though. He could have come any other day and not much would have been going on..." When St. Claire's Hospital opened in 1963, it was a living memorial to Dr. Louise Caudill. It has continued to thrive and grow due to what Caudill terms "family spirit." It is very much a regional medical center, serving nine counties, and in 1993, it was named the Outstanding Rural Hospital in the United States.

Louise Caudill tells young people who ask her about going to medical school that they must like what they are doing from the beginning. She loved being a doctor when she started and, almost fifty years later, she stills loves it.

Above right) Nurse Susie Halbleib and Dr. Louise Caudill making house calls, c. 1957.
Photo: *The Courier-Journal*

(Right) A reunion of the University of Louisville Medical School graduating class of 1946.

(Below) Dr. Caudill and Nurse Halbleib during the early days when babies liked to come too often and space was too little.

Rowan's 1st female physician praises her predecessors

By KENNETH A. HART
Independent News Writer

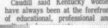
DR. C. LOUISE CAUDILL
Appalachian Celebration speaker

MOREHEAD — Characterizing the Appalachian woman as "strong-willed, independent and determined," Dr. C. Louise Caudill told an audience Monday that women have contributed greatly over the years to the development of the region.

Caudill, who has practiced medicine in Morehead for 41 years and was Rowan County's first female physician, spoke for about 20 minutes at a Morehead State University luncheon and symposium, part of the school's 13th annual Appalachian Celebration.

This year, the week-long event is focusing on the women of Appalachia and their contributions to economic development, education and politics.

Caudill herself has been instrumental in the growth and development of Morehead. After opening a family practice in 1948, she established the city's first health clinic in 1957, and was a key figure in establishing St. Claire

cine because "medicine was one of the easiest professions for women to enter, other than education."

Caudill said Kentucky women have always been at the forefront of educational, professional and

Terri Cecil-Ramsey

Holidays were always special on the family farm near Bardstown. Her family was poor, but she says she never knew what poverty was. In school, she loved sports; she was the first girl to play on the boys' basketball team in elementary school. "Sports defined who I was," says Terri Cecil-Ramsey. She was popular because of her participation in sports and because she was naturally gregarious. But she never really went to parties or dances in high school. Cecil-Ramsey was a female jock whose future was in sports.

The summer before her senior year, at age seventeen, Terri Cecil-Ramsey was in an automobile accident that left her paralyzed. She is considered a high-injury paraplegic. From day one neither she nor the rest of her family treated the accident like a tragedy. "When you grow up on a farm, everything is a challenge," she observed, "so my accident was just another challenge." She describes herself as being "hard-headed" during physical therapy. Once an attendant at the rehabilitation center handed her a huge pair of scissors, exaggerated in design, to help paraplegics like Terri Cecil-Ramsey learn how to dress themselves. Picking up each piece of clothing was awkward, and she managed to chip a tooth in the process,

so she found another way to dress herself.

She remembers the counselor made her future sound so bleak and terrible that she decided to do what she'd been taught to do and pray instead. At first Cecil-Ramsey refused to think of her paralysis as permanent. "Blissful ignorance," she says. "I always thought I'd walk again." Eventually she came to realize that she would "heal in a different way, in spirit and attitude rather than in body." By then, it was okay because she was further along in the rehabilitation process. "The rehabilitation center trains people to get around in a house that is 150% wheelchair accessible." she says, "but who has that?" Instead she went home and taught herself to get around in a world not easily accessible for someone in a wheelchair. When she married and moved into a house where nothing was accessible, her sense of humor helped her adjust. Ramsey continues to laugh at herself when she gets frustrated, and she also finds humor is the most productive response to unthinking people.

It was ten years before Cecil-Ramsey met another person in a wheelchair who didn't just sit at home. She not only did not stay at home, but she enrolled in classes at the University of Louisville and worked to put herself through college. "Everyone else worries about me much more than I do," she says. "If there's something a person tells me I can't do, I accept that challenge and figure out a way to do it, just to prove them wrong." She was awarded a degree in psychology, and

today she markets wheelchair conversions for vans. When told she makes everything look so easy, she replies, "If I can make you think it is easy, I've succeeded—because it's not!"

Giving up her dream to play college basketball was the hardest thing she ever did, but Cecil-Ramsey never gave up her love of sports. When someone mentioned wheelchair fencing, she went to watch the famous fencing coach in Louisville, Leszek Stawicki, who had added a wheelchair fencing division to his already popular fencing program. "He was not very helpful to me that first year," she observes. Then one night as they were preparing foils for the Paralympics, he began talking about growing up in Poland and his family. "Suddenly I saw him as a *person* , not just a teacher, and we became fast friends. I have tremendous respect for him and I would not be where I am today without his help."

Europeans begin fencing at age two, so their preparation is far more intensive than the eighteen short months Terri Cecil-Ramsey had spent preparing for the 1996 Paralympics in Atlanta, Georgia. Her whole family came to watch the Olympic competition and friends left e-mail messages of encouragement. She says she probably had fifty messages of luck and support every day. At the end of the rounds,

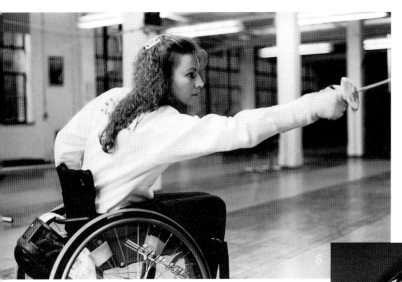

The highlight of Terri Cecil-Ramsey's life? Meeting Muhammad Ali! She says she understands why he threw his Olympic medal into the Ohio River. "An Olympic athlete not being served in a diner just because of the color of his skin?" she asked. No doubt, Terri Cecil-Ramsey would have thrown hers in, too.

(Left) Ramsey's wheelchair is strapped to the floor; she fences using only her upper body. (Below) 1996 Paralympic badges and passes.

Terri Ramsey was the #1 Female Fencer in the Paralympics and winning never felt so good. In retrospect, she thinks she might have won because she is the only female fencer in Louisville and fences against men. In Atlanta, she only competed against other women, and her unusual preparatory training had maximized her strength.

The Paralympics were "awesome, stressful, exciting," she said. She remembers getting to the top of the ramp and looking out over 85,000 people screaming "U.S.A., U.S.A." But having people expect you to do nothing just because you are in a wheelchair was even more emotional and stressful. Terri Cecil-Ramsey was accustomed to shining in sports, and she wanted to shine again. The pride and satisfaction that fencing has brought her is easy to detect in her voice. "This is the age of the disabled athlete," she said. "They are finally getting the attention they deserve and are being treated like other strong athletes."

With Cecil-Ramsey's inspiring levels of fortitude and fervor every year seems to be a banner year, but in 1997, she won the Ms. Wheelchair America pageant, a competition that selects the most accomplished and articulate female spokesperson for the disabled. She will take the message that the only difference between a person using a wheelchair and an able-bodied person IS the wheelchair. She's on her way to meet President Clinton at the White House and she will travel from Hawaii to New York in an effort to promote the dignity and productiveness of disabled citizens just like herself.

(Right) 1997-1998 Ms. Wheelchair America

Anna Mac Clarke

The Lawerenceburg train station where Anna Mac Clarke's casket came home to rest.

By First Sergeant John M. Trowbridge

*I*t was raining that April morning as the train rolled into the station at Lawrenceburg. It was one of those day-long rains that slows the world down and gives them time to reflect. They had been waiting to meet the train that was bringing her back home. Home to her final resting place. Anna Mac Clarke died just before her twenty-fifth birthday, but during her brief life she made enormous contributions to women, to African Americans, and as a pioneer in the United States military.

An athletic tomboy, an outstanding student and one who refused to settle for second best, she was raised by her maternal grandmother, who instilled the importance of high morals and values and the importance of having a good education. In 1937, she was one of three graduates of Lawrenceburg's Colored High School and that fall she entered Kentucky State College (now University). Among her eminent college friends and classmates were Whitney Young, Jr., who later directed the National Urban League, and Ersa Hines Poston, who became president of the New York State Civil Service Commission. Mary McLeod Bethune, who founded the National Council of Negro Women, delivered their commencement address.

Lawrenceburg offered college-educated Anna Mac Clarke the same jobs it offered other women of her race: maid, cook, seamstress. She refused to waste her education and instead took a summer job at a Girl Scout Camp in New York. But she believed life had more to offer and shortly after the bombing of Pearl Harbor she answered a challenge from Mary McLeod Bethune for "One Black WAAC." Bethune encouraged women to join the All-Volunteer Women's Army Auxiliary Corps, later the Women's Army Corps, and as "L-502251" Clarke reported to Ft. Des Moines for training. She graduated from the WAAC OCS Program in 1943, the only one of three black women who finished, and the only black officer in her class.

"No!" Anna's response was direct, brief, and unambiguous when asked if enlisted men could date female officers under her command at the Army Air Corps Field in Chico, California.

Despite her new status as an officer, she was chagrined that the post as a whole remained segregated. The swimming pool, for example, was opened to blacks just one hour a week, after which the water was purified. Despite such bigotry, Officer Clarke always believed the military offered more opportunities than the outside world, and her conviction proved true when she became the first black WAAC to command an all-white unit.

Anna Mac Clarke was a pioneer, part of a unique group of women who came together for one purpose, to help their country win a world war. She and her sister WAACs also fought another war at home, racism, but they began to break down the barriers of race and gender which eventually led to the civil rights movement.

At Douglas Army Field in Arizona, Clarke purposely chose a seat at the post theater outside the area marked "Reserved for Negroes." As a result of her protest, the commanding officer entered a lengthy order making it crystal clear that discrimination would not be tolerated on his watch. Anna's story was carried in newspapers around the country, supporting the national movements for desegregation and ending discrimination within the military. A month later, Anna became ill and complications of a ruptured appendix led to her death on April 19, 1944. A brother accompanied her body on the train back to Lawrenceburg, where a funeral was conducted with full military honors. She is buried in a cemetery in Stringtown, a small community near Lawrenceburg.

COMMONWEALTH OF KENTUCKY
UNITED WE STAND
DIVIDED WE FALL

ANNA MAC CLARKE (1919-44)

This Lawrenceburg native was one of the first black women in Ky. to enlist during World War II. She joined Women's Army Auxiliary Corps in 1942, and was commissioned a 1st Lieutenant the next year in newly named Women's Army Corps. While stationed at Douglas Air Field, Arizona, she led fight to desegregate base theater.

Presented by Ky. African American Heritage Commission

1996   KENTUCKY HISTORICAL SOCIETY   KENTUCKY DEPARTMENT OF HIGHWAYS.   1870

Historic marker in honor of Ann Mac Clarke located at the Court House in Lawrenceburg.

Laura Clay

By Claudia Knott

A major issue in American political life has been the question of who has the right to vote. The women's suffrage movement, once relegated to the historical periphery, now holds a more central place in our history. A Kentucky woman who was a key figure in this movement was Laura Clay. It can be said that she was born and grew old with the movement.

Born in Madison County in 1849, one year after the Seneca Falls Convention launched the woman's rights movement, Clay was in the forefront of suffrage organizing in the South, founding the Kentucky Equal Rights Association in 1888, which was the region's first permanent suffrage organization, and she served as an officer in the national association from 1896 to 1911. Clay died in 1941, twenty-one years after ratification of the Nineteenth Amendment.[1]

As a suffrage leader on the local, state, regional, and national levels Laura Clay occupied a pivotal position within the movement and participated in nearly every controversy it faced. One of the most significant issues within the movement, indeed, within American society, at the turn of the century was the 'Negro problem,' a white euphemism for the clash between Southern blacks' aspirations for full citizenship that emancipation and Reconstruction had nourished and Southern whites' determination to curb or extinguish those aspirations.[2]

The suffrage movement first emerged in the South in the 1890s, the very decade when whites began to "solve" racial conflict with 'Jim Crow,' an extensive system of *de jure* segregation and disenfranchisement. Many Southern white suffragists, including Laura Clay, used a statistical argument for woman suffrage, predicting that women's enfranchisement would further protect, not weaken, white supremacy, because in the South, whites outnumbered blacks. Most Southern whites, however, feared that black women with ballots could undo Jim Crow laws.[3]

As a border state, Kentucky resembled and diverged from the Deep South's racial patterns and politics. Clay's suffragist and the K.E.R.A.'s policies, which she influenced heavily, reflected Kentucky's racial complexities and contradictions. Consequently, Laura Clay left us with a mixed legacy of women's rights and racial injustice.

Clay and Kentucky's white suffragists operated within a complex racial context. Although Kentucky, exempt from Reconstruction, never ratified the Fifteenth Amendment, black men did begin voting in 1870 and never lost that right. A low black population statewide and a small Republican Party had given white Democrats a firm control over most of the state from the Civil War onward, and they never disenfranchised black men.[4]

It was within this setting of secure, white Democratic control that Clay founded the K.E.R.A. and that the legislature granted school suffrage in 1894 to all women in the state's second-class cities of Newport, Covington, and Lexington. Clay often claimed that Kentucky had no "Negro problem," but the reality was that racial politics simply had a different configuration there. In Kentucky's former slave belts in the southwestern part of the state and in the Bluegrass, black populations ranged from twenty to fifty percent, and in Lexington where Clay lived, African Americans were thirty-eight percent of the population in 1900.[5]

While Clay used the statistical argument for woman suffrage in the rest of the South, interestingly, she never seems to have used it at home, no doubt because the Democratic party enjoyed a wide margin of control there. The Fayette County Equal Rights Association, which Clay also helped found and over which she presided, actually sought to register black women for the school board elections. This strategy was most concerned with instituting suffrage without disturbing white supremacy. Clay and the city's white suffragists presumed black women would be voting, but they took steps to preserve the racial status quo. The Fayette Association used the superintendent of Lexington's black schools, a Democratic appointee generally unpopular with black Republican voters, as their main contact with the black community. Furthermore, all women's registration and polling sites were located in white homes.[6]

Despite impediments many of Lexington's black women voted in the city school board elections from 1895 to

Laura Clay,
Lexington,
Kentucky.

1901. When the Kentucky legislature suddenly repealed the women's school ballot in 1902, an uproar ensued and suffragists looked to Clay for an explanation.

To Clay's credit, she felt that the repeal was "a grievous loss," and she did not single out black women voters as the troublemakers. In fact, when the repeal controversy first arose, both the F.E.R.A., and the state association under her leadership initially defended black women voters as good mothers concerned about their children's educational welfare. Clay's official version of the defeat as written to NAWSA historian Ida H. Harper put the blame on partisan bickering and machinations.[7]

But in the heat of the repeal fight, Clay did abandon black women. When repeal seemed imminent, Clay and her white colleagues shifted their tactics to defend their own efforts on behalf of white supremacy in contrast to the Democrats, who they charged with upsetting the racial order by moving the women's polling sites from white homes to barber shops, livery stables, and "Negro cabins," all for partisan advantage. Clay never explained to Ida Harper that black women had consistently turned out for the school board elections, often in higher percentages than the white women. By soliciting black women suffragists but then minimizing and ignoring their actual role in the woman suffrage movement, Laura Clay was a bold advocate for women's rights, but as was true of most white suffragists in the Deep South, she helped perpetuate racial injustice.[8]

Laura Clay at the Democratic National Convention in St. Louis, 1916.
All photos courtesy of the University of Kentucky Library.

Laura Clay was overshadowed in politics by her father, the abolitionist Cassius M. Clay. Born at White Hall, a 2,500-acre estate in Madison County, she was propelled into the suffrage movement after her father divorced her mother, leaving her no property rights, under Kentucky law. She supported herself and her activism by becoming a farm manager on a 300-acre farm leased from her father. Clay was also active in the Kentucky federation of Women's Clubs and the Women's Christian Temperance Union as part of her advocacy efforts for women and children. She believed in the rights of women to participate in church leadership and was instrumental in gaining female membership on the vestry and synod of the Episcopal diocese of Lexington.

Jane Burch Cochran

and purchased a 3,000 square foot loft in Cincinnati which Cochran still maintains. "It is my city connection," she says. It is also the place where she has attended a weekly drawing class with the same group of artists for fifteen years. That support network is important to her. She says it is the "most Zen thing I do in my life."

Cochran is especially influenced by her mother and her grandmothers. "Strong but gentle women have been a constant in my life from my grandmothers, great aunts and especially my mother, Mildred James Burch," she describes. They instilled unconsciously in Cochran "the pleasure and love of the arts be they music or visual." In a statement to the art quilt, "For All Our Grandmothers," she wrote, "I have always felt close to my grandmothers and cherish the times I was able to spend with them. One of my grandmothers died at age 98. She was a painter and started me on my pursuit of art. Their gifts and our bond overwhelm me." The multi-textured, appliqued quilt features new and found objects, shiny and matte-finished fabrics, painted canvas, and beads. It pays homage to the first American grandmothers with a photo-Xerox icon of Native American women in beaded clothing. Below the icon is a nine-patch quilt Cochran uses as background for mementos and objects she obtained from her own grandmothers and great-grandmothers as well as the grandmothers of several friends.

For hundreds of years, quilts stayed on the beds. Most quilts were considered utilitarian labor, not art. Quilts have always been regarded as "women's work," she said. Women made them for a daughter's hope chest. Some women created their family history on story quilts. But when art quilts exploded on the quilt market, Jane Burch Cochran was one of the few

Deviled eggs, lemon pie, cantaloupe, papaya, shish kabob, nachos, and a Chinese rice dish—this tantalizing, multicultural display of foods appears on a quilt aptly named "Pot Luck," which was sewn, painted, and embellished by artist Jane Burch Cochran. It was the only quilt by a Kentuckian to appear in the exhibition, The Quilt Connection All-Stars, held at the Museum of Folk Art in New York City and then brought to Louisville in 1993. Since people often cook and enjoy the foods of different cultures, Cochran used this smorgasbord image to make a statement about race relations. On one side of the quilt was stitched a black glove that reaches across to a white glove on the other side, but there is a wide space between.

Jane Burch Cochran lives in the idyllic community of Rabbit Hash, Kentucky, in a log house overlooking the Mason-Dixon line. Despite her Kentucky birthplace and current residence, she grew up in the Midwest and Northeast, which may have broadened her artistic scope but she still returns to her Kentucky roots in many of her quilts. She came back to Kentucky to get her B.A. from Centre College in 1965 and then studied painting at the Cincinnati Art Academy from 1966 to 1970. When her car burned, she took the insurance money

One of Cochran's favorite dogs is honored in "Looking for God."

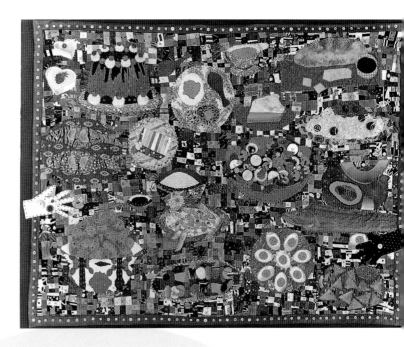

Pictured at left is Cochran's quilting creation "For All Our Gradmothers." Above is the quilt "Pot Luck."

art quilters in America. A buyer would never use one of Cochran's quilts as a bed coverlet. They are exquisite wall hangings that "portray emotion, love and anger in every piece," she said.

She has certain symbolic elements, like ladies' gloves and Native American iconography, that repeat themselves in different quilts. Finding the gloves is like going on a treasure hunt among her quilts. "The gloves (hands) are reaching and searching for both questions and answers about race, the environment, and the human psyche," she says.

A viewer can luxuriate in the intricate hand bead work and know that her years as a jewelry maker were good preparation. These quilts are highly embellished with beads, buttons and paint that "enhance the narrative with a unique and personal texture." Cochran's art quilts take months to create and she makes very few in one year. "I could probably make a living producing costume jewelry," she said, "but I do art that takes a *long* time."

In 1979, five contemporary quilters who had been meeting in Athens, Ohio, helped develop a cultural art center in an old dairy barn. Thus began Quilt National, the world's first juried art quilt

show. Cochran has exhibited several times in the biennial show, which has become the premier international showcase for contemporary quilt buyers and gallery owners. Cochran says that being featured on the cover of the Quilt National program in 1987 catapulted her into fame. Her work has appeared in shows all over America as well as England and Ireland.

In between working on other quilts, Jane Burch Cochran produced "Coming Home: Kentucky Women Quilt." A booklet that fits into a pocket on the back lists the names and accomplishments of over 200 famous and not-so-famous Kentucky women. "Often I would be reading the obituaries and there would be a woman who had raised lots of children and done good things for the world. I didn't want her to be forgotten." The names are stamped on individual strips with paint over fabric. Then the quilt was adorned with beads, buttons, paint, and found objects. She chose the name "Coming Home" because "while working on it," she says, "I became more connected to my roots and wanted to honor Kentucky's women."

After finishing this name quilt,

Cochran began thinking of a quilt using dog names. People need to understand that the Cochrans have "his and hers" Labrador dogs, and *they* own the Cochrans, not vice-versa. It is such an enviable devotion that most visitors have visions of being reincarnated as a "Cochran Lab." Short of that, people can enjoy several quilts which honor her dogs. Jane Burch Cochran had "sketched and pondered and dreamed of" doing a quilt about her studio companion, a black Lab named Barker, for thirteen years. Finally she used the background from another quilt already entitled "Looking for God," whose central image she had not been able to find. She used dog names she'd collected from friends and family and beaded the head of her current Lab, Belle, using a baby dress as the body. "My husband asked, 'Why the pot holder?'" She answered, "It represents the un-known."

It was a healing quilt for Cochran, who had recently lost two close friends to cancer. She had just completed a quilt for the show, "Sewing Comfort Out of Grief," to honor the children in the Oklahoma City bombing. "I needed to laugh," she said. And somehow the title fits since she figured that, "after all, dog *was* God spelled backwards."

Martha Layne Collins

By Barbara Hadley Smith

On the day Martha Layne Collins was inaugurated as the Governor of Kentucky she rode from downtown Frankfort to the ceremony in a horse-drawn carriage. The carriage began the five-block approach to the Capitol. In an automobile the incline is not very noticeable, but in a horse-drawn carriage it seems considerable. Seeing how hard the horses were working, the carriage driver, Dinwiddie Lampton, a friend of the Governor said, "You know, it sure is a long, steep climb to the Capitol." Martha Layne Collins looked at him and said, "Dinwiddie, you have no idea how long...and how steep."

As a child growing up in Bagdad, Kentucky, Martha Layne Hall did not dream of becoming Governor. There was no grand plan for her future. She had a traditional upbringing in a small, rural community as the cherished only child of Everett and Mary Hall.

Martha Layne Hall's father operated a funeral home and ambulance business. It was a business where service to people was the order of the day. Family meals were often interrupted. He was on call 24 hours a day, seven days a week.

"I grew up with a clear understanding that life is uncertain," she recalled. "I saw the unpredictability of life firsthand, and that made an impression on me. With that background, I learned that you should do as much as you can, as fast as you can."

After graduation from the University of Kentucky and marriage to Bill

Collins, Martha Layne began her career as a school teacher. She gave birth to two children, and the family moved to Versailles where Dr. Collins set up his dental practice and Martha Layne taught school.

When Wendell Ford decided to run for Governor, he asked Martha Layne Collins to do volunteer work for him. One campaign led to another and, after several years, politics became a full-time occupation. After exhaustive efforts on behalf of other candidates, she decided to run for office herself.

In 1975 Collins successfully campaigned statewide to become clerk of the Supreme Court. She was elected lieutenant governor in 1979 and four years later, won the race for Governor. She was the first woman Governor of Kentucky, and, at that time, one of only three women in the nation to ever hold that position.

Governor Collins decided to empha-

size education and economic development. "I saw education as the key to improving the quality of life for Kentuckians," she said. An educated work force will attract economic development. But the first step was to convince people to increase our investment in our schools."

The Governor formed a coalition of former governors, legislators, business leaders, civic groups, educators, sports enthusiasts, media—anyone who would agree to join was put to work. They took the show on the road and traveled across the state to convince people of the need for education improvement. The result was a $300 million school improvement package which Governor Collins considers one of the most important accomplishments of her administration. This step forward helped develop support for the massive Kentucky Education Reform Act, which won legislative approval in the next administration.

The second major focus was to increase the number of jobs available to Kentuckians through both new and existing industry. An aggressive recruiting campaign resulted in a stunning success with the location of Toyota Motor Manufacturing, U.S.A., Inc. in Georgetown, Kentucky. "Competition was fierce among the nation's governors to land that plant, and I was determined to get them to choose Kentucky," Governor Collins recalls.

"On the final evening of the inspection team's final visit, I hosted a dinner at the Governor's Mansion. We planned it meticulously with special courses of favorite foods and entertainment including the Stephen Foster Singers from My Old Kentucky Home in Bardstown. The finale was to be a surprise: a grand display of fireworks over the capitol which is across the street from the mansion and in the

middle of a residential area. The finale was scheduled for 9 p.m. However, our guests lingered over dinner, and then made a great number of toasts, which were certainly appreciated but time-consuming. By the time the singers were finishing 'My Old Kentucky Home' it was closer to 11 P.M. The fireworks went off with great, resounding noise...absolutely beautiful in the dark sky...and all over Frankfort children screamed and people leapt out of bed. Some said later they thought the town was being bombed."

Whether or not the fireworks clinched the deal, Governor Collins and her administrative team succeeded in bringing Toyota to Kentucky and changed the face of economic development in the state. In the decade after its opening, Toyota increased its work force from the original 3000 to 7500 people. In addition to the Camry, the plant now produces the Avalon and will begin production of a new mini-van.

Governor Martha Layne Collins received some criticism in 1987 for offering Toyota a $147 million incentive package. Ten years later the critics are silent as Toyota's investment in Kentucky has grown to $3.4 billion, and the company chose Kentucky to be the home of its North American Manufacturing Headquarters which employs another 550 people.

Looking back at her administration, Governor Collins said, "Four years is a short period of time and I believe we accomplished a lot in diverse areas, not only in education and economic development, but in human services and in meeting the needs of local communities for bridges and roads and other infrastructure. We created teams, not just top management, but throughout the ranks," she said. Many of the unique programs established, such as Governor's Scholars for the Arts, Bluegrass State Games, and Champions Against Drugs continue today because groups of people invested something of themselves in making them happen.

After leaving the Governor's office, Martha Layne Collins served as president of St. Catherine College for six years. Today she is Director of the International Business and Manage-ment Center, Carol Gatton College of Business and Economics at the University of Kentucky. She also has her own consulting firm, serves on several national boards, and enjoys the company of four grandchildren.

Cartoon, top: Linda Boileau for The State Journal.
Top right: The Governor looks at a Kentucky history quilt made by students.
All photographs, Kentucky Libraries & Archives

Martha Purdon Comer

Bob Warner for *The Ledger-Indep*

ome is where the heart is. If it hadn't already been written thousands of times, Martha Comer might have written it herself. But a journalist of her caliber would never allow such a hackneyed phrase into her lexicon. Heart and home commingle in Comer so well that it's hard to resist drawing the parallel.

For Comer, they have always been in Maysville, Kentucky; at *The Ledger-Independent*, the newspaper she edited and published for more than forty years; among her community fighting for public housing and anything else to make Maysville a better place to live; and, especially, at Woodlawn, the Gothic Revival house on her farm.

It was luck, some of it bad luck, that got Martha Comer into the newspaper business. By the time she was a high school senior, her father was at the helm of *The Ledger-Independent*. She had a job there the summer she graduated and she collected the Associated Press news that came over the wire from Cincinnati. That meant sitting in a small closet wearing headphones and deciphering an assortment of national news. The sweltering summer heat didn't help, but the real problem was that Comer didn't always know what she was listening to.

"God, girl, don't you read or know anything?" one man asked her in amazement.

"I didn't know how to spell all those long Russian names, but I got up the next morning and I learned. It was a real lesson."

For a time she attended college but she returned to the newspaper to continue her life as a reporter and married the hometown boy she'd met at fourteen. Then came tragedy. Comer's brother died unexpectedly on the operating table, and suddenly, Comer found herself taking over his responsibilities as editor of the newspaper.

In no time, she was running the show and life got very interesting. Comer's career at *The Ledger-Independent* gave her access to people and information that few women in her day shared. She was one of the first journalists invited to John F. Kennedy's White House. She traveled with a contingent to Germany to convince them to do business in Kentucky. A lifetime as a newspaper woman would have been enough for most. Enough to do, and enough of an accomplishment.

But not for Martha Comer. "I guess if you were to ask me the one thing I've done in this town that I take a great deal of pride in, it's public housing." Public housing was more than giving people a home, it was part of the effort to integrate the town. And it was a fight that met resistance. Despite what she calls a "terrible burden of criticism," Comer had to respond. "I actually saw places where there were holes in the floor of the kitchen and people urinated right into the ground. And it just burned me up." She was not to be stopped. She lived as she believed she ought to, and left it at that.

"I think I was born writing. The only reason I'm still not writing is

Martha Comer

Retired editor, Maysville Ledger-Independent and Daily Independent; served for 42 years. Continued to write regular column at age 87. Started work at newspaper in 1924. Steadfast proponent of community and industrial development, especially in advocacy of public housing, floodwall, county health department and community college. Co-founder of Maysville-Mason County Development Association and original member of the Maysville Community College Advisory Board. Outspoken supporter of civil rights, job creation, education and social equity. Chosen First Lady of the Year in 1953 by Beta Sigma Phi. Maysville's Most Distinguished Citizen by the Chamber of Commerce in 1976 and Distinguished Alumni of Maysville High School in 1979. Long associated with historical restoration in the community. Held leadership positions in numerous civic and community efforts, as well as St. Patrick's Church.

Kentucky Journalism Hall of Fame

1995

Presented by the University of Kentucky Journalism Alumni Association.

the arthritis in my hand. Here I am a woman 90 years old and dying to go back to work!" The name of her column was "Do You Know?" and she's proud of how much she could say in so few words. She hasn't much praise for long-winded reporters. And she also likes to tell you what radio and television did to newspapers: "It's made all those people scramble, looking for sensational pictures."

She loves Maysville like it was another child, but she laments people deserting its downtown for the sub-urbs. "Wal-Mart is the worst thing that ever happened to this country!" So she worked tirelessly to build a new library downtown, anything to keep downtown Maysville from dying.

Martha Comer may be most proud of her work in pubic housing, she may be Maysville's best booster, and she was the editor of the newspaper when her stands on community issues made her controversial. But it is her home, Woodlawn, that will be her legacy. Ironically, when she and her

family moved there after the 1937 flood, she soon realized that two working parents and two school-age girls did not make for easy country living. Not until 1970 did she decide to renovate Woodlawn and restore the house to its original glory. And then her heart and home were under one roof.

Previous page, bottom left: Her plaque from the Kentucky Journalism Hall of Fame.
Below, a tribute in the Congressional Record.
Bottom, her home in Maysville.

Congressional Record

United States of America

PROCEEDINGS AND DEBATES OF THE 104th CONGRESS, FIRST SESSION

Vol. 141   WASHINGTON, TUESDAY, APRIL 25, 1995   No. 67

Senate

TRIBUTE TO MARTHA COMER

● Mr. McCONNELL. Mr. President, I rise today to pay tribute to an outstanding Kentuckian who has been selected for induction into the Kentucky Journalism Hall of Fame. Mrs. Martha Comer of Maysville, KY, is devoted to her profession, to the Ledger-Independent, formerly the Daily Independent, and to her community.

Martha Comer was born in 1906, the same year that her father founded the Daily Independent. It is not surprising that Martha displayed her journalistic qualities at a young age. She served as the editor of the school annual at Maysville High School. Upon her graduation from high school she began working on the editorial staff of the Daily Independent. She assumed the duties as editor in 1935, although her name did not appear as editor until 1941.

In 1968 the Daily Independent was sold to the Maysville Publishing Corp. and became the Ledger-Independent.

At this time Martha became the editor and was responsible for publishing both the morning and afternoon editions. Although Mrs. Comer retired on January 7, 1977, she continued to remain on as an editorial consultant. For many years she continued to write a daily column and editorials. And to this day, Martha Comer still writes editorial commentary two or three times a week for the Labor-Independent.

Mrs. Comer's editorial involvement allowed her to become actively involved with her community. She has campaigned tirelessly for many organizations and causes, such as advocating public policy and teaching in the literacy program.

Mr. President, I would like my colleagues to join me in paying tribute to Martha Comer, a new inductee into the Kentucky Journalism Hall of Fame. I am positive that Mrs. Comer will continue to display the great qualities in which she has in the past. I know that her community appreciates her involvement and dedication.●

47

b. 1915

Helen Crabtree

Two out of every three girls probably go through a horse or ballet idolatry. Librarians place books in their hands about a black stallion, relatives give them horse stationery or scarves, they may even dream about winning the Kentucky State Fair Horse Show. This was especially true for Kentucky girls growing up in the 50s and 60s when Helen Crabtree swept them off their feet and taught them everything they wanted to know about American Saddlebred horses.

As a child growing up on a farm in Illinois, Helen Crabtree was a self-taught rider. The smallest person in the class, she won her first riding show in 1919. Even at age four she had a sense of aesthetics, for she still remembers that she was wearing a pink organdy dress on a beautiful black pony. But she doesn't know where her *compulsion* came from. She does

remember that when she brought in the milk cows on Jack, the family's old farm mule, she'd make him carry his head high. No one taught her that either; she just wanted her mule to look wonderful.

Crabtree carried this love of riding to Illinois College, where she convinced the administration to offer riding classes for physical education credit. In 1939 she graduated and headed to MacMurray College where she coached undefeated riding teams. She learned as she taught, not from books but from combining intuition about style with trial and error.

Helen and Charles Crabtree moved to Louisville so that he could manage Rock Creek Riding Club. After four years they bought 32 acres in Simpsonville and started training American Saddlebred horses and teaching equitation riding. Crabtree Farm eventually grew to 200 acres with

five separate operations and over 100 horses in training, at one time the largest stable in the world of American Saddlebreds. "We were the first to come to Shelby County, and now it is the saddle horse capital of the world," said Crabtree proudly.

To house the girls who came to Crabtree Farm to train, the Crabtrees built a sixteen-bed dormitory above the garage and soon students were coming to Kentucky from all over the country to spend summers becoming "Crabtree Girls."

Crabtree's trademark as a riding instructor was a psychologist's understanding of both horse and rider. "I am interested in your child as a person," she told parents. "How they ride, that's secondary." Quick to praise but also a perfectionist, she challenged her young charges to become the best riders without losing sight of the inherent fun.

Another Crabtree signature was the uncanny ability to match horse and rider, which inevitably resulted in a winning combination. Still another was taking a look at the way judges scored equitation competition and figuring out how to make her girls stand out. Early on she made sure they rode better quality horses than other riders and the horses always wore red brow bands to let judges identify her riders.

What Crabtree really accomplished was to change the way equitation riders *look* forever. She altered the style of the riding habit, adding color to the basic black as well as opening up the front of the riding jackets and lengthening the sleeves. With an eye for detail, she tailored each habit individually so that it would be the aesthetic compliment to *both* horse and rider. One of her Grand Champion protégées, Lynn Girdler Kelley, had Titian red hair and Crabtree designed a handsome rust-colored habit to match. No one had ever seen such stylish ensembles in the Saddlebred industry, but soon other trainers followed suit and copied everything she did! She adds with a twinkle, "My girls always looked like diamonds in a coal bin."

When she realized that every rider had a different conformation, she invented adjustable stirrups and the result was The Crabtree Saddle. "Too bad I didn't patent that idea," she laments.

And the judges rewarded her hard work, ingenuity and creativity. "Once at a show in Illinois, there were twelve riders left in the ring for the Grand Championship. Four were eliminated and the eight left were all Crabtree Girls," she remembers proudly. Mary Ann O'Callaghan Cronan's family bought her a 5-gaited pony and her father wrote on the check: "for everlasting joy." It paid off. At age 14 she was another Crabtree Grand Champion.

Helen Crabtree was the first woman trainer of American Saddlebreds winning against men in the ring. "I invaded a territory," she said. "I kept my eyes open, my mouth shut, and went in the ring and beat the heck out of them." In 1965, she was voted "Horsewoman of the Year" by the American Horse Shows Association, and in 1978 she was the first woman to be named "Trainer of the Year." She was awarded an honorary doctorate along the way and invited to bring sixteen American Saddlebreds and riders to participate

in a presidential inaugural parade. In 1989, she was inducted into the Kentucky State Fair Saddle Horse Hall of Fame.

She has given clinics from Alaska to England to South Africa; written authoritative books on saddle seat equitation and an autobiography. At the age of 82 she still writes a monthly column for *Saddle and Bridle Magazine*, and she awaits release of her next book. If all of this makes you dizzy, you might assume Helen Crabtree welcomed retirement with open arms. Not so.

One may think that being a horse trainer is the hardest job in the world. No doubt about it, it is tough, but not being a horse trainer is even more difficult. That lonely Maytag repairman with his sad-eyed Bassett hound has nothing on a horseless retired trainer. Retiring is for the birds.[1]

And so she's back in the trainer's seat and everyone who was ever a "Crabtree Girl" knows why—because she's the very best.

The Courier-Journal

49

Joan Dance

The bold look of Dance! Sounds like an advertisement for a ballet company, but Joan Dance is a primitive painter. She epitomizes the famous quote from Pablo Picasso:

Once I drew like Raphael, but it has taken a whole lifetime to learn to draw like a child.

Basic shapes, balanced delight, expressive colors—all rolled into an innate ability that Joan Dance controls by telling stories on canvas. Her visual reminiscences of wash boards and non-electric irons are seen by some as politically incorrect, but she says she is making historical statements that should not be lost on future generations.

It is an art form born of a desire to speak through painting. Dance may be filling a hole in the psyche that some of her friends and her husband try to forget. Not Dance— *"One's identity cannot be overlooked,"* she said. This artist feels an urgency to go back and lift up African American history and put it into her compositions.

"Neighborhood Watch 'Old' Style" is the result of Dance's special concern for children, particularly African Americans, who are growing up today. "I regret the lack of support among neighbors who used to take collective responsibility for the safety, good behavior, and care of each other's children." She wants neighborhoods to live out the African adage, "It takes a village to raise a child."

Painting with watercolors, markers, and acrylics Joan Dance has developed a pared-down style that is sophisticated, developed with an intuitive eye over a schooled eye. She draws with Shaker simplicity of line but not of color or content. Bold primary colors explode across the canvas. Subjects that appear to be familiar scenes of jump rope or hopscotch are actually windows on the subtle relationships between children as they play those games. Joan Dance is telling viewers that "play" is an important learning experience for child development.

One's identity cannot be overlooked— Joan Dance is a religious woman whose church is a large slice of her life. A sense of God's presence gives her grace that shields her from the typical feelings of too many artists: isolated, undervalued, and unable to survive on art work alone. Being black and female in a community that is only 6% African American compounds the lack of ability to *feed* herself and her work, literally and figuratively.

Joan Dance grew up in Paducah within a few blocks of her present house—*one's identity cannot be overlooked.* "Spring Cleaning," "The Old Clothes Line," "Two Women and a Quilt," are straight out of her memory's neighborhood scrapbook. Work, in household and garden, is especially significant. She is reminding us that many occupations have been traditionally earmarked as male or female. When women are the topic, Joan Dance paints with her trademark wry humor and warmth—the relationship between mother and daughter; the unadulterated joy between women having as much fun as the women in *Waiting to Exhale*; hats galore in "Easter Sunday" evoke memories of an era when women did not enter churches without a festive wide brim atop their heads.

An outspoken artist on canvas and in real life, Joan Dance minces no words as she describes the flowering of her art. Painting came late to her but when the strong urge hit three years ago, she began painting neighbor-

"Three Women of Color"

hood churches on cloth. "I thought if I didn't paint, I would die." But she wonders if her community takes her art seriously. "People still think of me as doing *nothing*—and that's hard." Being a new female artist "at my age" (people think she should be retired), and espe-

cially since she "works from the home, people don't see that as working." When people ask Dance what she is doing, she does not tell them she's an artist. "I'm somebody's wife or mother or I'm a member of Clay Street Church and so I leave it up to the people to decide

whether I'm an artist or not."

Joan Dance's social commentaries are pictures out of the African American cultural history books—*One's identity cannot be overlooked.*

Mary Desha

DAR Magazine

On April 30, 1890, at the first Congress of the Sons of the American Revolution, held at the Galt House in Louisville, Kentucky, the members voted to exclude women from their ranks. The move drew criticism from one woman named Mary S. Lockwood. She wrote a strong Letter to the Editor, published in *The Washington Post* asking, "Were there no mothers in the Revolution; no dames as well as sires whose memories should be commemorated?"[1]

Lockwood's query inspired another woman to speak out. "I come from good old fighting stock," she wrote Lockwood in response, "and it made my blood boil when I read the report of the convention's action."[2] That woman's name was Mary Desha, and within six months Desha, Mrs. Lockwood, and two other women founded the Daughters of the American Revolution (DAR). By 1973, there were 3,000 chapters and approximately 196,000 members in the DAR. Any discussion of the daughters joining the sons had long since been put to rest.

Mary Desha gave twenty years of service to the society she called her child. So devoted was she to the cause of patriotism and the DAR, that she would undoubtedly be heartsick were she to hear its well-known claim to infamy. In 1939, the DAR prevented Marian Anderson, the famous contralto, from performing in Constitution Hall in Washington, D.C., because she was black.

But that was not the DAR Mary Desha knew or wanted to build. The organization was created to honor the men and women of the American Revolutionary period through the collection of historical artifacts and records.

These were eminent American women like the kind of women to whom Desha was related. History shows that her paternal great-grandmother, Katherine Montgomery Bledsoe, "on one occasion, during the Revolutionary War, carried important dispatches through the British lines to the patriot army."[3]

Mary Desha was born in Lexington in 1851 to a doctor and his wife. The Deshas lived a comfortable life, but the

Civil War cost Dr. Desha his fortune. The War also sent young Mary from her Kentucky home for two years. She, her siblings, and her mother were forced out of Lexington due to her father's Confederate leanings.

The Civil War changed Mary Desha's life. Among other things, she had to work. She began teaching, but in 1885, she moved to Washington, D.C., to take a government position. Three years later, at the age of 38, she accepted an assignment to teach in Alaska. As one of the first American women teachers there, Desha's year in Alaska proved enlightening. She was appalled by the condition of the Native Indian groups and the prejudice against them. Upon her return she felt compelled to make a report to the government and a federal investigation of the territory's schools followed.

It was typical of Mary Desha to take action to change things in Alaska after her experiences there. A revolutionary at heart, she was passionate and believed anything right and just was worth fighting for. She was not the type of person to alter her beliefs for the comfort of friends. "She never permitted friendship...to blind her to the faults of others or to make her bow her head in obedience to the judgment of others, did not her own judgment coincide."[4] Although she may have made enemies, it was this very intractability that made her great, and all who knew her well understood that.

Mary Desha was a woman who had the courage of her convictions. When she

died on January 29, 1911, mid-stride on her walk home from work, Desha's beloved DAR closed its offices for an entire day. The flag on Memorial Continental Hall was ordered placed at half-mast, and she was honored with the first memorial service ever to be held in the Hall. A train took her body to Lexington where she is buried.

Desha's obituary in the official DAR publication summarized it perfectly: "Rarely has a woman been so honored by women."[5]

(Above) Diamond and sapphire-studded Founders Medal awarded to Mary Desha.
Courtesy *DAR Magazine*

(Below) Langham Hotel, Washington, D.C., site of meeting where DAR was founded in 1890.

Julia Dinsmore

By Hannah Hume Baird

Julia Dinsmore was a child of nine when her family moved up the Mississippi and Ohio Rivers from Terrebonne Parrish, Louisiana, to their new home in the Belleview Bottoms section of Boone County. She was the middle of three daughters of James and Martha Dinsmore.

Her sister, Isabella, married a first cousin and died shortly after the birth of their second child, and the father sent these children to the farm in Kentucky to be raised by their Aunt Julia. Julia's younger sister was drowned in a boating accident. Thus, by the time her father died in 1872, Julia Dinsmore had lost all of her immediate family and was left with two nieces to raise and a mediocre farm to manage. The work was rough and hired help often tried to cheat her. She was discouraged often in those early years alone. Her journal of 54 years revealed her various moods.

Sept. 23, 1873
Came home more discouraged than usual and rode along in the dark and mud crying.

December 31, 1873
I have been so bothered and felt so discouraged to-day that I have been right unhappy. God grant me a happier year this next.

January 21, 1875
...I drudge and worry to no avail, lose money and temper and hope. I feel so unlike a lady in my externals that I have no doubt I shall be less of a lady in reality...never having one day of leisure or pleasure in which I can be my own old self again. Lord send me a fool who wants to pay a good price for this place.

Time proved to be a healing agent and Julia settled in to raise her nieces and see that they received an education as good as Julia and her two sisters had enjoyed. She became accustomed to farm work. Her diary of 1879 recorded the rhythm of her days:

January 4
(14 below zero @ 8 a.m.) Tom tried to haul wood but broke an iron on the sled. Went to Bellvue for mail. River is frozen over.

Jan. 21
I spent most of the day in a crusade against mice.

February 24th
Found two new lambs and one old ewe down to die apparently...tried to count the lambs - made out 85 in all...

Feb. 27
Found one dead lamb in the pen and one we had in the kitchen. Charlie and Tom both worked, put rings in the hogs and pigs noses. Hauled a load of barrels to the wine house...

May 23

...I put fire in 2 stumps...Killed copperhead on my way home to dinner...

June 29

Went to Rising Sun to see Uncle Jillison (a former family slave) - found him dying and he died while I sat by him. Poor old man-I wish him a blessed rest. Got Mr. Whitlock to go and attend to him-bought clothes, ordered coffin, etc. and came home.

June 30

Twelve years to-day since sister Belle (Isabella) closed her eyes on this world. - 'Love's not Time's fool' Thank God...Tom Nettles took a spring wagon down to the ferry to meet Uncle Jillison's coffin in the hearse and to bring it out home.

December 28

One of 7 little pigs dead. Went to church in evening. (Another time Julia writes that she was late getting to church - got there at Putting-on-Hat-Time.)

As the girls grew up and married, Julia Dinsmore maintained the farm as home, as a haven for rest, for childbirth, and for sickness and dying. All the time she recorded her day book and kept up a lively correspondence. In her leisure after age fifty, Julia Dinsmore began to write poetry, and her *Verses and Sonnets* was published by Doubleday in New York City in 1910. In 1926 she suffered a fall that eventually led to her death. She is buried in the family graveyard at Dinsmore Farm.

MAMMOTH CAVE

SILENT, reverberant, like some vast shell
  Its unknown occupant at last outgrows,
Lies the dark labyrinth. No longer flows
The rushing river whose obstructed swell
Clove these wild ways, and dashed along pell-
These rugged rocks, and in its mighty throes
Burst these wide caverns, and in domes arose -
Then, desperate, down these black abysses fell
All vanished, - save the still, small secret stre
Amid whose gloom the prisoned echoes fly -
And in its empty course we glide today,
Glancing like fireflies with the lanterns' gleam
Strange visitants, to vanish by and by,
As the lost, nameless river passed away.

(Previous page) The Dinsmore Homestead.

(Top, this page) Pages from her journal.

(Above right) Dinsmore and another generation.

(Right) Dinsmore and her two nieces.

Alice Allison Dunnigan

By A. G. Dunstan

In too many cases and too many instances, the stories which Alice Allison Dunnigan reported while she served with the Associated Negro Press were the only newspaper accounts both of injustices against the African American population and of progress made in civil rights by the same population in the twentieth century. Her job, her life's work, was to tell the true story of the ex-slave population as this group struggled to gain equality in the midst of racism and injustice.

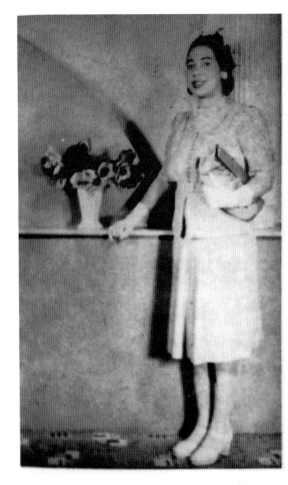

Born in Russellville in 1906 to poor and unlettered parents, Dunnigan began writing one-sentence items for the *Owensboro Enterprise* at the age of thirteen. After she completed the teaching course at what is now Kentucky State University, Dunnigan taught Kentucky History in the segregated Todd County School System. When she noticed that her students were not aware of the contributions of African Americans to the health and welfare of the Commonwealth, Dunnigan prepared "Kentucky Fact Sheets," which she gave to students as supplements to the required text. By 1939, these articles had been collected into manuscript form but no publisher was found until 1982 when *The Fascinating Story of Black Kentuckians: Their Heritage and Tradition* was published by the Associated Publishers, Inc.

After moving to Washington, D.C., during World War II, Dunnigan worked as a clerk typist for the War Labor Board, as an economist for the Office of Price Administration and as a part-time reporter for the Associated Negro Press. In 1947 she became chief of the Washington Bureau. She also became the first African American female correspondent to receive White House credentials. By 1951 her reputation in newspaper circles and across the country was solidly built on her "no-holds barred" way of reporting both the progress being made in civil rights as well as the instances in which corporations, individuals, and organizations demonstrated their racist ideology.

Probably no other Black female journalist broke so much ground for those who followed, and it was just such a celebration when she was recognized by President John F. Kennedy at his first press conference. It is a jolting commentary on the reality of race relations in 1961, but it hit the pages of every major newspaper. This is the way *Jet* magazine described the event:

For his first nationally televised press conference in Washington, President John F. Kennedy quietly scrapped a long standing White House policy. It was: to ignore veteran correspondent Alice Dunnigan at press conferences. For two years, grandmother Dunnigan bobbed up and down at press conferences to get the eye of ex-President Eisenhower. She was skipped, passed over, and ignored...Cause of the obvious slight was a question Mrs. Dunnigan asked Ike regarding a reported "retiring" of Negro Assistant Labor Secretary J. Ernest Wilkins. The ex-President reddened, denied such action, but two weeks later Wilkins was "out" of the job. Earlier, the ex-teacher and native of Russellville, Ky., got in Ike's hair twice on civil rights matters—revitalizing the Contract Compliance Committee and ending of segregation at schools on military bases. Following Mrs. Dunnigan's pinpointing of the conditions, the administration took action.

Alice Dunnigan comes to Washington in 1942.

> *Her job, her life's work, was to tell the true story of the ex-slave population as this group struggled to gain equality in the midst of racism and injustice.*

In her autobiography, *Alice A. Dunnigan: A Black Woman's Experience*, she recounts some of the many indignities she suffered while traveling on behalf of President John F. Kennedy's Committee on Equal Employment Opportunity. On one such occasion she was in Frankfort, Kentucky, in 1963 and was tossed from one hotel to the next trying to obtain a room. Even when she confronted the room clerk with the obvious racial discrimination, she was told "No vacancies," so she spent the night sitting up in the bus station. Perhaps because she never gave up and never lost her sense of humor was she able to describe a reception at the Russian Embassy in 1959. Dressed in a gold dress as fancy as any other female guest, her taxi driver still assumed she was a servant and warned her not to let anything happen to the food for Khrushchev. Standing outside the Embassy, one of the local society page writers assumed that a Black woman appropriately dressed was obviously the wife of a diplomat! "Nobody," she writes, "seemed to think that a Black woman could attend a white diplomat affair as just an ordinary guest." [2]

Alice Allison Dunnigan received over fifty national and international awards for news reporting, including an honorary doctorate degree from a Colorado college. Nationally and internationally she was a pacesetter for Black female news reporters as she chronicled the progress, or lack, of American civil rights. But back home in Kentucky she will always be remembered for her documentary series during the 1930s, "The Achievements of the Kentucky Negro," which became a book, *Fascinating Story of Black Kentuckians: Their Heritage and Traditions.*

(Top) Graduation day.

(Right) Dunnigan's assorted press passes.

Mary Edith Engle

by Barbara Ward

If Mary Edith Engle had never developed a talent for standing on her tiptoes, this story would read quite differently. For if not for trying to make herself appear an inch taller, Engle would not have become an airplane pilot.

Engle, who grew up in Jackson but has spent most of her eighty years in Lexington, served in the World War II Women Airforce Service Pilots, or WASPS, a program in which women flew military planes, often new (and untested) from the factories, all over the United States, to bases where men could train with them. "We wanted to help. I felt really good about it. I was having a great time," she said.

Engle and her husband, William "Billy Bob" Engle, already were accomplished pilots by the time war broke out in 1941. Soon after Pearl Harbor, Billy Bob volunteered for service, and it seemed natural to Mary Edith to volunteer as well. With her flying experience, she was quickly accepted into the newly formed female pilot's group, except she nearly flunked the physical, since the minimum height was 5 foot 2 and she was an inch shorter. After practicing balancing on the balls of her feet, she squeaked by.

The rest, as they say, is history. From 1942 to 1944, about 1,073 WASPS logged sixty million air miles, flying new planes and war-battered aircraft, a perilous task that took the lives of 38 of the women. Not having military status, they paid for their own transportation and housing during training. In 1943, Mary Edith Engle graduated from training in Texas and spent more than a year flying planes all over the United States and Canada. She flew anything from tiny cub fighters to the B-29 bomber, at that time the biggest plane in the war effort. "I didn't care which one it was, just let me go," she said.

In a letter to her mother in 1943, she wrote:

I'm at 10,000 feet between Cheyenne, Wyoming, and Great Falls, Montana. I'm on top of a layer of clouds and with the sun shining on top of them and the sky so blue over me, it makes a very specially pretty world.

It never really occurred to Engle that what she was doing was all that extraordinary for a woman in the 1940s. "I didn't bother about what everyone else was doing. I was just having a great time."

Indeed, conventional thinking seemed a waste. When she entered the University of Kentucky, Engle at first planned to become a doctor like her father, not a nurse like her mother. Mary Edith Engle went on to get a master's degree in psychology from the University of Kentucky and also did work toward a doctorate.

After the war, when the couple settled in Lexington, Mary Edith stayed busy rearing three daughters. But that wasn't all. She served in numerous organizations, took up painting, raced and trained saddlebred horses at The Red Mile and stayed active in Lexington aviation groups.

"It was neat growing up with the attitude in the house—she was very forward thinking about how women can do anything," said the youngest daughter, Robin Gornto.

The couple traveled around the world in the 1960s and came home with the idea of buying a Chinese junk, a round-bottomed, high-stearned sailing vessel once common to the Far East. After the junk was carried from Hong Kong to New Orleans on a freighter, the whole family spent the summer sailing it up the Mississippi and Ohio Rivers. "We're crazy—anything that's different," Mary Edith Engle said.

Mary Edith Engle was among a group of WASPS who went to Washington in the 1970s to lobby for some overdue respect. Despite being such an integral

part of the U.S. war effort, WASPS never had military status or benefits and were not considered veterans until 1979.

In 1997, Engle was one of five aviators inducted into a charter enshrinement of the Kentucky Aviation Hall of Fame. She looks back on it all now and smiles: "We've had a great life...I don't think I'd do anything different."

"My mother to me was just my mother, not anything special," said daughter Mary Gail Engle. "It wasn't until I was an adult I realized not everyone's mother did these things."

WASP
"Songbook"

WAR DEPARTMENT
HEADQUARTERS OF THE ARMY AIR FO
WASHINGTON

Miss Mary Edith B. Engle
210 Catalpa Road
Lexington, Kentucky

Dear Miss Engle;

It is a pleasure to send you with this
tificate of Honorable Service and Servi
you as a member of the WASP.

May I take this opportunity to thank yo
contribution you have made to the WASP
the Army Air Forces, and to the war eff
sidered it a great privilege to be asso
fine group of girls, and an honor to ha
the WASP.

Hearty good wishes to you for the futur

Sincerely,

JAC QUELINE

2 Incls
otf
pin

INDIVIDUAL FLIGHT RECORD

(2)NAME ENGLE, Mary E. (3)RANK W.A.S.P. (4)AGE 1916
(6)BRANCH Army Air Forces (7)STATION Love Field, Dallas, Tex
ATC 5th 601st
(11)ORIGINAL RATING & DATE
(13)FLIGHT RESTRICTIONS None
(14)TRANSFER DATE

(17)MONTH October 1943

1:45
3:20
:50
1:50
2:05
1:55
1:50
1:15
1:10
1:30
3:25
2:10

CERTIFIED CORRECT
RICHARD C. SHULTZ
2nd Lt., Air Corps
Ass't Oper. Officer.

COLUMN TOTALS 22 1:30 28:05

	(42) TOTAL STUDENT PILOT TIME	(43) TOTAL FIRST PILOT TIME	(44) TOTAL PILOT TIME
(37) THIS MONTH	28:05		29:35
(38) PREVIOUS MONTHS THIS F.Y.	50:15	16:15	71:20
(39) THIS FISCAL YEAR	50:15	44:20	100:55
(40) PREVIOUS FISCAL YEARS	120:05		120:05
(41) TO DATE	170:20	44:20	221:00

Janey Fair

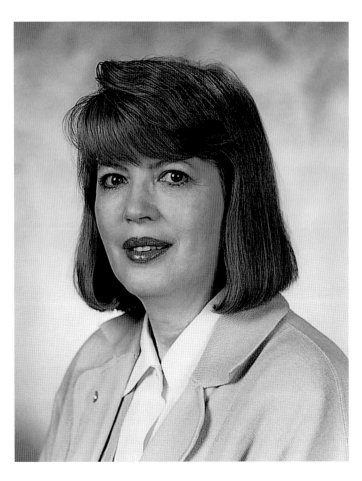

A dazzling collection of crystals, geodes and fossils greets the visitor to Janey Fair's home in Radcliffe, Kentucky. The many-faceted crystals catch the colors as sunlight plays through each prism. It is an unexpected sight that is a reminder of the world of nature. Nature had little to do with the tragedy that struck Janey Fair and her family in 1988 but, as with her crystals, she has turned her life over in many directions until she found a different way of looking at it.

Most Kentuckians remember the tragic bus crash in Carrollton, but not like Janey Fair. Her 14-year-old daughter, Shannon, was killed that night and her death changed the lives of her family forever. The First Assemblies of God Church bus left Radcliffe the morning of May 14,1988,

Shannon Fair 1974-1988

filled with 67 persons going on a fun-filled day to King's Island, an amusement park near Cincinnati. After a drunk driver hit the bus that night, 24 children and 3 adults had been killed and many others seriously injured.

When midnight came and Shannon still wasn't home, Janey Fair was pacing the floor when the telephone rang and she was asked to come to the church. She knew the news was not good when she saw satellite media trucks in the church parking lot. It was mid-morning before accurate information reached the anxious families. Half the victims had military connections and when the General was informed, he stepped into the chaos to bring a semblance of order to his families in need. The commanding officer arranged for dental records to be flown to Carrollton and for three vans to transport the numb military families there. Shannon Fair was the last person identified and her family took her home to East Tennessee to be buried. The next Saturday there was a memorial service at the North Hardin High School for 6,000 persons to pay their respects .

Shannon was the child who "had it all together. She was very mature for her age. Very intelligent...in the gifted and talented class—all A's in school. She played the saxophone and had just won second chair in the District Competition. She didn't want to play a girls' instrument—very much a feminist and independent. Exciting for me," Janey Fair explained, "because I always wanted her to be a feminist, but sometimes kids don't do what we want them to do."

Janey Fair was born and raised on a small farm in Johnson City, Tennessee. Her father was a long distance truck driver and her mother ran the farm with her grandfather. Her grandfather was also a Latin and math professor so education was an expectation. After high school Janey attended business school in Florida and went to work for a county attorney. Little did she know that the legal knowledge she gained there eventually would earn her the respect of Kentucky legislators and enhance her abilities as a victims issues advocate.

Janey's marriage to a hometown career Army man kept her on the move for 20 years. Although she did not join her husband on his tour of duty in Korea, she moved with him four more times. In 1981 when they were assigned to Ft. Knox, Kentucky, she was determined that the family would identify with the community of Radcliffe, not the military base. She wanted their children, Shannon at age seven and Donald at age ten, to experience the "real world—not a post where everyone is within a 20-year age span and everybody is able-bodied,"

SITE OF FATAL
BUS CRASH
MAY 14, 1988

(Left) This sign was installed beside the north-bound lanes of Interstate 71.

(Below) Memorial Garden in Radcliffe.

said Janey Fair. They bought a house in town, and the family became participants in Radcliffe's activities, organizations and church as if they had lived there for generations.

In the aftermath of Shannon's death, Janey Fair was thrown into the spotlight because she was an articulate spokesperson and because she could interpret the legal jargon that it would take to change Kentucky's drunk driving laws and increase its bus safety. One organization Janey had little to do with until 1988 was the fledgling Hardin County chapter of Mother Against Drunk Driving. "It was a way of coping," she remembers, "but it was also a way not to forget the kids. It was the best memorial I could make."

The national office of MADD sent its first crisis-intervention team to work with the families of the crash victims in Radcliffe and the police and rescue personnel in Carrollton. Janey Fair liked what they provided and what they stood for, especially in the field of advocacy for victims.

Today, thanks to the dedication of women like Janey Fair, Kentucky's buses are among the safest in the nation though the state's laws on drunk driving need further revision. The defense bar finds new ways to fight drunk driving charges, judges sometimes ignore existing law and it is tough to win victories in a legislature so vigorously wooed by Kentucky's liquor industry. Janey Fair's course is

slowed down neither by these realities nor the accusation that women involved with the crash are "reactionary and hysterical."

No one would ever describe Janey Fair as "hysterical." She is thoughtful and careful, always thinking before she speaks. She is so altogether that you know exactly where her beloved daughter, Shannon, inherited her own mature responses at age fourteen. Among the fossils in Janey Fair's collection is a bit of amber which holds the remains of a creature trapped inside eons ago. Like that creature, Janey Fair might have been immobilized from the telephone call every parent dreads. Instead, her life has become a tribute to her daughter as she dedicates her time, talents, and energy to changing Kentucky and the nation so that tragedies like the one that killed 27 innocent people in 1988 cannot recur.

LET ALL WHO VIEW THIS MONUMENT COUNT OUR DEAD AND KNOW THE TERRIBLE LEGACY OF DRUNKEN DRIVING.

THIS MONUMENT IS A GIFT FROM THE MEN AND WOMEN OF THE COURIER JOURNAL IN MEMORY OF THOSE KILLED ON MAY 14, 1988 IN THE NATION'S WORST DRUNK DRIVING CRASH.

Sharon Fields

"I ate humble pie," said Sharon Fields, as she talked about breaking her thumb last year. "It taught me patience, humility, and to depend upon other people." She couldn't tie her shoes or cut up her food, but the experience gave her insight into the everyday life of disabled citizens. It is typical of the former director of the Leadership and Cultural Diversity Center at Midway College to take a personal hardship and turn it into a learning experience that would enable her to help other people. She finds that people of today are "tolerant of diversity but not embracing diversity." One of her goals is to teach young people how to get along with one another. Fields wants young people to appreciate that all people don't think like they do *or* even like their parents think. "Each small step changes attitudes," she said, "and widens the circle of exposure to include people not 'like me.'"

Midway College is the only women's college in Kentucky, and although night classes are now attended by men, it is still a supportive environment for female students, allowing them to focus on learning in small classes without having to compete with men. Fields says that schools and churches have important roles to play in bringing about gender equity and opportunities for women. Many Midway students are the first generation to go to college, and though some families are proud, others fear their daughters or girlfriends might come to think of themselves as "better than the rest of the family." Most Midway College students have never been outside Kentucky and are unfamiliar with people from other parts of the world. It has only been in the last thirty years that African American women could be Midway students.

Before coming to Midway College, Fields taught in the Paris County school system and served on the Paris City Commission. While studying for her Master's degree in Public Affairs from Kentucky State University, she learned how each level of government influences the other. She was the first black female ever elected to the Commission, and she remembers that the elected officials did not always agree with one another, but they respected each other's opinions and skills.

Her family has not always been supportive of Fields' political involvement, but only "because parents want to protect their children from antagonism." Her father, Robert Fields, worked as a horse groom for Spendthrift Farms. Her mother, Meliva Fields, has been the biggest influence on her life. As the nurturer of two children, she always did day work and whatever other jobs could add to the family income. Sharon Fields recognizes that it was stifling for her mother to be born during her era because although she graduated at the top of her high school class, there was no money to send her to college. When Sharon Fields was growing up, her mother was an active church woman and Fields came to realize that without black women there would be no black church. Black churches have "served as places of fellowship and places where black people could experience leadership and develop their talents. By day you might be a janitor in a local bank, but on Sundays you were a deacon in church with a powerful, influential voice," she said. "A housekeeper with the lowest paying job in the county would be a respected Sunday School teacher on Sunday mornings."

Sharon Fields is currently a Disciples of Christ minister at Second Christian Church in Midway. When she first got "the call" she was not sure what it meant, but she decided to pursue her intuition. She gave up her secure job with the Paris schools and attended Lexington Theological Seminary. Her classes were filled with people seeking second careers—

lawyers, doctors, engineers—"an energizing group," she said. She was forty years old at the time and her standard of living plummeted, but "I was never hungry," she said wryly. Fields became a full-time pastor on July 1, 1997, and is one of three or four female Disciples of Christ pastors in the state. She remains affiliated with the Midway College teacher preparation program.

Since Midway is a retirement community, her congregation is an older population. After World War II most African Americans left the area and went to bigger cities up north to seek better employment opportunities. "There are no black people coming in for me to evangelize," she observed.

Amigos Ministry in Woodford County has opened up new involvement for Sharon Fields and her congregation. Every year, ten to twenty thousand Hispanic migrant farm workers arrive in the surrounding three counties and stay to pick crops from spring until fall. Fields wants her congregation to become active in this ministry because she sees it as "an opportunity to help widen the circle of our communities, our schools and colleges, our churches, our children, and our friends."

Sharon Fields has been a proven teacher and politician with a commitment to making Kentucky a better place to live and work. Today she widens her own circle and speaks out from the pulpit in an effort to better the lives of all those around her.

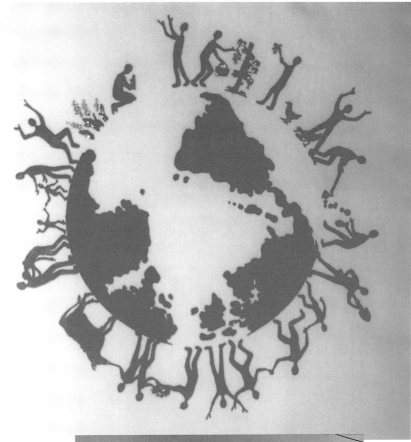

"Each small step changes attitudes," she said, " and widens the circle of exposure to include people not 'like me.'"

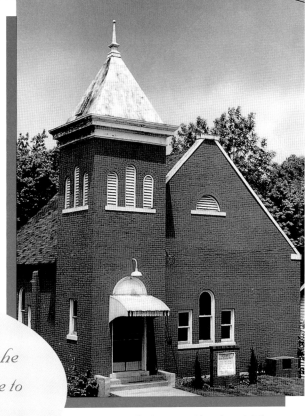

Second Christian Church in Midway.

Mary Elliott Flanery

the Ashland *Daily Independent* and also contributed to various newspapers throughout Kentucky and neighboring states, using her columns to advocate social causes.

Flanery was friends with suffragist Madeline McDowell Breckinridge and as a

CHRISTMAS GREETINGS

Mr. and Mrs. William Harvey Flanery
Catlettsburg, Ky.

I can hold my own with the boys when I get to Frankfort," said Mary Elliott Flanery in 1921, when she became the first woman to be elected to the Kentucky Legislature.[1] Flanery entered the race as a Democratic candidate in the Republican district of Boyd County on the heels of the 1920 ratification of the Nineteenth Amendment, which extended to women the right to vote. She managed to oust the Republican incumbent because she appealed to the things the "good people back home needed: hard roads and plenty of them, good schools and more of them, and a real Eastern Normal School."[2] Flanery followed in the footsteps of her grandfather, who served as state senator for two terms.

Mary Elliott Flanery was born in 1867, in a part of Carter County that would eventually become Elliott County. After attending college in West Virginia, she graduated from the University of Kentucky and then began teaching in Elliott and Carter counties. From 1904 to 1926, she worked as a journalist for

member of the Kentucky Equal Rights Association, she worked diligently for women's suffrage and educational reform. She especially wanted to promote higher standards of living for women and children, and she was concerned with Kentucky's marriage and divorce laws. While in office she introduced the bill that created Morehead State Teachers College and sponsored the Sheperd-Towner Maternity Act. A year after her election, she was named Kentucky's Most Prominent Woman by the Kentucky Historical Society, and in 1924, she was elected a delegate to the Democratic National Convention. She was asked to be the first person ever to announce a roll call over the radio.

In addition to her busy career as a journalist and state representative,

Flanery also took care of a large family: four daughters, one of whom died in childhood, and a son. The following excerpts are taken from letters written to her children. They combine commonplace motherly concerns with words of love, encouragement, and affirmation, and they answer the question headlining a *Huntington Herald Dispatch* article on November 20, 1921:

"Can women be real mothers as well as good delegates?"

To a daughter, Nov. 20, 1914
Your card announcing your grades...I am satisfied...I am still betting on you for the future...am expecting you to be head and shoulders above anything in all this country when you get through. It may reduce my 'worldly possessions,' but you will be rich in intellectual exploits and founded well in character...Don't neglect your gym work...You must have a strong body—health, to have a strong & active mind.

To her daughter, Dawn, Nov. 20, 1924
Am in the midst of the greatest convention ever held...I was the first alternate Gov. Fields appointed this morning...I sent you a box of Smith Candy that was given me at New York Woman's Club breakfast...Am having time of my life. They almost have riots. It is great.

To her son, Elliott, undated
...I miss you so and can't get used to your being gone. Send your clothes home to be washed...if I were you whatever I joined I would use my violin, for think of the several years you took lessons...it is the favorite of all instruments...Do you know where your green bordered sweater is? Love from Mamma

A picture of Flanery and her son, Elliott, as a State House page made newspapers around the country for, although there

"Elliott Hall" residence of the W. H. Flannery family Cattlettsburg, Kentucky.

had been plenty of father-son teams, there had never before been a mother-son team.

After Flanery's death in 1933, a permanent bronze marker was place at her "No. 40" seat to memorialize her service and distinction in the Kentucky General Assembly. Mary Elliott Flanery was revered by Kentucky friends, suffragists, and Democratic party members alike as a pioneer in public service. She in turn loved the state whose interest she worked so diligently to represent. "In all the world it would be impossible to find anything more beautiful than our own Kentucky in its spring garb," she wrote, "when the hills and valleys are purpled with violets and yellowed by dandelions."[3]

VOTE FOR

Mary Elliott Flanery

Election, Tuesday, November 8th, 1921

Election, Tuesday, November 8th, 1921

Democratic candidate for

REPRESENTATIVE

OF THE 89th LEGISLATIVE DISTRICT

Your support will be highly appreciated

(Above) One of Flannery's campaign posters. (Left) Telegram giving her daughter the victorious news.
All photographs courtesy of the University of Kentucky Library.

Elizabeth Beatrice Cooke Fouse

By Jennifer L. Pettit

One of Lexington's most prominent social activists, Elizabeth "Lizzie" B. Fouse, worked within local and national networks of club women to expand the opportunities of black Americans and to promote racial equality. Many details of her life would remain a mystery to her admirers if not for two account books she and her husband, Professor William H. Fouse, conscientiously recorded for twenty years. Between 1898 and 1918, the Fouses entered grocery lists, insurance premiums, bank deposits, tax payments, household and consumer expenditures, utility and medical bills, tithes, cultural activities, and costs for entertainment and transportation. The ledger recorded weather forecasts and natural disasters, celebrated their achievements, and remembered their contact with and loss of friends and relatives. By revealing Mrs. Fouse's contributions to the household economy, the crumbling pages and faded entries of this ledger also suggest new ways of thinking about class and racial identity, for Fouse helped manage her family's finances to overcome the barriers imposed by racial discrimination.

The ledger helps historians understand how Lizzie Fouse perceived herself as a black middle class woman. A unique window through which to view their daily activities, this important primary resource traces their evolution from hard working and socially active young adults into respected community leaders and property holders. Documenting the first ten years of their marriage, the first account book outlines their acquisition of property and household goods and lists their accounts with local merchants. In the second book, they added to these familiar entries money collected from renters and boarders. Throughout these two decades the Fouses maintained

meticulous records of their expenditures and daily activities. For example, during the fourth week of May, 1918, as the nation neared the end of World War I, the Fouses allotted:

$3.25 patriotism
4.57 table
.40 luxuries
.69 church
.42 household necessities

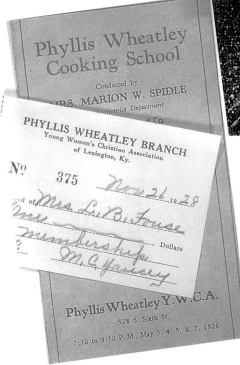

While the ledgers enable us to study the private lives of an African American couple who lived in Lexington at the turn of the century, Mrs. Fouse's civic activism or her "club work" offers a view of black female leadership in action. Although Fouse retired from salaried labor in 1903, she perceived her volunteer work as a full-time job that brought community respect and leadership opportunities rather than material rewards. Fouse and other

African American club women of this period devoted themselves to improving material and spiritual conditions in their communities.

Mrs. Fouse founded the Phyllis Wheatley branch of the Y.W.C.A., presided over the City Federation of Colored Women's Clubs, and served as an officer in several organizations that included the Acme Art and Culture Club, the Women's Improvement Club and Day Nursery, the women's auxiliary of the Emancipation League, and the Baptist Women's Educational Convention. As president of the Kentucky Federation of Colored Women she established a scholarship loan fund, a project she directed for over forty years.

Leadership in the federation led Fouse into the National Association of Colored Women (NACW). A minor officer in the NACW, she traveled across the country attending biennial conventions,

executive committee meetings, and promoting NACW objectives and programs. As the coordinator of the committee for the Mother, Home, and Child Department, Fouse established herself as an expert on child welfare issues and she coordinated the NACW's Better Homes Movement, a project dedicated to "making home a better place in which to live—better in the sense of being more commodious, more convenient, more sanitary, more beautiful."[1]

By participating in these organizations, Fouse joined her co-workers adopting the motto, "Lifting As We Climb," an ethic that guided her commitment to social reform and racial equality. In opposition to discrimination, segregation, and limited public assistance, she followed a strategy that encouraged self-help, self-sufficiency, and respectable behavior. Although it served the community, club work also allowed black women to cultivate leadership skills and to establish a base of organizational strength.

Through their civic activism, women such as Lizzie Fouse created and sustained institutions that enabled the black community not only to survive racism, but also to demand civic and political rights.

CONSOLIDATED COACH CORPORATION
INCORPORATED

GENERAL OFFICES:
LEXINGTON, KENTUCKY

October 27, 1931.

Mrs. L. B. Faust
219 North Upper,
Lexington, Kentucky.

Dear Madam:

I have your letter of October 25th, in which you enclose me your statement for damages incurred on July 7, 1931, when you were a passenger on one of our buses. I note that the damages set out amount to $52.90.

While, of course, I know that the payment of this amount would not compensate you for your embarrassment and humiliation, yet without consultation with any of the officials of the Company, I am willing to pay you this amount in settlement of your claim, and if this is agreeable with you if you will advise me I shall be very glad to forward you our company's check.

Very truly yours,

Wallace Muir
GENERAL ATTORNEY

(Above right) Meticulous records were kept in the Fouse's daily Ledger. (Center) In resisting legal segregation on a public conveyance, Lizzie Fouse challenged the driver, the police officer who forced her to move, and the lawyer who initially denied her claim. (Above left and bottom) Receipts for purchases made by the Fouses.

Laura Freeman

ALL WE ADD IS OUR NAME

As visitors turn into the driveway at Mount Folly Farm in Clark County, a striking contemporary metal sculpture is juxtaposed against the façade of Laura Freeman's traditional Kentucky farm house. The contrast seems to symbolize Freeman's refreshing new concept of raising reduced-fat beef cattle on what used to be a traditional factory farm.

Freeman represents the fourth generation of female farmers in her family and the seventh generation of family farmer, yet her unique way of raising cattle flies in the face of the traditional farming practices handed down to her. She never expected to be a farmer and has never been to agricultural school. In fact, after graduating summa cum laude with degrees in philosophy and political science from Duke University in 1978,

she worked as a journalist for four years. Thus it is not surprising that Laura Freeman brought to cattle farming a fresh perspective that looked at problems from a different end of the telescope.

"When mother inherited the farm from an aunt in the 70s, the University of Kentucky set it up like a little factory raising the calves up to a certain weight and shooting them to feedlots. We never had any contact with the customer or any control over the end product. And there was no incentive to the farmer to raise better cattle because they all went into this great maw."

The way it had always been done just didn't seem reasonable to her. "In the past it seemed *normal* to have these little calves on low-grade antibiotics and use steroids. They put bug juice on the alfalfa fields and the birds were flying over the fields and dropping dead." Well, none of that seemed *normal* to Laura Freeman. She "got the idea of raising drug-free cattle right off the bat." The story goes that she went to the doctor after giving birth to her daughter, Alice, seeking help in losing the weight she had

gained. He told her to stop eating meat, an interesting challenge for a cattle farmer. Actually, it was just the right challenge given to just the right young woman. One time she'd parachuted out of an airplane on a dare so she was always up to a good challenge.

She went to the University of Kentucky in 1984 to learn how to raise low-fat beef, and "they thought I was out of my mind." She wanted a quantitative measurement for the very leanest beef, as comparable to chicken as possible and no reprocessed animal tissue. Fortunately, one man helped her design the early product, which hasn't changed much since. Her mother, who knew that Laura needed something new to make the farm profitable, was so supportive that Freeman jokes about her mother and all her friends who kept her in business that first year. "But my grandmother is a little bit more traditional and the idea that a woman would get into this business and have her *picture* in the grocery store really mortified her, and I have yet to live it down."

At first she sold sides of beef straight off the farm from newspaper advertisements. Those were the days when she was barely sustaining the operation, but when she walked to the mailbox she could always count on there being at least one fan letter telling her that reduced-fat beef was the greatest idea anyone ever had. Those letters were from consumers and they sustained Laura Freeman through the birthing years of "Laura's Lean Beef." She knew it was a market-driven economy and she was on to something big, so she approached supermarkets. In 1986, "Laura's Lean Meats" were placed into the Kroger grocery stores but she couldn't raise enough cattle on her own farm to meet the needed volume.

Today the cattle are raised elsewhere and her products are in Kroger stores and nationally in grocery stores from Texas to New York. Freeman spends a lot of time on the road, speaking before health groups and those who advocate sustainable agriculture. She is an active board member of Mothers and Others for a Livable Planet, and she serves on the advisory board of Partners for Family Farms. In the January, 1997 issue of

Laura's Lore, her company newsletter, she writes that "some of the most important changes we can make are small ones. Buy naturally raised foods and support a way of farming that benefits the environment. Make our communities better places to live...and recycle." She adds that "if we rely on our common sense and collective wisdom we can find the solutions we need."

Laura Freeman is a Kentucky female entrepreneur whose success story comes from a combination of hard work, creative spirit and down-to-earth common sense. The contemporary sculpture planted in the front yard of her family farm reminds us that the best of tomorrow comes from using our collective wisdom to blend yesterday with today.

Three generations of female farmers.

Ruth Mae Geiger

From a river rat to the "Lady of the Lake" is a descriptive transformation that indicates only one facet of Ruth Mae Geiger's dual professional life. The name comes from the late Joe Creason, who published an article in which he called Geiger the "Lady of the Lake."[1] But getting there was down a long hard road.

Born in Munfordville, her parents died while she was still a baby and when she was six, the orphanage sent her to live with a family who needed a work hand. She lived in a two-room cabin by a brook and often caught fish that she traded for other food staples. That's how she learned to fish. The couple never allowed her to go to school because there was too much farm work for her to do. On her eighth birthday the foster couple gave her

a shotgun and told her to hunt for food and furs that could be sold for money. Because they spanked her if she missed any game, "I learned to make every bullet count."[2] Bullets were expensive and she taught herself to kill game with one shot.

At 13, she left looking for work in the city. With only a second-grade education she finally worked for a boss who encouraged her to go to night school. During the Depression hard times fell on most people and Geiger turned unusual job skills into real money makers by raising mice and rats and taming snakes for laboratory use. As sideline ventures she also made greeting cards and baked over 1,000 fruitcakes to support herself. She was young, but she was self-sufficient.

As the first licensed female commercial

fishing and hunting guide in Kentucky, she set an example for her lifelong respect for nature. She was a top-notch hunting guide and could "drop a deer, string it from a tree and field dress it before most men could get the procedure started."[3] Taking hunting parties out on her 300-acre farm was her idea of enjoying the outdoors, but she never bagged more than she could eat.

What began as a week-end and summer house by the lake eventually became a permanent address. But how does someone get from teaching kids to water ski for fun to becoming a professional fishing guide? Not intentionally! When the manager of Lake Cumberland State Park asked her to take out a group of fishermen, they came back so impressed with her prowess, that afterwards

Lines From The Lady of The Lake

June-27-68

The Louisville Times
April 14, 1960

Fishing this week was very slow in the main lake on black bass. Some were caught on deep-running lures.

WHITE BASS — caught casting the jumps, but jumps were few.

TROUT — good. Nice catches, both day and night on both sides of the dam. Some were caught casting Rooster Tails, others on worms and cheese.

I enjoy feeding the birds and squirrels. I have four gray squirrels and eight flying squirrels. The flying squirrels will eat out of my hand.

Do you know a bird has to eat most all day to live? Why not make a feed box & enjoy these little friends? Just a little sunflower seed and bird seed is all it takes, or bread scraps, and water.

If you want quail and doves, throw some of the seeds on the ground by the feeder, as these are ground feeders.

Flying squirrels feed at night.

And you farmers — did you notice in "Ruby's Column" in the Courier Journal last week were you would get adult quail for $1.25 per bird for stocking purposes? Why not get one or two pair for your farm?

he suggested that she take out a guiding license. Thus began more than 20 years of making fishing customers happy.

With a lifetime fishing license, Geiger was probably the best guide on Lake Cumberland, and always one of the most requested. Instinctively she knew where the fish were hiding— "I know where the tree tops on sloping banks are."[4] In one five-day period she caught 48 good bass. Just to properly envision women fishing before the late 60s, most ladies still wore skirts, not pants, in boats!

She remembers a somewhat unorthodox method used for catching big Ohio River catfish: "We would swim down along an overhanging bank, locate a cat and bring him to the surface by running our hands through his gills and out his mouth."[5] (Such practices are now illegal.)

With a hard scrabble beginning, Ruth Mae Geiger became almost one of a kind among women as a guide hunting in the woods and fishing on the lakes. Such a distinction made her one of a kind among women in Kentucky.

Mrs. R. H. Geiger and five bass that weighed 27 pounds 4 ounces. On the right is her 8-pounder in the middle a 7¾ and on the left 7½. A 2½ pounder is second from the right and a 1½-pounder second from left.

Mrs. Geiger Tells Secret Of Success

"The larger the minnow, the larger the bass."

That seemed to be the secret of the highly successful five days of jig-fishing Mrs. R. H. Geiger of Shepherdsville was telling me about.

"I have a summer home on Lake Cumberland near Jamestown and I've just come back from a week's stay during which I fished five days and caught 48 good bass.

"My best day was last Friday when I got my limit of 10, the string weighing in the neighborhood of 40 pounds. In it were the three biggest fish I caught all week, an 8-pounder and two that were not much smaller, 7¾ and 7½. The others were from 2¾ down to 1½.

"All told I must have caught easily 120 pounds or so. I was using large minnows, 2½ to 3 inches long, in the milky water of Beaver Creek.

"SOME TIME ago, I served in that area as a fishing guide, so I know where the tree tops on sloping banks are. That is where I found them last week in from 3½ to 4 feet of water.

The 51-year-old grandmother limited on Monday, Wednesday, Thursday and Friday, by fishing from about 9 a.m. until dark. On Saturday, she fished only half a day, but caught eight. She did not fish Tuesday.

Only one day did she have any help in sculling her boat. On Wednesday, she 'most wore out her arm, so she had a boy to handle the boat on Thursday.

The jiggers were having the most success around Jamestown while she was there, but casters were getting a few on dollflies, helldivers and Paul Bunyans, casting the coves where the clear water comes into the lake.

Most of the bass caught by casters were between 3 and 5 pounds, but one helldiver thrower had a 6-pounder.

Janice Holt Giles

By Dianne Watkins

*J*anice Meredith Holt was born around eight o'clock on the "bleak, blowing morning" of March 28th, 1905. She weighed nine pounds and ten ounces! She was named for the title of a two-volume romantic Revolutionary War novel, which her mother had been reading while waiting for her birth. Even though they had a very close relationship, mother and daughter had a clashing of wills from the day of Janice's birth "because we are as much alike as two peas in a pod," wrote Giles in *A Little Better Than Plumb.*

I am not my mother's daughter for nothing. She had no use for weaklings and leaners and she reared her children on pungent jabs calculated to make them self-reliant...Stand on your own two feet...Figure it out for yourself... where there's a will, there's a way.[1]

A permanent move to Kentucky in August, 1941, began a long professional career and eventually marriage. What began as a chance meeting on a long bus ride from Kentucky to Texas progressed

to a long-distance romance chronicled in the 634 letters between Henry and Janice Giles when he was a soldier in Europe. They were married and later moved to their first small farm in Adair County 822 days after their first meeting.

With success as the established author of "The Piney Ridge Trilogy," she turned to historical fiction in which her ability to use real and imaginary characters in historical settings was extraordinary. "I write history because it fascinates me and because I find in history an explanation of the present," she wrote. "I am trying to present the westward movement in a form that many readers find more palatable than the texts of history."[2]

By 1955, Janice Holt Giles wanted to move her chronological mind into "the time of the great religious awakening which swept like a storm over Kentucky. This book would have its setting in the Shaker community located at South Union and would deal with a strong woman serving the community as eldress told by a young Sister. Giles was especially curious about the Shaker's

"peculiar belief in celibacy. How did they expect to replenish their communal lives if husbands and wives were separated from each other?"[3] Commenting on her thought process for this book, **THE BELIEVERS,** she wrote,

I have brooded considerably on how it must have felt to either party of a married couple, if, say, only one became converted... I have thought how it would be if Henry did such a thing...

I do not believe I could bear to give him up entirely ...

This has to be another woman's book, of course. And the woman must tell it herself, for she must know and feel this great agony...

I have made a beginning: My name is Rebecca Fowler. I grew up in Lincoln County...[4]

It would not be difficult to suppose that Giles' very close relationship with her own daughter, her painful divorce and later happiness in a second marriage greatly influenced the strong family ties found in roles played by the women who shared Rebecca Fowler's room at South Union. In her writing notes she says, "I hope it will turn out well. I mean to end it happily. She will either save her husband and bring him out of that community with her, or she will find some other man worthy of her love who will take her out of it."[5] It was not that Giles had no feelings for the communal life or an appreciation for the Shakers. "I have had great respect for the Shakers. They were a gentle, dedicated, innocent people, though in their dedication and innocence they perpetuated great wrongs because of their fanaticism. That is what this book is about."[6]

Janice Holt Giles overcame an unsatisfactory first marriage which produced Elizabeth. In "My Darling Daughter," she wrote:

Mothers should have lots of children, of course. But if fate decree otherwise, if they give to a woman only one child—let her be a woman-child—a sister under the skin.

A lifelong devoted relationship developed between this mother and daughter and it is reinforced by much personal correspondence because Knifley, Kentucky, did not have telephone service until 1961. Among the letters:

Dear Mom,
This is a thank you note...for writing
HANNAH FOWLER.
It is a warm, loving strong book....once again a reader finds himself transported right into the center of that time, living with the people..you are an artist at smooth dialogue.[7]

In a letter written three months after their meeting, Henry Giles wrote: "...I almost asked you if you ever tried writing poetry. Or writing stories of any kind, but somehow I decided not to. *It seems you could write almost anything.*"[8] In the 36 years of their marriage, Janice Holt Giles wrote 24 books which sold in excess of 3 million copies. Janice Holt Giles is gone now. But she gave to us through a talented pen, a timeless and honorable literary legacy. Neither will be forgotten.

Log house in Adair County where Giles wrote many of her famous books. Photographs courtesy of The Courier-Journal.

Sarah Ogan Gunning

Folk-Legacy Records

S he was a particular kind of artist—a pure Appalachian ballad singer—a kind many people have never even heard of. And she was a creation of the Eastern Kentucky hills where she was born and raised. Sarah Ogan Gunning mastered one of this country's genuine original art forms, and she infused it with a message of tough vitality as devastating and inspiring as her own life.

Sarah Ogan Gunning was born into the singing Garland family which included the traditional and protest singers Aunt Molly Jackson and Jim Garland. Her mother passed on a large collection of ballads, hymns, love songs and stories to her fifteen children. Sarah's father taught her spirituals and how to sing them. Their lessons informed Gunning's style and technique, but the content of her work was the result of a cruel life of oppression in the early 20th century Matthews mine camp near Ely, Kentucky. By the time Sarah was born, her father had left behind an early career as farmer and minister to enter the mines.

His son, Jim, remembers that he became a miner "not out of choice but necessity" and "he was a very bad miner because he hated it so much."[1] The necessity was hunger, and it forced him back into the mines repeatedly. Folklorist Archie Green says that "she lived through the deepest change in the region's economy and the most devastating accommodation to such change."[2] But it was more than hunger and the grueling life of the mine worker that fired Gunning's creative spirit.

Near the turn of the century, her father joined the Knights of Labor, later the United Mine Workers of America. Sarah's entire life was touched by the union movement, and it was there that her music had its biggest impact.

Andrew Ogan, Sarah's first husband, was a miner and union member. The picket line was a brutal place and many died. Countless others were lost to starvation because even when they worked, some miners could not earn enough to feed their families. This was the overwhelming reality that colored Gunning's songs. Armed with words, she was as dangerous to the anti-union forces as any gun-carrying union member. And it was more that just being poor that bothered her. It was the inherent greed she recognized in the capitalist system.

Sarah Ogan Gunning's repertoire included original songs, well-known mountain tunes to which she wrote original lyrics, and spirituals, all sung in a mountain acappella, with no instrumental accompaniment, style. She had a great diversity of expression, and was best known for blending the traditional, old-fashioned ballad- singing style with a fervent, contemporary message. "I Am a Girl of Constant Sorrow" and "I Hate the Capitalist System" capture both the style and content that made her unique.

Gunning's life was not a fairy tale but she was widely recognized as a woman of spirit, courage and conviction. During the 1930s, ballad singing took on a cultural chic. It represented the struggle of the common man that became so intense during America's Great Depression. Gunning happened to be living in New York City's lower east side when Woody Guthrie, Pete Seeger, and Burl Ives brought popularity to her art form. In the Appalshop video, *Dreadful Memories*, Pete Seeger remembers her:

I meet Sarah Ogan—pretty as a picture, golden curls, blue eyes, snub nose...lived in a little walk up flat..just enough room...they ate their same old southern food. It was like stepping into a little piece of Kentucky when you stepped into their apartment. And full of jokes, full of laughter. Sarah had a raffish, rakish sense of humor...

Gunning wrote much of her protest songs in New York City, after she had left the troubled mining picket lines of Kentucky. "I Hate the Capitalist System," originally recorded as "I Hate the Company Bosses," was one such original composition. She described its origin in the album brochure:

This song I composed about my own life when I first went to New York from Kentucky. One of my children had starved to death in Kentucky and I had to take the others to New York to keep them from starving too. I first called this song "I Hate the Capitalist System," but people said that it was too radical sounding. I really didn't think that much about it so I changed the name to "I Hate the Company Bosses." But I thought about it later and decided that it really was the capitalist system that I hated after all—the system that starves little babies and children to death and where the capitalists have all

the money and I don't have any.[3]

After her first husband died, she remarried and moved to Detroit. There she lived, in the basement of an apartment slum, in relative obscurity. She was out of the popular music scene for decades, but she was rediscovered during the 1960s. Folklorist Archie Green persuaded Sarah Gunning to come to a studio and cut her first LP and she began singing in concerts in Carnegie Hall, the Smithsonian Folklife Festival, and the Newport Festival. Archie Green remembers asking Gunning about meeting Joan Baez in Newport and her reply was, "Well, Joan was a nice young lady but she

sure couldn't sing. If I just could have worked with her for a little while, I could have taught her Appalachian style."

Sarah Ogan Gunning knew how to sing music Appalachian style. And she never forgot. One of the singing Garland clan until her last moments, she died at a family songfest in 1983.

Photo John Gaventa for the Highlander Center

DREADFUL MEMORIES

WORDS: SARAH OGAN GUNNING
MUSIC: "PRECIOUS MEMORIES"

EXPRESSIVO

Dread—ful mem'ries, how they lin-ger, How they ev-er flood my soul, How the work-ers and their child-ren Died from hun-ger and from cold.

© 1965 by Folk Legacy Records

Dreadful memories, how they linger,
How they ever flood my soul,
How the workers and their children
Died from hunger and from cold.

Hungry fathers, wearied mothers
Living in those dreadful shacks,
Little children cold and hungry
With no clothing on their backs.

Dreadful gun-thugs and stool-pigeons
Always flock around our door.
What's the crime that we've committed?
Nothing, only that we're poor.

Oh, those memories, how they haunt me
Makes me want to organize.

When I think of all the heartaches
And all the things that we've been throu[
Then I wonder how much longer
And what a working man can do.

Really, friends, it doesn't matter
Whether you are black or white.
The only way you'll ever change things
Is to fight and fight and fight.

We will have to join the union,
They will help you find a way
How to get a better living
And for your work get better pay.

Gunning singing with Tillman Cadle, Lois Short, Nimrod Workman, Hazel Dickens and George Tucker at the Highlander Center, 1980. Photograph by Candie Carawan for the High-lander Center.

Eula Hall

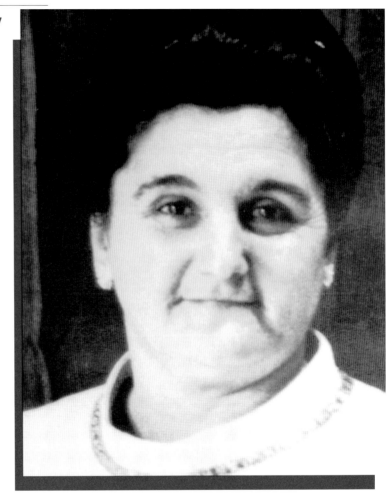

*I*n 1976, the American Public Health Association gave two awards of commendation, one to Betty Friedan, the feminist writer, and one to Eula Hall, the Eastern Kentucky activist. "Now I like Betty, but I talked to Betty just before the award presentation," said Eula Hall. "I told her she did her thing on paper, but I did mine out among the people, where it really counts." For decades Eula Hall has been bearing the torch for her Grethel community and they in turn have been inspired by Hall's belief that everyone has health rights. She educates others to become social activists, focusing on environmental and economic issues vital to community health.

Eula Hall grew up off Greasy Creek in Pike County, the oldest of seven children in a sharecropper family that grew corn, sold eggs to buy flour and beans, and kept pigs. She remembers her mother almost dying with the last baby. "We had to let the last hog go to get the doctor from Pikeville to go out and deliver mama."[1] But the baby died and her mother almost did, too. When she was grown, she realized that simple health

care like antibiotics or tetanus shots or sewers would have made such a difference in their preventive health care. She remembers doing everything possible to take care of somebody sick and they'd still just die. "All my life I thought 'this was ridiculous that good people have to suffer and die for the lack of money."[2]

During World War II food was rationed. "I was pregnant with my first child and you couldn't go to the store and buy what you wanted. There was such a shortage—no electricity in this area and no refrigera-

tion, and the food we'd get was not good wholesome food for a pregnant woman. I remember walking to the company store at Ligon, where they did have electricity, and buying vegetables and fruit from the company store in the winter...probably a seven mile walk each way...get as much as I could carry...and pregnant..."[3]

Her daddy thought girls didn't need to go to school. "You're going to be married to somebody, learn how to cook and sew and be a housewife. It didn't matter whether you learned anything in school or not, we were working for other people for a quarter a day." Hall's formal education went through the eighth grade, which she finished in five years. At age 14, she lied about her age and went with her brother to upstate New York to work in a canning factory. There she gained her first taste of labor activities by helping to organize a strike to protest working conditions. She was arrested, her real age discovered, and she was sent back to Kentucky.

For almost 40 years, Eula Hall has been a community organizer in Eastern Kentucky. In the mid-60s she helped found the Eastern Kentucky Welfare

Rights Organization, instigating a flurry of activity beginning with free school lunches for poor children and culminating with the opening of Mud Creek Health Clinic, which she created and has directed ever since. Volunteers documented federally funded programs from the War on Poverty and realized it wasn't meeting the peoples' needs, so they got the program defunded! Then she tried to get some of the same money redistributed to the volunteers, but when that wasn't successful she founded a clinic herself. In 1973, the clinic was housed in her own house while she moved next door to live in a trailer. Eula Hall and another woman stocked the pharmacy by taking out a personal loan; they didn't have a lab, so they sterilized baby food jars to use to send out specimens. Even after arson destroyed the clinic she never lost the driving spirit. Under Hall's leadership the community raised $102,000 to receive matching funds from the Appalachian Regional Commission and in July, 1982 she opened an up-to-date, fully-equipped facility with a modern laboratory and pharmacy on site. With inordinately high rates of black lung, diabetes, hypertension and poor nutrition, Eula Hall had found a way to provide affordable health care and the people's dream came true. Patients pay according to their income, and *no one is turned away*. As you enter her office, there's a sign over the door that reads "Social Director," and that speaks volumes. On any given day, she finds clothes for a homeless family, money for someone to turn on the heat, takes people

to Pikeville to apply for food stamps or other benefits. From experience she knows the devastation of physical abuse, and her hope is that the community will establish a spouse abuse center. In between she's taking constant phone calls, always responding like a best friend or at least a grandmother. Eula Hall knows everybody in Mud Creek, they count on her, and she takes her role seriously.

Eula Hall knows

that sometimes money has been funneled into the wrong hands, whether it's been to politicians, school superintendents, doctors, or coal operators. And in some cases she knows that the community might grow old waiting for legislation, so she always believes that if strip mine operators can move mountains, so can the people. For example, when it comes to stripmining, "I can't come up with

> anything but people to stop a strip mine. I think if there's enough people you can stop anything."[4] *Coming from the people* is an honorable strain in Eula Hall's philosophy and it is the key to her success.

In the 60s, Hall worked with VISTA and joined the Appalachian Volunteers. She learned all about community organizing. In 1973, she and other women helped block the road to the Brookside mine to prevent non-union miners from breaking a strike. She led another group in Knott County to protest the destruction of homes and family graves by coal companies. She is ready to join other women to picket utility rates any day of the week.

"The women keep the mountains going. They may have to do it

behind the scenes and the men may get credit for it. I think women have really proven themselves, that they'll hang with it until it's done, regardless of the cost." It's no surprise that Eula Hall received a "Wonder Woman" award given to women over 40 who display characteristics like the comic book figure. For her living legacy, Mud Creek Clinic, she is a true Kentucky wonder woman.

Nhi Nguyen Hearn

*W*omen are the stories they tell and Nhi Nguyen's story of immigrating to America is the story of lost childhood and found courage that sought new beginnings in Louisville, Kentucky. Nhi's mother told her that "America was the greatest place in the world and that if she ever got there, the rewards would be worth the cost." Her dreams and nightmares became all wrapped up in coming to America and America did not disappoint her. Nhi Nguyen's story is so eye-popping on the surface that the results sound deceptively simple. Born in Danang, Vietnam, her father worked for the United States government. When the Vietnam War was over officials of the new government took her father to jail and came for her mother and four siblings to take them to a re-education camp. But her quick-witted mother bribed the driver and they ended up on the streets of Saigon instead. Nhi Nguyen lived there until 1987. By then her mother had been able to scrape together $2,000, and she arranged for Nhi, age twelve, to be smuggled out of Vietnam to Cambodia, and eventually to Thailand. But her ultimate goal was always America. Her mother's parting words were "I know I will never see you again. But I hope someone will take care of you so that you can have a better life. Get to America—it is your only hope."

In a group of 16 to 18 other people, her trip through Cambodia was harrowing: jailed three or four times, often afraid for her life, but always bent on surviving. Trudging through the jungles across Cambodia, she finally took a boat to Thailand. Her wise mother had sewn valuables inside her clothing and along the way she bribed her way out of tight situations. When Nhi Nguyen arrived in a Thailand refugee camp she made contact with the American delegation and in 1989, Catholic Charities made it possible for her to come to Louisville, Kentucky, where her sister already lived.

Iroquois High School was enormous; she spoke no English; students laughed at her. Driven to America by the circumstances of a controversial war, she had to fight overwhelming cultural misunderstanding and racism. But there was an extraordinary teacher named Mary Lou Hearn, who took a special interest in Nhi Nguyen, and soon she was living with Mary Lou and Lewis Hearn and their children. The Hearns became her legal guardians and when Nhi Nguyen became an American citizen in 1995, she took the last name of her Louisville family. Gaining citizenship was an informed adult decision that culminated years of struggle and achievement. It was almost like a present to herself.

(Above) Hearn in Vietnam.

Nhi Hearn says that as she struggled to learn English she "began to appreciate deaf and mute people who have similar challenges when trying to communicate with the hearing and speaking world. Students had little patience with my inability to speak their language." But she was highly motivated and once she learned, she was off and running. Nhi took nothing for granted, she worked hard, and she was rewarded. In less than 2 1/2 years Nhi Hearn was the valedictorian of her graduating class, named a Governor's Scholar and received a Presidential Scholarship to Centre College in Danville, Kentucky. It was at Centre College that she met her peers on common ground, savoring every day she was there. Centre College was a small, personalized school where "I could walk into the President's office and sit down to talk—not just about academics but on any topic. Professors were not only my teachers but became my friends." And she made close friends with other students who became a support network in her studies and play.

In 1994, she traveled with a college group back to Vietnam and visited her mother, who still thought of Nhi as her twelve-year-old child. Although her mom "had a hard time accepting me as an American, she was also very

proud and she had to accept the new Nhi."

When asked about her choices, she is quick to point out that some Vietnamese people believe "I have become too Americanized." But Nhi Nguyen arrived in Louisville, Kentucky, completely cut off from her parents and already bonded to America. She was no longer attached to a Vietnamese community and she was not leading her life as a traditional Vietnamese young woman. Today, some might think she is caught with one foot in each world, but not Nhi Hearn.

Nhi Hearn's declaration of independence to become an American citizen characterized her unembarrassed idealism about this country. She literally percolates with optimistic fervor. In fact, she is so connected to America that it makes people ask themselves what it really means to be an American. Her grateful thanks to the Hearn family reminds us all that we *are* our sister's keeper.

(Left) Hearn with friends on her graduation day from Centre College. (Below) Hearn in Vietnam.

Josephine Kirby Williamson Henry

By Aloma Dew

*I*f you own property or have credit in your own name and you are a married woman, you should thank Josephine Henry. Until the late nineteenth century married women in Kentucky could not make wills, be the guardian of their children, receive wages earned, or own or inherit property. Upon saying "I do" at the marriage altar, a woman became chattel property, not even owning the clothes upon her back. By 1890, Kentucky was the only state in which such laws still existed. Henry observed that in the eyes of Kentucky law, "It is almost a crime to be a married woman..."[1]

Josephine Henry, a dynamic speaker and powerful writer from Versailles, worked tirelessly in the political arena as an advocate for Kentucky women, especially in the area of property rights. Although largely overshadowed in histories of the Kentucky women's movement, it is clear that Henry was a major player in the fight for women's equality. Her greatest accomplishment was the Married Woman's Property Act, or the Husband and Wife Bill, passed in 1894. Henry regarded the property act as the first step toward women's suffrage because she understood the importance of economic independence and security. She called for women to no longer be "treated as outlaws and all their property confiscated at marriage."[2]

After years of speeches, articles and lobbying, the Married Woman's Property Act, though criticized as anti-family and unladylike, finally passed the General Assembly and was signed into law.

Henry was the first woman in Kentucky, and indeed the South, to run for state office. She was the 1890 Prohibition Party candidate for Clerk of the Kentucky Court of Appeals and received nearly 5,000 votes. She was also nominated in 1894 for State Superintendent of Public Instruction and was discussed as a possible candidate for President in 1900.

In 1895, publication of Elizabeth Cady Stanton's *The Woman's Bible* fueled fires of dissension within the ranks of suffragist organizations. Josephine Henry, an agnostic, signed on as a member of the international revising committee for the book and wrote two commentaries. Her participation in the controversial project severed her longstanding friendship with renowned suffragist Laura Clay and led to Henry's ejection from the Kentucky Equal Rights Association as "an undesirable member."[3] In her books, *Marriage and Divorce* and *Woman and the Bible*, Henry described the *Bible* and those who taught it as repressive of women. Her

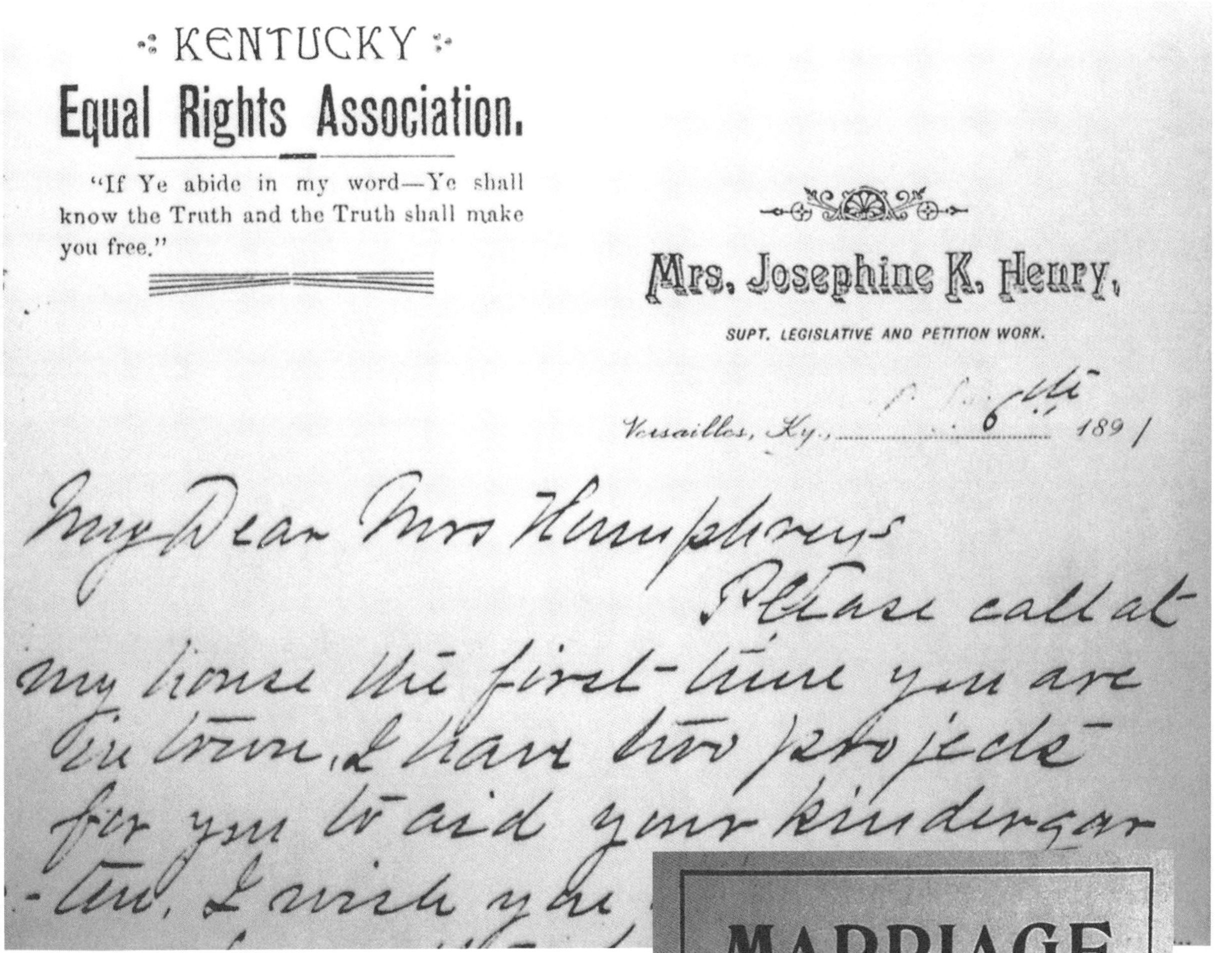

KENTUCKY Equal Rights Association.

"If Ye abide in my word—Ye shall know the Truth and the Truth shall make you free."

Mrs. Josephine K. Henry,

SUPT. LEGISLATIVE AND PETITION WORK.

Versailles, Ky., _____ 6th 1891

My Dear Mrs Humphreys

Please call at my house the first time you are in town. I have two projects for you to aid your kindergarten. I wish you...

Photographs courtesy of the Woodford County Historical Society.

If you own your own property or have your own name and you are a married woman, you should thank Josephine Henry.

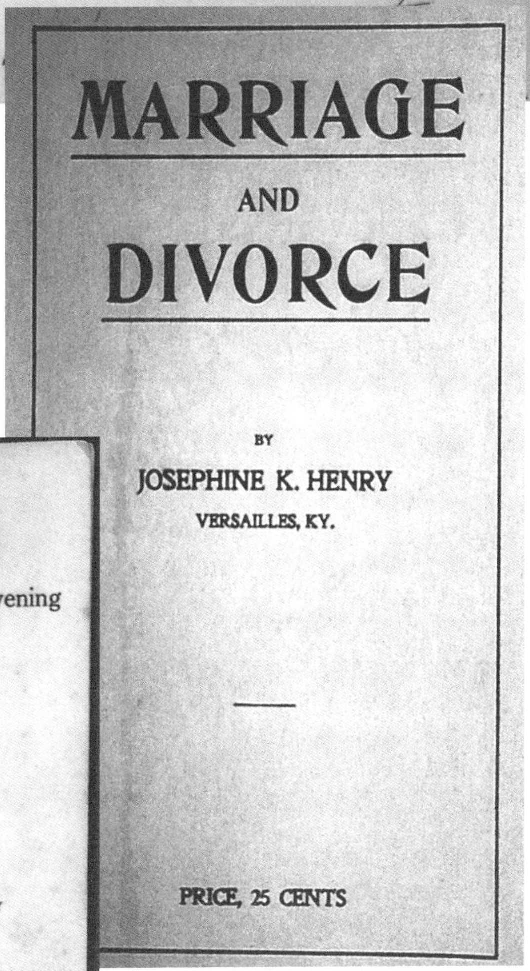

Musings in Life's Evening

by

JOSEPHINE K. HENRY
Versailles, Ky.

MARRIAGE AND DIVORCE

BY

JOSEPHINE K. HENRY
VERSAILLES, KY.

PRICE, 25 CENTS

writings reflect anger and frustration at a male dominated religion which she believed legitimized cruel and unequal treatment of women.

Far ahead of her day, Henry questioned the male controlled values of the time and discussed topics such as divorce, restoration of the maiden name, birth control, dress reform, finance and economic security, and sex education. A woman of courage and conviction, Josephine Henry dedicated her life to the pursuit of justice and equality for the women of Kentucky. Although largely forgotten or unknown a century after her liberating work, Henry's legacy continues.

Nelle Pitcock Horlander

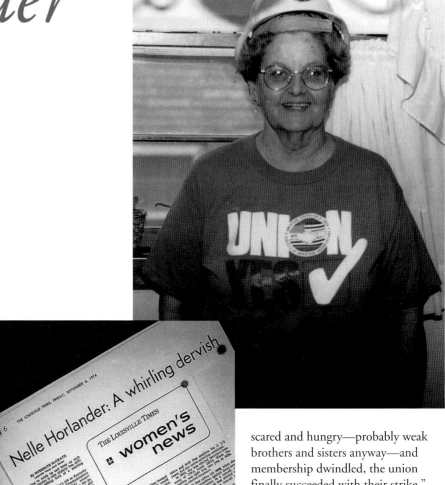

Nelle Horlander: A whirling dervish

THE LOUISVILLE TIMES
women's news

Talking with Nelle Pitcock Horlander is like visiting with a real-life Rosie the Riveter, surely one of the most popular heroines of every young woman. Born in Dry Fork, Kentucky, Horlander came of age during the critical years of World War II. Married and single women entered wartime industry and support services in droves, taking up the slack caused by American men going overseas. Though thankful for the opportunity to prove themselves, many gladly went home after the war to husband and hearth. But the die had been cast, and others continued to work outside the home, usually out of necessity or the desire to contribute something and to stretch and prove themselves in the working world.

Horlander's family moved to Louisville when she was fourteen, and after graduating from high school in 1946, she attended college for two years. At age twenty, she began working as a "Number, please!" telephone operator for the Shawnee exchange of Southern Bell. Although unions have a history of excluding women, especially from leadership positions, Horlander was active in the local union from the beginning, serving first as Steward, then Secretary ("You know, women are the only people who can write," she quipped.), then Treasurer, and finally President from 1969 to 1974. She made her voice heard.

From 1974 until her retirement in 1996, Nelle Horlander worked full-time as Kentucky's state director of the Communications Workers of America (CWA). Its membership is unusual in that fifty-two percent are women. She administered contracts and grievances, handled arbitration, serviced the locals, trained stewards and officers, and organized units. She says she filled the job of two people and liked hearing

people say to her, "You won it for me, and I'll never forget it."

When the union went out on strike against Southern Bell in March, 1995, Horlander was Secretary and in charge of the defense fund, which had begun in 1952 at 50 cents per member per month. "It was an awful experience," says Horlander. "I was single so I didn't have a family like the others." The president of the local union and over 200 others across the country were fired, but the top officers kept things together. The strike lasted 72 days. At the time they didn't belong to the Greater Louisville Central Labor Council, where all the unions meet to support one another. They joined after the striked was settled.

Though people got "nervous and

scared and hungry—probably weak brothers and sisters anyway—and membership dwindled, the union finally succeeded with their strike," she said. They only paid survival bills like health insurance, house payments, and food coupons from Kroger, and since women were then, and still tend to be today in the clerical jobs, the union would not cover them. That's the reason why historically there have been few women in unions in Kentucky.

Horlander remembers the days when Louisville was called "strike city." The workers at General Electric, for example, continually called strikes for better contracts. Today, however, the relationship between management and workers is much better. Perhaps the gains unions made in the past have enabled young people to be apathetic about joining them today. Their parents built up the benefits such as vacation days, hospitalization, shorter work week; they got safety regulations put in place. "Unfortunately," she says, "the older men didn't educate the younger men and placed no emphasis on bringing them in and training them."

But Horlander has trained her family well. She reminds them that, sadly, no televisions, no baseball gloves, no tape recorders are made in this country. She urges them to leave foreign-made goods on the shelves. And her grandchildren all know that if they find a toy made in America, grandmother will buy it. Nelle Horlander walks the talk.

Horlander was also the first woman hired as a communications consultant with Southern Bell in 1965. It was a top-paying craft job, and when she went to their training school in Atlanta, she says, "they tried to flunk me out. It was a hard class." In addition to always being on the front lines educating women about the connection between their economic roles and political consciousness, her longtime activity with the Democratic Party as district chairperson has given her political connections that enabled her to become a community leader. Her biographical résumé lists two pages of political experience and appointments and community service.

Armed with the belief that women are equal to men, Horlander is a hardworking role model dedicated to serving people, especially women and minorities. She says they have a lot of catching up to do, but they can do something about the inequities they face. Today, Nelle Horlander sees women as the future of unions. "Hospitals, health care industry, service, clerical—that's where growth lies." The image of the post-war happy suburban homemaker was shattered by Betty Friedan's book, *The Feminine Mystique*. Women like Nelle Horlander bought into "the problem that had no name," and her wish is that "I live long enough to see women in the Constitution." Women and unions—it's the story of her life work.

Betty Howard

Since 1990, the women of Benham, Kentucky, have transformed the town, literally and figuratively. What began as a show of support to help pay for a state-of-the-art fire truck ended with a côup d'état of the town's political offices. Today, Benham is run by a female council and headed by a female mayor, Betty Howard, who unleashed a different framework for governing small towns in Kentucky. They are known affectionately as "The Petticoat Mafia."

In 1985, International Harvester Company turned over the deed to the city of Benham to its citizens for $9. The population was 1,500—today the population is 716. To appreciate the seriousness of this property conveyance is to understand what "company-owned" meant. The coal company told you what street you'd live on, and in the case of African Americans, in which section of town you would live. Your children attended company schools and families went to company doctors. The company owned the fire trucks, the utilities, the houses (two families per dwelling), the garbage trucks, the streets, sidewalks, water system (no sewers), all the land, and all the buildings. Everything from haircuts to furniture was bought in the company's commissary store. Suddenly, all that reverted to the citizens and it was bedlam, not Benham.

The City had to be incorporated into a sixth-class city and a political structure formed, but no one knew how to write job descriptions because "no one ever saw a politician except on election day or tax time," said Howard. The company had run everything *for them*. No Benham woman ever dreamed of becoming a politician and the newly-formed government was filled with all men.

Now the city needed a new fire truck and they ordered the Cadillac of all fire trucks, but the City Council did not pay attention to little details. Remember, the company had always taken care of everything. When the bill arrived for $133,000 plus 7 percent interest financing every man on the Council looked at his shoes.

The women of Benham said, "Well, what about a yard sale?" Thirty-seven

[signature: Betty Joy Howard]

BETTY J. HOWARD
MAYOR, CITY OF BENHAM

women showed up to organize the sale and it developed into "This-n-That," a used clothing store. Of course the roof leaked one day and the women had to take all the clothes home: wash, dry them and rehang neatly in the store. This happened over and over again. Only another woman could appreciate their wash woman dilemma, so the female head of the Community Action Agency offered free labor. And finally they found someone to lend them money for the roofing materials and the women signed the note.

Another bright-eyed Pollyanna resurrected the Garden Club to clean up and spruce up the town. But they needed a place "to meet." City Hall was beginning to feel a little threatened by all the visible accomplishments of "the ladies," and they had no suggestions. Never underestimate the power of a woman. One cold January day they called CSX railroad and inquired about an excess caboose. In February they received the

bill of lading. One small detail hadn't been ironed out yet: where does one *put* a caboose? "Can't put it in your pocket book," quipped Betty Howard. And that's how The Coal Miner Memorial Park came to pass. They asked for help.

Whether for yourself or family member, this is an excellent opportunity to become a permanent part of a lasting memorial and tribute to the nation's coal miners. Order your brick today. Print name as it will be engraved.

With fierce determination, the women of Benham took up their wheelbarrows and coal shovels and built the park themselves. Sweeten the pot with honey bun cakes and chicken and dumplings and you've got enough goodies to feed the spirits, too. The day the caboose arrived, there was no place to turn it around. Coming down the tracks, the caboose was in front of two big engines. "It looked like the little red caboose wanted to come to Benham so bad, it was pulling the engines yelling 'Goin' to Benham, Goin' to Benham,'" remembers Betty Howard.

All this time, of course, the men of Benham had been laughing and watching, never dreaming that any of the blood, sweat, and no tears would produce anything like this cherished place of honor. When it came time to buy the black granite marker, the women sold enough pinto beans, wieners, and corn bread until they collected $5,700 to pay for it. For the women of Benham, it's strictly "cash and carry."

When election time rolled around there was little doubt that the women should be in charge. Betty Howard had been the city clerk for more years than she cared to remember so running for Mayor was a natural. James Goode, a former council member, sums it up best: "We'd had a whole history of mayors and male-dominated councils. It's not that they didn't do anything. But they didn't have this kind of vision."

And vision it is. We aren't talking about a Mayor who has to worry about wetlands or nuclear reactor plants or noise pollution. We are talking about a Mayor who focuses on reunions, renovating the old theater, and keeping the doors to the Coal Mining Museum open. Reunions build memories and Howard figures they must be doing something right. Former Benhamites come home summer after summer from all across America to the Benham Reunion. They remember a night in high school; the day one of them watched her father struggle to breathe from black lung; the nights the company

*(Above) The Petticoat Mafia.
Lexington-Herald-Leader.*

'Petticoat Mafia' gives Benham, state lesson in leadership

BY KAREN SAMPLES
HERALD-LEADER STAFF WRITER

BENHAM — They have their own T-shirts, they're in demand on the speaking circuit, and letters have been pouring in from across the state.

Benham's Petticoat Mafia — six city councilwomen and one councilman known as "the Godfather" — is on a roll.

"It's been a big joke," said Betty Howard, sporting a custom-made "Benham's Petticoat Mafia" T-shirt. Howard is the first female mayor in this tiny city, which used to be a coal town for miners and their families. The Herald-Leader published a story last year about the women's dominance in city government and their efforts to boost community spirit.

Since then, the Benham City Council has received an award from the Kentucky League of Cities for its work in human development. Benham High School's class of 1945-46 collected $3,000 to finish the town's gazebo, and workers with Harlan County's community action agency provided the labor.

City council members also have been asked to share their secrets with various leadership organizations.

"Yes, the Petticoat Mafia will be here," said Lindsay Campbell of the state's Commission on Women, which is putting together a conference on women's history at Kentucky State University in March.

City council members already have spoken to several groups stay-

See BENHAM, B4

official came to tell them their husband or father or brother died in the mine; or they share one of grandmother's treasured recipes; or take a bite out of Council member Lacey Griffith's best ever chocolate cake.

In Benham, the female need for personal interest and relationships intersects with public policy. It could be said there is a decidedly female nature to some of the topics and the responses. The Council members feel like the citizens have a right to a responsive government, one in which the Mayor listens to the individual. That's why Howard

set up a coffee station just inside the door of City Hall. Come in, sit down, put your feet up, and stay a while. And while you're at it, have a cup of coffee with the Mayor. She's sitting at one desk among many other desks not far away. There's no "Mayor's Office," per se, anymore. She's *accessible*. The Petticoat Mafia won the 1996 President's Award for Excellence and they stay on the speakers' circuit with their message: *women, get involved.*

Betty Howard is indomitable, warm, straight forward, and likes nothing better than good old-fashioned fun. With luck, determination, and sheer grit, the women of The Petticoat Mafia have rebuilt the spirit and dignity of a tiny town in Kentucky named Benham.

Helen Humes

Humes singing at Joe's Palm Room, Louisville, 1980.

Joy Mather for *The Courier-Journal*

(Above) The Helen Humes Award given annually to the person who has contributed most to jazz in Kentucky.

By Victoria Norman Brown

Louisville was never more than a trip away for Helen Humes. Some cautioned that her inability to break ties with home would hold her back. And indeed, some of her contemporaries (like Ella Fitzgerald, Leslie Uggams, Billie Holiday) did move on to greater fame and fortune. Humes preferred to use her high-pitched melodic voice singing funny blues rather than sad blues. Her mother and father *and Louisville* made Helen Humes happy.

Her mother was a school teacher but never worked after Helen was born. Her father was one of the first black lawyers in Louisville. She had happy memories of popping popcorn and making ice cream and playing games. Born in Louisville in 1913, she got her love and gift of song from her parents, who often performed duets together at church and social functions. By the age of five, Humes was singing and performing in Bessie Allen's Marching Band for children. At 14, Sylvester Weaver, one of the band's former members who recorded the first blues man/guitar recording, "Guitar," introduced Helen Humes to a producer

at Okeh Records. She recorded several tunes, including "Cross-Eyed Blues," but her recording career was cut short by her mother's insistence that she complete her studies at Louisville's Central High School.

After graduation, Humes worked for a short time in her father's law office as a secretary, singing locally in the evenings. By 1937, her aspirations to perform had

taken her as far away as Albany, New York. While performing with the Al Sears band at the Cotton Club in Cincinnati, Humes was spotted by "The King of Swing," Count Basie. He invited her to replace Billie Holiday and join his band as a singer, but she declined because she didn't want to venture too far from home. The following year, Count Basie again invited her to join his band, and

(Above) Message from Ella Fitgerald. Fitzgerald pictured on the left, Humes on the right.

this time she accepted.

Helen Humes left the Count Basie Orchestra in 1942 and settled in California. She worked with various bands and wrote and recorded "Be-baba-leba," which was a commercial hit. Humes recorded tunes for films and television and appeared in the Hollywood production of Langston Hughes' play, *Simply Heaven*. In between projects, she came home to Louisville, occasionally staying for months at a time.

Humes returned to jazz, performing on tour in Australia several different times. She also made a successful European tour and lived abroad for almost a year.

In 1967, Humes returned to Louisville after her mother became gravely ill. Upon her mother's death, Humes sold her records and piano and resolved never to sing again. She stayed in Louisville taking care of her father and working odd jobs, including a stint at an ammunitions plant in Indiana. In 1973, music critic Stanley Dance asked her to appear with Count Basie at the Newport Jazz Festival. With her father's consent, she went.

Slowly she resumed her career and during the late 1970s Humes enjoyed a second career hiatus. Her good humor and sheer love of "swinging" made her a favorite with audiences. Fellow musicians dubbed her one of "jazz's nicer people." Critics admired her way of "making the blues sound ladylike," without destroying its authenticity. In 1981, she died in California.

(Below) Humes always kept in close touch with her parents.

Louise Gilman Hutchins

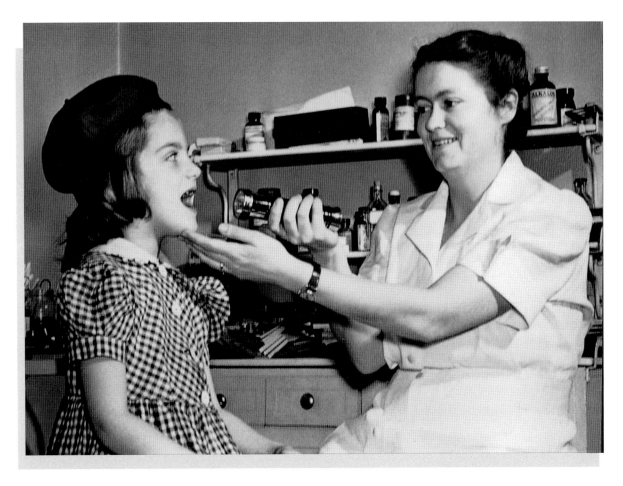

A professor at Yale University Medical School thought that Louise Gilman should be dropped from its rolls when she married Francis Hutchins. He doubted that a married woman would ever practice medicine. Fortunately for thousands of people on two continents, who became Dr. Hutchins' patients over the next six decades, he was overruled. Although women physicians were a rarity when Louise Hutchins earned her degree, she was encouraged by her family to pursue her chosen career. She took them at their word, and devoted most of her life to her credo, "better health for mountain mothers."

Her family history can almost be measured by some of China's rebellions and revolutions. Gilman's missionary mother arrived in China in 1901, one

year after the Boxer Rebellion in which many missionaries were killed. Her father, grandfather and great-grandfather had all been Christian ministers so the meaning of serving humanity was simply taken for granted. Louise Gilman Hutchins was born to her ministering parents in Changsa, Hunan province, China, so it came as no surprise when she later chose to complete her medical school internship there. As a child, she may have been teased about her blond braids and large feet but when she was able to answer back in Chinese, the taunting children were amazed and she was pleased.[1] Their house in Kentucky became filled with Chinese artifacts as a legacy to her childhood homeland. China was a cultural experience that very definitely influenced Louise Hutchins's life.

Louise Gilman came to America when she was 15 and graduated from Wellesley College, where professors inspired her to take chemistry and physics. But she was often lonely living in a country where she had no family and she continued to visit her parents in China during school holidays. Later, she married Francis Hutchins and they moved to China so that he could direct the Yale-in-China program and she could complete her medical training. Louise Hutchins found pediatrics in China frustrating because children were fed rice water and often had typhoid, but penicillin was not yet available and sulfur drugs were just being introduced.[2]

When the Japanese invaded China in 1939, she and their young daughter survived some rather harrowing experiences and they went to live in Shanghai.

Francis Hutchins remained in dangerous Hunan province, the birthplace of Chairman Mao. Missionaries and the international community, however, supported Generalissimo Chiang Kai-shek's nationalist guerrillas and it was to everyone's advantage that they stay in relatively safe Shanghai. When Francis Hutchins accepted Berea College's offer in 1939 to become its president, he wanted his wife to develop her own work interests. Louise Hutchins came to Kentucky with a deep social conscience ready to bring medical care to the people, and Francis Hutchins followed in his father's footsteps to become president of Berea College. They were a most unusual couple-in-service who made Kentucky their home for life.

Louise Hutchins' medical care was much needed in the mountains. Poverty was rampant. Families with a dozen or more children lived in tiny, drafty cabins, most without indoor plumbing, roads, or electricity. Measles and whooping cough took children's lives too soon. Tuberculosis was a major health concern. Hutchins worked tirelessly to bring the benefits of medicine's latest developments to her patients. She insisted, for example, that the local dairy pasteurize its milk and in collaboration with another physician, she ensured that oral polio vaccinations were available in Berea and Richmond.

Although she was a pediatrician for twenty-eight years through Berea College, it was in the area of itinerant family planning that Louise Hutchins left her lasting imprint on mountain health care. Hutchins was no stranger to women having large families. She'd seen Chinese women bear as many as twelve children and too often they died. Her view of family planning was that it would come with an educated public. In the meantime she wanted to make contraception available to everyone who desired such health service. She arrived just after it was legal to send contraceptives through the mail, and "plain, brown wrapper" took on a new meaning. Eight hundred women became dependent upon Dr. Hutchins for contraceptive supplies via the mail. As director of the once-fledgling Mountain Maternal Health League, Hutchins became one of Kentucky's trailblazers in family planning. Her fierce determination was borne of a creed that *every woman of whatever race, religion or economic status should know all the facts of family planning, and*

then should choose for herself what method she would use or whether or not she wished to use any.[3]

To understand her dedication and bravery in promoting contraception in the early decades of this century, it must be remembered that mere mention of the word "contraception" was almost taboo. In Connecticut, for example, it was illegal for married couples to use birth control until 1966. Although contraception was legal in Kentucky, the state health department balked when Dr. Hutchins asked that county health departments provide it. She found two women county health officers who understood the extreme need of offering family planning services to improve the health status of the people of Eastern Kentucky. In 1961, thanks to these officers, health departments in ten mountain counties began offering family planning. A year later, the Commissioner of Health gave permission for all county departments to follow suit. It was Louise Hutchins who gave the first speech on contraception to her peers in the Kentucky Medical Association.

In 1967, Francis Hutchins retired from the presidency of Berea College and the couple moved to Hong Kong for three years. Her fluency in Chinese enabled her to spend their sojourn there as a family planning advisor to hundreds of women. But they returned to their beloved Berea where she was invited to serve as Family Planning Clinician for the

Photographs courtesy of the Berea College Archives

state. Her longstanding dream of a mobile family planning unit to serve Eastern Kentucky was arranged, and from 1970-1987, Dr. Hutchins saw 87,413 patients in the mobile unit and in 22 county health departments. For this, she received the Helen B. Fraser Award and countless other state and national awards.

Her childhood home was never been far from reach. In 1985, she was invited by Emory University School of Medicine to visit the Peoples Republic of China as part of an American delegation of health professionals. But she loved the Commonwealth and once said in the *Berea Citizen* newspaper that "I've lived more than half my life in Kentucky, which is where I'd rather be than any other place in the world." Louise Gilman Hutchins died in 1996, a woman of compassion, courage, and energy who made incomparable contributions to the quality of life of thousands of Kentuckians.

Eleanor Jordan

Durell Hall, Jr. for *The Courier-Journal*

In 1980 an African American woman from Louisville testified before a state legislative committee in Frankfort. "Nobody on the other side of the table looked like me," she recalls. Her observation was particularly disheartening because she had experienced the same phenomenon as a 12-year-old student visiting the State Capitol. Today Eleanor Jordan is on the other side of the table, having been elected in 1996 to Kentucky's House of Representatives.

Women who were "firsts" in the Kentucky Legislature like Georgia Powers aand Mae Street Kidd created their own histories about African American achievement in Kentucky politics. Eleanor Jordan represents the second generation African American female politician and she brings a new tone of voice that is politically astute and energized by her life experiences. She speaks with knowledge and confidence, particularly on issues affecting women and cities.

Being truthful about where she came from is important to Jordan. She becomes very serious when she talks about being an unwed mother at seventeen, and later being "out on my own with three

children and no credit because everything was in my husband's name. I know what it's like to start over and build a credit record, buy a car, buy a house," she says. Eleanor Jordan knows what it is like to be on welfare, stand in a food stamp line, and feel the financial pinch of trying to pay for child care on a meager salary.

Luckily she had some personal tools that helped her face such challenges and a lot of credit goes to her mother, Ruth Marion Allen. She "taught us to respect literature, read poetry, and how to dream. Twice a week she marched us to the library to check out books and then she made us give oral book reports. I could read before I got to first grade," Jordan said. What she really appreciates most about her mother is that she taught her daughters that there wasn't anything they couldn't do because they were girls or black or poor. Ruth Marion Allen was a domestic housekeeper who also wanted to expose her children to the finer things and "every Sunday we ate with china and crystal and silverware. We had to set the table with full place settings even if we were having smoked sausages and cabbage. We still had to put out the salad fork, butter knife, shrimp fork,

soup spoon. We learned because it was important to her."

Eleanor Jordan does what she believes is important. Disappointed in the performance of her alderman, who had been in office 12 years, she ran against him in 1993. A neophyte? Yes, but she came within 97 votes of winning her first political contest. In 1996, when Representative Leonard Gray left his post, he handpicked Jordan to take over. She laughs, "I didn't even know what a state representative *did*." Her family wasn't thrilled with the idea of another election, but she won the special election. Then it was trial by fire because the legislative session had begun and she had an opponent waiting in the wings who figured she was a speculative bubble that would pop. Not quite.

Luck came in the guise of a poorly conceived child care bill. "My personal interest," she told her colleagues eloquently, "is for the child who shows up at day care with cigarette burns, not just a child who lives in a two-parent family with a white picket fence." Jordan understands child care like no other legislator. Not only had she struggled to pay for child care as a young divorced mother, more recently she had served as executive director of Iroquois Child Care Center in Louisville which, under her watch, captured a $397,000 federal grant to work with parents. Being a freshman legislator didn't stop Jordan from filing an amendment to gut the child care bill. Legislators listened and Jordan's amendment passed. She got good press.

Her biggest media coup, however, came the last day of the legislative session. A color photograph and front-page newspaper story about women in the Kentucky General Assembly introduced Eleanor Jordan to the whole state. Gritty realism and her personal frame of reference again garnered praise and got results. She ran in the spring primary and the November election and won both.

Jordan wants to develop a women's agenda for Kentucky. "Women must work together," she says. "Republican and Democratic women should join hands to further their interests. There are so few women politicians in Kentucky (only Alabama has fewer) that we can't afford *not* to get together." She also knows that one of her tasks is getting more women to run for pubic office and the task won't be easy. "Getting more involved means more than sitting back and saying to women, 'the door's open, come on in,'" she says. "You have to physically go get women and ask them to shadow you for a few days and send

messages to them that being a female politician is a good thing for Kentucky."

Kentucky needs more politicians and leaders like Eleanor Jordan. She is doing her part to make sure Kentucky's children are learning the truth when they are taught that government is "of the people, by the people, and for the people." Her mother told her years ago that nothing should stand in the way of her dreams, and nothing has stopped Eleanor Jordan yet.

(Right) Jordan as a young girl. (Below) Jordan at the microphone. Photograph by Pat McDonogh for The Courier-Journal.

Elect
Eleanor
Jordan
DEMOCRAT
State Representative 42nd District
A Proven Leader!

2ND Annual Glitz & Glamour Gala
The Friends of
Eleanor Jordan
State Representative
42nd District
Cordially Invite You to Experience
"HOLLYWOOD NIGHTS"
on
Saturday Evening, May 10, 1997
8:00 until 12:00 Midnight
Jay's Restaurant
1812 West Muhammad Ali Blvd.

Food   Dancing   Monte Carlo   Cash Bar
$25/Person

"Dress to Impress"

Paid for by the Committee to Re-Elect Eleanor Jordan, Terrie Looney, Treasurer

"Glitz & Glamour"

91

Elizabeth Kizito

*K*IZITO had never eaten a chocolate chip cookie before coming to Louisville, but she thought they were the best things she'd ever tasted. Soon she realized she could make her own and sell them, so she made cookies for fellow workers and they wanted more. With $20 worth of cookie staples, she baked enough to start selling heavenly chocolate chip cookies to people in downtown businesses. It seemed like everyone had a sweet tooth. Someone offered a vendor cart and Elizabeth was off and running, hitting street corners and festivals with a Ugandan basket atop her head laden with **KIZITO** cookies and brownies.

Only running your own business was quite different from making a few cookies once a week. After reading health department regulations, she realized this was a serious undertaking. Undaunted, she began baking for mass production in restaurant ovens she found idle from 4 to 7 a.m. By this time **KIZITO** was a single parent, and the

cookie business *had* to be a success. When she wanted to open a store on Bardstown Road, she had no history of borrowing nor owning property so nobody would lend her any money. Not to worry! In piecemeal fashion she added a new floor, commercial mixers, and paint. Soon whiffs of peanut butter, oatmeal, and chocolate chips fluttered out the door tempting passerbys. Maybe it's a success story because she is a wild card with unabashed optimism and props to match non-stop creative energy.

Newspapers get a lot of credit for making **KIZITO** a success story, she is quick to say. Colorful articles and pictures got her face before the public and soon she found a line waiting for her arrival—serious cookie monsters. Her big break came when she developed wholesale niches out of state.

Growing up in the village of Nansana in Uganda, Elizabeth **KIZITO** had 36 brothers and sisters, the offspring of her "father's five or six wives," Kizito explained. But her mother was the main wife, so she enjoyed a comfortable lifestyle. Like father, like daughter. "He

owned a bakery much like Rainbow," she said. With mixed emotions she described being sent to a very strict Roman Catholic boarding school run by a Canadian nun. Although she understood that education was the way to get ahead, she only came home every three months and she was horribly homesick. Besides, Elizabeth **KIZITO** had never done house work. The school was self-sufficient and students were required to grow all the food, clean rooms, wash and iron the clothes. She had to work harder than she'd ever been expected at home. Looking back, she credits that discipline and strict lifestyle for providing strength when she needed it most.

As she talked about Uganda under Idi Amin she described the devastation of the family home which "was ruined just like Tara. It was a civil war that lasted two years and lots of family were killed. That's why I didn't go back home; it was too scary for me when I finished college in America. They took everything we had, even stole doors and windows out of the house. I took a year's profits to my mother for her to restore the house."

All of her life she has been fascinated with the United States. "I dreamed about it. I befriended an exchange teacher at boarding school and within a month I was on my way to finish high school in Denver, Colorado." She arrived in New York City bewildered by cross-cultural differences and a language barrier. Since the words "Denver" and "Geneva" sound alike, she found herself on a flight to Geneva just long enough to miss the Denver plane. But she tells memories on herself in a laugh-with-me attitude that make her miseries seem almost enjoyable.

Elizabeth **KIZITO** has accomplished great things against great odds because ambition born of desperation was the key motivator. She invented her own winning routine that brings a touch of Uganda to the streets of Kentucky. Actually she is a textbook study in the choreography of selling: hats, baskets, street corners, infectious smile—a veritable whirlwind of fast talking, joyous exuberance. Elizabeth **KIZITO** found a new world in America bathed in chocolate chip cookies. Kentucky welcomes her with open arms.

Sarah Gertrude Knott

The Princeton Times Leader

By Michael Ann Williams

"As the frog said to the tick, you got hold of something big."[1] These were the words Pulitzer Prize-winning playwright Paul Green wrote to Sarah Gertrude Knott in 1933, in response to a letter sent to him explaining her extraordinary idea. With Green's encouragement and the endorsement he secured from President Franklin D. Roosevelt, Knott's dream became reality when the first National Folk Festival was held in St. Louis in May, 1934. This festival was the nation's first major multicultural folk festival and

Knott remained its director until her retirement in 1971.

Sarah Gertrude Knott was born on January 31, 1895, in the community of Kevil, Kentucky, on the border of Ballard and McCracken counties. Not content with rural life in far western Kentucky, Knott aspired to be an actress. After high school, she picked up drama training at various institutions and in the mid-1920s ended up in North Carolina, eventually working for the Bureau of Community Drama under the direction of Frederick Koch at the University of North Carolina.

During this period Knott fell under the sway of the idea of "folk drama" as promoted by Koch, Paul Green and others.

At the beginning of the Great Depression, Knott moved to St. Louis where she continued her involvement in community drama. "When we started the festival," Knott stated in a 1971 interview, "I wasn't dedicated to folk song and dance. In fact, I knew nothing about it. I was trained along dramatic lines and...I got sold on the idea of rural drama, of simple natural drama that grew out of the lives of people...I had this other experience that made me appreciate the honest-to-goodness culture, the natural culture, and the natural need that people have for some kind of an artistic outlet."[2]

Unlike other festival promoters of the day, Knott wasn't presenting the folk culture of a single group or region. From the outset, her festival featured cultural diversity and always had strong African American and Native American components. The key to the success of the festival was that Knott relied on the expertise of the noted scholars and collectors of folklore of the day, as well as the help of prominent literary figures such as Paul Green (who served for many years as president of the National Folk Festival Association) and folklorist/author, Zora Neale Hurston.

The National Folk Festival became

National Council for Traditional Arts

Program book cover from the Third National Folk
Festival, Dallas, 1936

*"I got sold on the idea of rural drama,
of simple natural drama that grew out
of the lives of people."*

Second
NATIONAL
FOLK FESTIVAL

Different Program Every Afternoon and Evening

May 14-18
MEMORIAL AUDITORIUM
CHATTANOOGA

Knott's life work. As friends noted, she "ate, drank, breathed, and slept" the festival.[3] She poured all her energy and resources into it. The festival under Sarah Knott never was totally financially secure. Knott moved it and herself from city to city seeking support. In the late 30s and early 40s, the National Folk Festival found a semi-permanent home in Washington, D.C., with the financial support of *The Washington Post*. Soon America's involvement in the war effort would again send the festival on the road. Although Knott maintained strong connections to her family in Kentucky, the National Folk Festival has only been held in her home state twice (Covington in 1963 and Florence in 1964).

In the 1960s a new era of folk festivals came into being. Sarah Knott was somewhat at odds with the new generation of folk enthusiasts, including those within her own organization who felt that the festival had become stagnant and old-fashioned. Even with her official retirement in 1971, Knott was reluctant to let go of the reins of the festival. She returned to Kentucky to live with her sister in Princeton, but kept involved in the festival for several years until ill health forced her from such activity. Even after retirement, she remained an active promoter of folk arts; in her own words, "pestering" people to start up or continue festivals throughout the country. Knott died in a nursing home in 1984, as one family friend put it, still talking of the National Folk Festival.[4]

The National Folk Festival continues today. During the 1970s the original association became the National Council for the Traditional Arts and the festival underwent a considerable facelift. Still Knott's vision of a national festival featuring the scope of the country's cultural diversity remains intact. Although the orientation hardly seems radical today, Sarah Gertrude Knott was a visionary during times when most festival promoters believed that only the supposedly "pure" Anglo-Saxon traditions were worthy of presentation and preservation.

Helen Lew Lang

"One never does things alone," says Helen Lang, quickly naming dozens of friends and family she credits with making Crane House an internationally recognized center for learning about Chinese culture. Yet it has been Helen Lang's vision, dedication, and at the beginning even her personal possessions, that made Crane House a reality.

She was at an age when most people might narrow their interests to grandchildren and retirement pursuits when she decided to create a non-profit organization that promotes understanding about the country where her parents and eldest brother were born.

Lang's mother and father, who immigrated to Seattle, Washington, in the early part of the 20th century, instilled in her a love of China. As a young woman, who learned to speak Cantonese at home, she was inspired by a visit to the China Institute in New York City when she worked with the Chinese delegation to the United Nations. Her degree in Far Eastern Studies from the University of Washington deepened her knowledge and understanding of her own ancestors.

Lang's love of history only adds to her credentials as the guiding light for an institution which promotes multicultural appreciation and respect.

When Crane House opened its doors in Louisville in 1987, the resources were almost immediately in demand. Today, students of all ages, business people, and the general public attend educational programs, taste Chinese dishes, use the library (which now has over 1,000 volumes), and ask question after question. Kentucky is not a state with rich diversity in its population which might tend to make us insular and provincial. Because we lack a vibrant ethnic and racial mixture it is perhaps *more* important that we educate our children and ourselves to develop cultural openness. When succeeding generations encounter a world wider than Kentucky they will need to know how to interact and respect people of many cultures.

"In the beginning, Helen Lang worked every day without pay," according to Gladys Horvath, Executive Director of Crane House.

Self-effacing Helen Lang sees it differently. "I love what I do," she says simply. "We must learn to respect our differences."

Professional volunteering has long been a way of life for her, primarily in causes associated with Asian culture and multiculturalism, but she also has contributed her interests and talents to such disparate groups as government task forces, jazz societies, and her children's schools. Even before establishing Crane House, Helen Lang's culinary skills were well-known in this region. "Cooking is an art form like writing a symphony," says the master Asian chef who studied *tai pei* in Taiwan and who is always learning more dishes during her frequent visits to China. Each trip to China results in additional resources and new educational ideas for Crane

At her wedding on the arm of her brother.

House which is already overflowing with artifacts and creativity.

Young people are our future," says Helen Lang, who believes opportunities are greatest for those who recognize that ours is a global society and economy. To play an effective part in the world of tomorrow, she suggests that young people learn a language, join an international organization, and travel. To become culturally literate about China, begin by reading books about the Chinese people— their fairy tales, history, and traditions. It is the next best thing to traveling there, and

Growing up with her family in Seattle, Washington.

Lang at the Summer Palace, Beijing.

Helen Lang supplies all Kentuckians with the gift of a China connection.

The recipient of numerous awards, Helen Lang is particularly pleased that Louisville's Trinity High School presented her with its 1997 Peace Award. She firmly believes that promoting multicultural understanding and respect is an endeavor which contributes to world peace. She encourages Kentuckians to express a need for worldwide peace through an awareness and sensitivity to other cultures.

Working quietly and without any desire for personal recognition, Helen Lew Lang continues to draw an ever broader base of support even as Crane House broadens its scope to include all of Asia. Its official name is now the Asia Institute, but the organization will always be known informally as Crane House.

It seems appropriate that the crane is an ancient Asian symbol for longevity and that Helen Lang's greatest wish for the organization she founded is exactly that— longevity. With the solid footing and caring guidance Helen Lang has provided, there is little doubt her desire will be fulfilled.

Lily May Ledford

ily May Ledford grew up the seventh of fifteen children in the Red River Gorge section of Powell County, with its "wealth of giant ferns, laurel, dogwood, and redbud." Her family farmed corn and sorghum cane; raised vegetables to be dried, canned, and pickled; always kept a few farm animals; and supplemented their produce with wild greens, rabbits, berries, nuts, and fish.

"Our papa," she wrote, "as well as being one of the best banjo pickers and fiddlers I ever knew, was talented in woodwork and carpentry." But "Mama believed in work and plenty of it as a cure-all for everything," she said. With such a large family the only way to survive was for everyone to do her share of the work, which did not leave Ledford much time for playing the banjo.

When she was twelve, the family moved down river where there were other farms and lots of young people, and the musical Ledfords fit right into this new world of church singing, square dances, tobacco settings, and other festive events. Some of the Ledford children and a neighbor boy soon formed a band called the "Red River Ramblers" that played for events outside the valley, usually with Ledford doing the fiddling. Soon, an audition was arranged for Ledford with WLS radio in Chicago, and at nineteen she was on the train with a ticket paid for by a pig her father had sold.

John Lair was the music librarian for WLS and Ledford was on several radio programs, but now she was playing the banjo, not the fiddle, in a rare, frail-style (or claw hammer style). Lair became her agent, concocted the Coon Creek Girls and staged their stereotypical Appalachian image. Then he took them to a radio station in Cincinnati and finally to his lifetime dream of a radio program and Barndance show, which he built at Renfro Valley, Kentucky. Along the way, Coon Creek Girls Lily, Rosie, Violet, and Daisy had a hard row to hoe. Lily May had already been teased by fellow Chicago musicians about her mountain accent and had become the subject of a running cartoon entitled "Lily May."

The impresario Lair gave them the opportunity of a lifetime to take their music out of the mountains to the big city, and they became wildly popular for generations of radio listeners. But it was at a price, and the price did not include a good pay check.

Granddaughter Cari Norris, who looks disarmingly like her grandmother and is herself an artist and musician today, explained that John Lair controlled their image by projecting them as naive young women who went to church every Sunday, who were upstanding and very well-chaperoned. "The first all-string female band in America," she pointed out, "was on the cutting edge and Lair knew he had to balance their image with the public's traditional expectations of

women during the 1930s-1950s. And he did a good job. They gained a national audience for their music."

The Coon Creek Girls had a fiery, energetic, foot-stomping style usually reserved for men. In the Kentucky mountains, women did not play the music. They sang ballads and religious songs while the men did the stomping. The music of the Coon Creek Girls sounded like square dance tunes, the kind that make you move your feet automatically. That always reminds granddaughter Cari Norris of the White House story. First Lady Eleanor Roosevelt invited the Coon Creek Girls to be part of a concert of American music which she had organized in honor of the first visit by the King and Queen of England. The Coon

shadowed by the upstart Grand Old Opry. But what makes Ledford's story even more amazing is that she had a renaissance.

In 1967, a recording company gathered the Coon Creek Girls together again for a just-for-old-times-sake reunion. Against a backdrop of an American folk music resurgence, as much the result of the 60s peace movement as anything else, came Lily May Ledford. After a few years with

And He was called
    the Rose of Sharon
This son, God gave us all
And life like a rose,
    starts just a bud
And toward its end,
    the petals fall

Lily May Ledford Pennington
March 17, 1917
July 15, 1985

Services
Wednesday
July 17, 1985
2:00 PM
Berea Baptist Church
Rev. Randy Osborne

Burial
Berea Cemetery

Creek Girls joined Alan Lomax, Marian Anderson, and others, and Lily May Ledford told her granddaughter how much she loved being dressed up in an evening dress, riding in a limousine, and being served caviar sandwiches and raspberry punch. Ledford remembered that everyone was smiling "but the King, with rather a long-faced dour, dead-pan look, worried me a little. Then as I glanced down I caught him patting his foot, ever so little, and I knew we had him."

But expectations prevailed and Lily May Ledford left the show in the late 50s to marry and raise a family. Not a bad time to exit because radio was being eclipsed by television and the Renfro Valley Barndance was becoming over-

the Coon Creek Girls again, she went out on her own. A grant from the National Endowment for the Arts made it possible for Ledford to join Berea College in a music residency. Her new image was tied to performances that educated the public to appreciate traditional Appalachian music and its roots, and she was

amazed at the interest.

Lily May Ledford and the Coon Creek Girls left a legacy of traditional Appalachian music that stretches all the way to the current Reel World String Band, another all-female Kentucky band. For the Kentucky woman with only an eighth grade education she became a star-studded performer not once but twice. Lily May Ledford resonated with a smoky, husky timbre as she sang and the people loved her.

(Top right) Cover of Standby magazine, publication of Chicago radio station WLS, c.1938.

(Left) Lily May in center of the Coon Creek Girls, c. 1950.

(Top left) Lily May on the fiddle with the Coon Creek Girls, c. 1938.

(Above, center) Funeral program.

Photos: Berea College Archives

Alma Wallace Lesch

By Diane Heilenman

In her Cape Cod house on a quiet street in Shepherdsville, Alma Lesch has a new textile portrait pinned and almost ready to stitch up. She works in her basement, which is her real studio. It is the place where design happens and that is the most fun of art. The back of her kitchen door is her gallery where she hangs works in progress.

She stitches things together in her living room, seated in a blue slipcovered armchair. "Stitching is the drudgery part of art," she said. Lesch is a meticulous craftswoman with an inventory of stitches as varied as the needles she keeps at hand. She works with the radio on; "I don't like TV very much," she said.

A five-gallon bucket of buttons is hidden upstairs behind her blue chair. Lesch is noted for fashioning button necklaces, strung with all the care of pearls. The basement studio is lined with stacks of old and antique clothes bought at auction or —now that she has been famous for several decades—sent to her.

Born in 1917 in McCracken County, Lesch calls herself an "accumulator." She is the undisputed grande dame of Kentucky textile arts and is nationally recognized as a pioneer of the contemporary crafts movement. It is, she said, a life that is a "product" of the people and teachers she has encountered. But she has also been influenced by people she knew only through their clothes. She remembers the moment that crystallized her role in contemporary crafts. "I was in the basement sorting...clothes (just bought at

an auction). It occurred to me, why not make a portrait...with clothes? They were so different. I was afraid to show them. I was afraid of ridicule." It was the 1960s and portraits from old clothes had never been seen.

University of Louisville textile professor Lida Gordon said that Lesch's work has been part of the acceptance of traditionally female processes as viable media for contemporary art. For Lesch it has all been a matter of doing what she wanted to do. She finished her first quilt at age 12, a quilt begun as panels when she was 5. "In grade and high school I made textile objects and designed and sewed part of my clothing. I later found out that this was art," Lesch said.

Alma Lesch received the 1987 Kentucky Governor's Award for Lifetime Contribution to Visual Arts and in 1996, she was the first recipient of the Rude Osolnik Award from the Kentucky Art and Craft Foundation. The Foundation recognized Lesch for her many years as an artist and teacher, author of a classic text on vegetable dyes and producer of 25 one-woman shows.

After retiring from teaching third grade, Lesch dove into civic work and auctions. Lesch said she would wait until the end and bid on the woman's button box. "You never knew what all would be in it," she said. It was not enough. "Eventually, I became so bored, I went back to school." She started taking art classes. "I just went crazy," she said. "It just exploded in my mind to see everything that was going on and I knew I could do it."

(At left) "Minutes of the Last Meeting," made from Lesch's own dress with the minutes in the pocket.

(Right, top) Recipe from Vegetable Dyes, *the classic text by Lesch.*

(Right) Award-winning fabric collages.

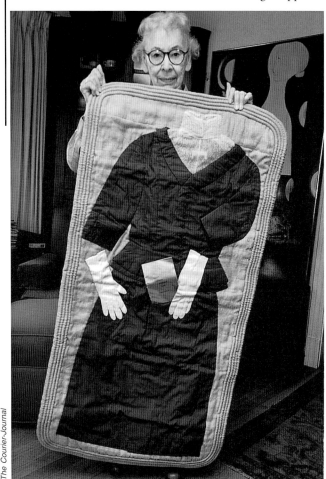

The Courier-Journal

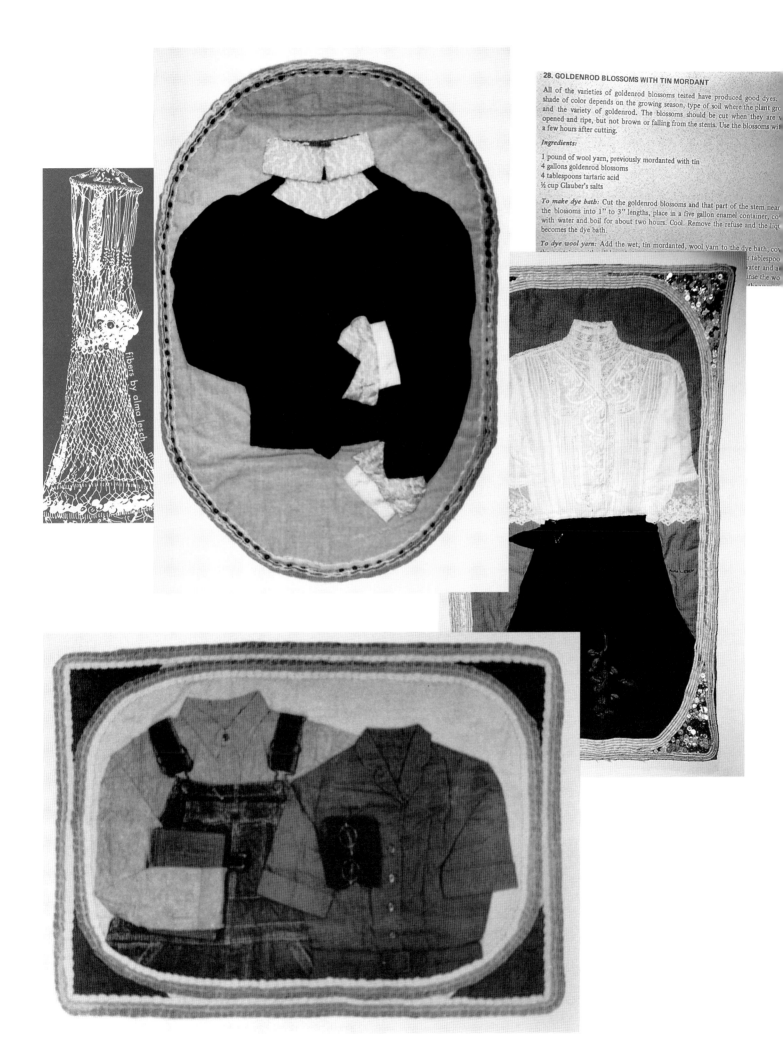

28. GOLDENROD BLOSSOMS WITH TIN MORDANT

All of the varieties of goldenrod blossoms tested have produced good dyes. shade of color depends on the growing season, type of soil where the plant gr and the variety of goldenrod. The blossoms should be cut when they are opened and ripe, but not brown or falling from the stems. Use the blossoms wit a few hours after cutting.

Ingredients:

1 pound of wool yarn, previously mordanted with tin
4 gallons goldenrod blossoms
4 tablespoons tartaric acid
½ cup Glauber's salts

To make dye bath: Cut the goldenrod blossoms and that part of the stem near the blossoms into 1" to 3" lengths, place in a five gallon enamel container, co with water and boil for about two hours. Cool. Remove the refuse and the liqu becomes the dye bath.

To dye wool yarn: Add the wet, tin mordanted, wool yarn to the dye bath, cov

101

Florida Slone Lovely

"*I always thought of myself as a bean being planted in a garden, then someone put a big rock on top of me so that I could not get out of the ground. There's so much in life you miss if you can't read or write.*"

After my husband died I went to the grocery store to buy some flour. I walked to the shelf and realized that I couldn't tell the difference between self-rising and plain flour because I couldn't read or write. I was 62 years old and my husband had always done the shopping. I just backed out of the store because I was too embarrassed to ask anybody to help me."

But Florida Slone, a deeply religious woman from Hindman, did not rest in her illiteracy. Bolstered by her faith and a determined spirit she not only went on to read, write and study for her GED, she also became a song writer and singer. The source of her fame is simply the fact that she is the genuine article—a good Christian woman.

"Saying 'I can't' does something to your body because you have no self-respect for yourself. Faith and 'I can try' gives hope to do it." Faith took Slone through the death of her first husband and the inevitable parting of six grown children. She had to stare down the same question many women do at 62: What next? Rather than rattle around alone in her house, Slone decided now would be a good time to learn to read. And while she was at it, she'd get her driver's license. Through classes at the literacy center of The Hindman Settlement School, she also learned how to write checks and read her *Bible*.

Slone's life has been a continual spiritual journey, and her experience with literacy no different. "The first book I read was about George Washington Carver. When it came to the part about the black man praying, it really helped me better than anything."

Slone was silenced as a child by an illness which rendered her unable to articulate. The shame of her speech pattern pushed her deeper into silence. Barely educated as a child, she was passed from grade to grade learning very little. Eventually she learned to speak, but not to read and write. She pushed her children toward education, as much because of her own missed opportunity as for their benefit. But as they grew and learned, she became even more painfully

aware of her own ignorance. "When they came home from school, they and my husband would sit and talk for hours on things I did not know about, and I did not feel like part of the family. I felt stupid and hurt."

She may have had little to say at those times, but all the while she was writing songs. She couldn't put them on paper, yet, but they were inside her head. "The Lord gave me the tunes and the words. Had them in my head long before I learned to read and write," she said in an interview on National Public Radio. Once she learned to write songs, her voice so long silenced, found its way. She wrote about all the things that matter deeply to her: God, family, regrets, and the ills of tobacco. Florida Lovely penetrates Kentucky's traditional reliance on tobacco with her genial, kindly presence of song. "'Chew Tobacco' is one of my favorites. I'm praying for hemp to take over tobacco. Feel sorry for farmers because they need to live good. But they need to raise something that don't kill people. My prayers are for everyone not to smoke."

Many songs seem evangelical at first glance, but actually they reveal a deep understanding of humanity. Slone speaks

of the "little church house way down in my heart." That tune is in part about her personal relationship with Jesus, and also about right thought and action in the most general terms. She says one thing true of all of us, "Every time I do wrong, I know it from the start." In fact, her little church is her own conscience. Florida Slone remarried in 1997 and daughter Christine observed, "Mom really fell in love, she's had a hard life, and she deserves this happiness."

Florida S. Lovely uses God's revelation and salvation not to teach a moral lesson, but to sing about a moment in her life that has particular integrity or meaning. Some women consider them moments of epiphany, but for Lovely her music is like moral meditation. Her tunes are simple and lyrics direct, but they are full of such

wisdom and often pithy wit that she has become a prophet of sorts, Kentucky's everywoman with a heart of gold. Her grandfather taught her life's guiding principle, that "being good is really what counts in a person's life," and Florida Slone Lovely has become a well-known Kentuckian because she is good, filled with a natural, warm, infectious love of life.

Loretta Lynn

*C*oal Miner's Daughter, The Queen of Country Music. By any other name she is still Kentucky's Loretta Lynn from Butcher Holler.

Married at thirteen, a grandmother at twenty-eight, Loretta Webb Lynn has never forgotten what it was like to be poor, to be country, to be regular. People lived just one day at a time, patching their houses and planting survival gardens, while city folk worried about things like the energy crisis. There were no cars, roads, or electricity in Butcher Holler, and Lynn says in her autobiography, *Coal Miner's Daughter*, that she first saw electric lights one year at Christmastime in Van Lear, a nearby coal mining town. The Webb's home was four miles further up the mountains at the end of a dirt road that ran alongside the creek.

Lynn considers her father an important influence on her life. He was the quintessential hard-working devoted father who labored his entire life to support their eight children, including going into the cramped confines of Kentucky's coal mines and breathing dust for years on end. She remembers him saving up for a battery-operated Philco radio. He'd make them save the batteries for Saturday night, when he was off work in the coal mines. "I still hear that great deep voice of Lowell Thomas today, and it makes me think of Daddy," she writes in her autobiography. "Then we'd get our favorite radio program of all—the Grand Old Opry." Unfortunately, her father died before she starred on the Opry.

Loretta and Doolittle Lynn moved to Washington state in 1959 and that's where it all began. At Doo's insistence she picked up a guitar and taught herself a few songs. Though she had not yet learned to read and write, or even read music, she was able to write and score songs. When an idea came to her she'd jot it down on a paper bag or napkin and stuff it in her purse. Then, usually late at night, she would sit down and work it out. In the morning she'd wake up with the complete verse and work the tune in her head. Someone else had to put the

Billy Reed for *The Courier-Journal*

notes down on paper, but the song was hers.

Loretta Lynn's songwriting is not unlike her approach to her autobiography, brutally honest and entirely familiar. She has none of the pretensions you sometimes see among the rich and famous. (But she refuses to give her exact date of birth.) That's probably why she has been so wildly successful as a country music star. Her fans don't live very differently from the way she did for years. Her ability to speak on the level with millions of Americans who love her music certainly helped make her popular. So did the fact that she was entirely devoted to her fans. Lynn spent decades of her life busing across America playing in every joint along the way. Before she could afford her own elaborate touring

David DeJean for
The Courier-Journal

Barbara Montgomery for *The Courier-Journal*

bus, she slept in the back seat of the car and changed clothes in gas station restrooms.

Time away and endless hours on the road did not come without a price. In fact, in her autobiography, Loretta Lynn laments the amount of time she has traveled in her life. For one thing, it kept her from her family. "It's a pretty emotional subject with me," she writes, "how I wasn't around when my kids needed me."

It also physically exhausted her. The singer suffered migraines just like her father and her lifestyle did not make things any easier. But she was born to sing and fatigue couldn't keep her from the stage. That was her place to shine.

Just about everywhere else, though, her late husband Doolittle Lynn had the upper hand. "When you love a man, you love him all the way," she wrote, "but I guess I always felt Doo was in charge of me, just like Daddy."

By the mid-70s Loretta Lynn had become the first woman to be named Entertainer of the Year by the Academy of Country Music and the Country Music Association. For twelve years she was voted Top Female Artist by country music fans. She became one of the most famous and well-loved country stars ever. She even performed at The White House.

It's a long way from Butcher Holler to 1600 Pennsylvania Avenue, but if you're Loretta Lynn, not much changes along the way. First and foremost, she will always be the little girl who grew up in Butcher Holler, Kentucky.

(Above right) Singing to benefit families of the victims of the 1971 Hyden mine disaster.
(Above left) Lynn hugs George Vecsey, author of Coal Miner's Daughter, at the premier of the film by the same name. At left is Phyllis George Brown and at right is "Mooney" Doolittle, Lynn's husband.

105

Lucille Parker Wright Markey

By Lynn S. Renau

The day she died, the flags at Belmont Park flew at half-staff. *The New York Times* headlined her July 26, 1982 obituary, "Lucille Parker Markey, 85, Calumet Farm Owner, Dies" and placed it in the coveted upper left-hand corner of the obituary page.

Even in death, it appeared that 93 year-old Lucille Parker Wright Markey had had the last laugh. Only Calumet's descent into bankruptcy in 1991 refocused public curiosity on Lucille Markey's life.

In fact, Lucille Wright Markey did not own Calumet Farm. She was a life tenant, bound by her first husband's will to keep Calumet intact for their son or sell it, with proceeds going into a residuary trust, which Warren Wright, Jr. or his heirs would inherit at his mother's death.

What was hers to do with as she pleased was her inheritance from Warren Wright. In the last years of her life, she gave $5.25 million to build the Markey Cancer Center at the University of Kentucky. The bulk of her $300 million estate endowed the Lucille P. Markey Charitable Trust, an unusually innovative arrangement Markey stipulated be dissolved fifteen years after her death. She wanted it directed by the trustees she named—such as her steadfast secretary, Margaret Glass, who understood her wishes and dictates. When the trust was dissolved in July, 1997 it had provided half a billion dollars—the largest charitable bequest ever

made by a resident of Lexington—to institutions nationwide and 113 Markey scholars, promising young researchers whose work, without Markey Trust support, might not have been possible.

Lucille Parker Markey's life was extraordinary, and eight years longer than her contemporaries realized. She came from Tollesboro, Kentucky (Lewis County), the youngest of seven children of a teacher-livery stable operator and his disabled wife.

Warren Wright, newly divorced heir to the Calumet Baking Powder fortune, met Lucille Parker in Chicago. They were married on March 25, 1919 and after an extended honeymoon in France, they returned to Chicago in 1920, a nanny and baby in tow. Warren Wright, Jr. was a sore disappointment to his mother; she distanced herself from him as much as possible, eventually referring to him as an adopted child. His remarkable resemblance to his father and grandfather led friends to believe otherwise.

Calumet Farm biographer, Ann Auerbach, wrote that Warren Wright "plucked (Lucille) from her working-class existence...and deposited her, securely, for the rest of her life, into the fairy tale-like world of a multimillionaire."

But Warren Wright was dour and self-centered. Wright's father, William Monroe Wright, had sold his company right before the '29 Crash and invested his fortune wisely—with one exception. He loved trotting horses; Calumet Farm was his dream come true. Warren Wright did not approve of his father's spendthrift ways, nor of his passion for such a blue-collar sport. At his father's death, Warren inherited Calumet. He bought Thoroughbreds and went to the races in style. After he took Lucille's advice and hired trainers Ben and Jimmy Jones, Calumet-bred horses dominated Thoroughbred racing. Wright loved accepting trophies in the winner's circle while his wife sat silent, seen but not heard in their box. The farm was their summer home. There, Lucille Wright did needlepoint, collected images of eagles and studied Christian Science.

Warren Wright died in 1950. Lucille Wright was then 62 years old. After a decent period of mourning, a new Mrs. Wright emerged. She went to Europe for a face-lift and to Paris for her wardrobe. She became Thoroughbred racing's vivacious grande dame. In September, 1952 she married thrice-divorced (from Joan Bennett, Hedy Lamarr and Myrna Loy)Hollywood bon vivant Gene Markey. She trimmed eight years off her birth date, making herself a year younger than her husband. Their fairy tale romance lasted twenty-eight years. The Markeys made their last public appearance together at the 1978 running of Keeneland's Bluegrass Stakes to watch her beloved Alydar run. He ran second to Affirmed in all three Triple Crown races that spring. There would be no ninth Kentucky Derby trophy for Calumet Farm.

Merry Christmas!

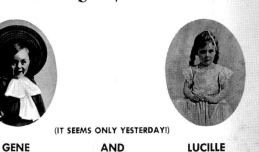

(IT SEEMS ONLY YESTERDAY!)

GENE   **AND**   **LUCILLE**

THE FLORIDA
TURF WRITERS AWARD

To The Owner Of The Outstanding
Horse Which Competed In Florida ---
1956-57 --- The Owner Of Bardstown

MRS. GENE MARKEY

(Left) A Caricature by PEB after winning the Turf Writers Award.

It was Gene Markey who persuaded his wife to donate that first million to cancer research. By then, she was estranged from her son—he died in 1978—and her grandchildren.

Markey died in 1980 and was buried in the Lexington Cemetery. In 1982, Lucille Parker Markey's casket was placed alongside her second husband's. Etched on the side of the mausoleum was her chosen name, Lucille Parker Markey, and the birth date 1896. She had the final say. The Wright name was nowhere to be seen.

(Above) The Markeys dress up in pioneer costumes.

All photos courtesy of the Kentucky Derby Museum.

M E R R Y   C H R I S T M A S

Rear Admiral and Mrs. Gene Markey

Judy Martin

Martin speaks at a Family Matters Conference in Washington, D.C.

"I'm the one who brought blankets to the women brave enough to work on the front lines," says Judy Martin. With self-confidence that comes with maturity, she generously gives away the power and credit to mountain women like "Eula Hall, Bessie Smith, or Helen Lewis who stood in front of bulldozers and got jailed for picketing," she remembers.

But history shows that women like Judy Martin are too self-effacing. Kentucky would be far poorer without this woman who has dedicated her whole life to making investments in "women who want something better for their kids. I help clear the path," she says. Women are conspicuous leaders in eastern Kentucky and at the close of the 20th century, their pride seems to be at an all-time high. Martin is an inspirational example of someone who began as a VISTA Volunteer with the War on Poverty program and thirty years later continues to involve the community in making change.

President Lyndon Baines Johnson sat on Tom Fletcher's front porch one spring day in 1964. He had come to Inez, Kentucky to declare war on poverty. Appalachia was a region with startling statistics that revealed an inordinate number of poor, uneducated people who relied upon a system that created dependent people and sustained local political machines. The War on Poverty program sent young Volunteers in Service to America (VISTA) into needy communities to help people at the grassroots level decide for themselves what changes were needed. The process was meant to inspire productivity, pride and self-reliance.

In Kentucky, summertime workers were called Appalachian Volunteers (AVs) and Judy Martin became an AV in 1964, when she was a student at Berea College. She taught in a one-room schoolhouse, but like other AVs she began to wonder what kind of system produced and sustained such dire poverty. AVs discovered that maybe people were poor because their land had been mismanaged and exploited by absentee coal and timber lords. Historically, government money never trickled down to the grassroots in eastern Kentucky because it did not get beyond politically influential officials like

Martin's beloved Grandmother and two daughters.

county judges, school superintendents and coal operators. AVs like Judy Martin became conduits of information and communication to grassroots people.

One AV fringe benefit for Martin was the opportunity to work with the Harvard University child psychiatrist Robert Coles and his all-male student research team who came to evaluate the effectiveness of the AV program. She was fascinated with the way his Harvard student assistants seemed to "have a way of fawning over him for his approval." She was not accustomed to a professor with an admiring entourage. They never treated her as a peer, even separating from her at meals, until Coles mentioned he was impressed with her writing. Overnight she gained their respect. Martin was especially valuable on the team, she says, " because I was a good listener and people told me things in their own way. Non-verbal communication is really important in the mountains. I was looking for what people wanted to tell me, not what I wanted to ask them."

Judy Martin was particularly effective because her family had been Kentuckians for generations. Many War on Poverty volunteers were from outside the state. But she had been raised in Cincinnati when mountain people like her parents left Appalachia seeking better jobs and wages during World War II. Her mom worked in a cookie factory and her dad in a war-related factory. She describes her parents as "feeling lost, the city was tough, and nothing was the same. We lived in a basement with no windows." Every weekend the family drove to grandmother's house in Clay County, Kentucky. It was still the home place.

Being a good listener who was interested in families, education, children, and women developed Martin into a dedicated worker with integrity and staying power. Today these are the same threads weaving in and out of her life. When she

left VISTA as the only female field coordinator in Kentucky, Martin worked for a short stint with Save the Children Federation. That led her to the executive director's position at Appalachian Communities for Children, a multifaceted, community-based group made up of low-income families in Jackson and Clay Counties, and she's been there ever since. It operates and is governed by the families of the communities it serves.

Martin's organizing and planning skills have come to bear fruit: tutoring partnerships with schools; *Women in Literacy* programs in partnership with churches, homes, libraries, and schools; *KY Homeplace*, a health care demonstration project; *Mountain Women Empowerment Project* , which helps women take charge of their own lives; and the only rural pilot site for the much publicized *Family Matters* program funded by the national Points of Light organization.

What are the origins of all this drive and caring? When you dig deeper, you find grandparents who were great influences. Grandfather Spurlock valued education to such an extent that he sent all eleven children from Bear Creek to Oneida Baptist Institute, "paying tuition with hog meat and loads of apples," she remembers. Grandmother Ibby Spurlock, who lived to be 102 years old, taught Judy how to work with a plain-speaking philosophy: "Do what you have to do and work hard for what you want."

She instilled in Judy that she "was *somebody*, that I was *dearly* loved," she remembers with fondness.

The land still holds Judy Martin, and she is rooted on top of a mountain near Berea. She can dig her fingers through the soil and know that it is the home place. "The comfort level is high here and this land is part of me," she says. Martin understands that families in Eastern Kentucky want to care for their own and she is still "bringing the blankets" to make sure that families don't have to leave like her parents did to find decent jobs, better education, and quality health care.

Martin's view from the home place near Berea.

Belinda Mason

Guy Mendes

AIDS took Mason's life, not her spirit

She was a poet. A playwright. A reporter. A wife. A mother. And one of the most interesting people you'll ever meet. But the headlines will say "AIDS activist dies."

KEITH LAWRENCE
Messenger-Inquirer

She was a genuinely funny person. The mountain dialect she brought with her from eastern Kentucky was frequently exaggerated for effect. And she could tell stories that would leave you giggling for hours.

But she will be remembered for a disease that snuffed out her life at 33. And that's so unfair.

But remember this: Belinda Mason was not a victim of AIDS. She was a mountain woman, too tough to be a victim of anything. The very sound of that word made her livid.

"Calling someone an AIDS victim is like calling a black person a nigger," she said once, trying to make this newspaper stop using the word.

AIDS took her life. But not her spirit. As she fought the fight she couldn't win, Belinda changed a lot of Middle Americans' attitudes about a disease they thought only happened to "bad people."

She was a grown-up poster child for the movement against AIDS at a time when few Americans cared. A cute 'n' cuddly mother of two who got the disease the "acceptable way" — through a blood transfusion, not sex or drugs.

She died in Nashville. For a

"I have a family. I'm white. I come from the South...easy to respond to...I look right. I got AIDS the right way. Most people with AIDS aren't like me. I'm palatable, like mashed potatoes and gravy, I figure."

In "Belinda," a video by Appalshop Productions, Mason tells why she was the perfect poster heroine for persons with AIDS.

By Anne Shelby

*B*est known as an eloquent and forceful spokesperson for those living with AIDS, Belinda Mason in the late 1980s lent her considerable writing and speaking skills to the cause of securing more humane treatment for the thousands of Americans infected with the HIV virus.

We are all in great danger from this epidemic, not of catching AIDS but of losing our humanity, and in all of history there has never been a cure for that.[1]

Mason co-founded the Kentuckiana People with AIDS Coalition, was elected president of the National Association of People with AIDS, and was appointed by President George Bush to the National Commission on AIDS, the first person with the disease to occupy a seat on the commission. At one of the Commission meetings in Washington, President Bush said he didn't see how he could really make much difference by just talking about the disease, but Belinda Mason wrote him a letter saying that indeed it was his job to speak out:

If we are to limit the toll that AIDS will take on our society, we must all work side by side in the clear light of reason rather than with fears and dark suspicions. Mr. President, those who come after me are counting on you.[2]

Mason worked with her father, Representative Paul Mason of Whitesburg, to write and sponsor legislation to protect the rights of Kentuckians with HIV infections. HB 425, "the AIDS Act," mandates AIDS education for health professionals in Kentucky and legislates against discrimination on the basis of HIV status. *Belinda*, a documentary from Appalshop Films, examines Mason's AIDS work and includes excerpts from her speeches and interviews.

Before contracting HIV in a blood transfusion in 1987, Mason had begun a career as a fiction writer. Her stories appeared in literary magazines and in the anthology *A Gathering at the Forks*. In addition to short fiction, Mason developed a one-act play, *The Gifts of the Spirit*, with Roadside Theater, and began work on a second play. Her unfinished writings include a dozen short stories and a novel, *Merle's Story*, about a teenage boy with AIDS.

Like her speeches and essays, Mason's fiction evinces a rare gift for language, sometimes startling insight, and a kind of celebration of the ordinary, a love for the everyday. One character from *The Gifts of the Spirit* puts it like this:

"Now there's plenty of 'em that would fault me on this, but if the good Lord hadn't meant for us to enjoy life He'd a took us straight to heaven when we was born and skipped over it."

Like their creator, Mason's characters are rural and small-town Kentuckians, who confront questions of meaning, values, perception against a backdrop of kitchen tables and vegetable gardens. "I grew up believing that being a Kentuckian was a special blessing," Mason once said. "Now that I have traveled, I know that what I believed all along was true."[3] Mason grew up in Whitesburg and earned a journalism degree at the University of Kentucky. She worked for the newspaper in Hartford where she lived with her husband and two children. Belinda Mason died in 1991, at the age of thirty-three.

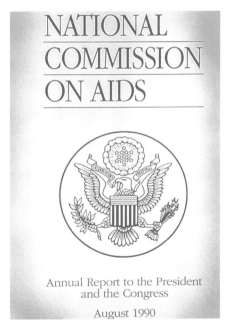

NATIONAL COMMISSION ON AIDS

Annual Report to the President and the Congress

August 1990

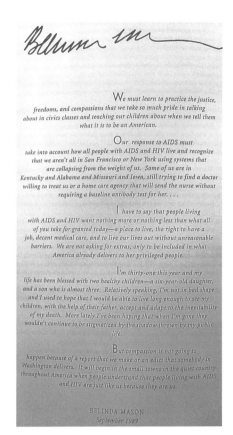

We must learn to practice the justice, freedoms, and compassions that we take so much pride in talking about in civics classes and teaching our children about when we tell them what it is to be an American.

Our response to AIDS must take into account how all people with AIDS and HIV live and recognize that we aren't all in San Francisco or New York using systems that are collapsing from the weight of us. Some of us are in Kentucky and Alabama and Missouri and Iowa, still trying to find a doctor willing to treat us or a home care agency that will send the nurse without requiring a baseline antibody test for her. . . .

I have to say that people living with AIDS and HIV want nothing more or nothing less than what all of you take for granted today—a place to live, the right to have a job, decent medical care, and to live our lives out without unreasonable barriers. We are not asking for extras, only to be included in what America already delivers to her privileged people.

I'm thirty-one this year and my life has been blessed with two healthy children—a six-year-old daughter, and a son who is almost three. Relatively speaking, I'm not in bad shape, and I used to hope that I would be able to live long enough to see my children, with the help of their father, accept and adapt to the inevitability of my death. More lately I've been hoping that when I'm gone they wouldn't continue to be stigmatized by the shadow thrown by my public life.

But compassion is not going to happen because of a report that we make or an edict that somebody in Washington delivers. It will begin in the small towns in the quiet country throughout America when people understand that people living with AIDS and HIV are just like us because they are us.

BELINDA MASON
September 1989

Bobbie Ann Mason

By Michal Smith-Mello

S cratch the surface of this gentle exterior and you discover a rebel whose energies have been unleashed in her acclaimed work as a critic, short story writer, and novelist. For Bobbie Ann Mason, art is an act of defiance, a rejection of the forms she might have been expected to fill in rural western Kentucky. Instead, she chose an altogether different life, that of an artist, but her defiance of convention did not stop with a choice of vocation. The style and the subject matter of her spare, minimalist prose break from a literary tradition that is in many ways as limiting as farm life.

After years of being unable to write, paralyzed by a lack of confidence, Mason finally determined to find her voice in fiction. After submitting nineteen stories, all of which were rejected, Mason received word that the *The New Yorker* would publish her short story, "Offerings." After the 1981 publication of that subtle, understated story, her work soon found its way onto the pages of the nation's top literary magazines.

Ironically, it is the people who live and work in the places Mason most wanted to escape—the farms and factories of western Kentucky—who have held her writing imagination. They work at K-Mart or the local Rexall drug store. They drive school buses, they play Battlestar Gallactica, they read *TV Guide*. They are often inhabitants of a provincial western Kentucky town who are caught up in a rush of change that is strange and incomprehensible. Roles, values, and even truths are being questioned and abandoned with startling rapidity. It is this encounter with change that is particularly acute for her women characters. But the women who inhabit Mason's short stories are more accepting of change, more willing to move with it, to explore, and to become.

"A repressive culture produces a great amount of creative energy. Slavery must have been incredibly intense to have produced energy behind the blues. The whole region (the South), in fact, has produced a great body of American music and writing."

Photographs: Pam Spalding for *The Courier-Journal*

Mason's memory of her childhood is one of being completely cut off from the world. "I had no playmates until I was six and started school." For Bobbie Ann Mason, series books for children and movies were doors to imaginary travel. Mason watched as many as twelve movies a week. Another vivid memory is that of listening to an early rhythm and blues radio station. "The blues which led to rock and roll originated in the Mississippi Delta. I feel like I was kind of close to that, having grown up in that corner of Kentucky so close by," Mason reflects.

Mason believes that early attitudes about rock and roll were intertwined with class consciousness in America. This spiritual connection to the roots of a musical form that broke every rule is akin to a political experience for Mason. She continues to follow rock music. "I'm not by nature a political activist of any sort, but I have a stronger and stronger anti-elitist feeling these days. In general

terms, the few who are privileged have the power and the money, and they are threatened by rising classes," she says.

Like many women, Bobbie Ann Mason eagerly expresses an enormous debt of gratitude to her mother, from whom Mason says all her stories come.

"I worship my mother," Mason offers with genuine reverence. "She was an orphan, raised by a huge family who made her work in the tobacco fields. Her most poignant memory was when the other girls got dolls at Christmas and she got only an orange. Knowing her background makes me care. To compensate, she sacrificed her whole life for her children, her family. She's a real earth mother who gives and gives and gives, a farm woman who is strong and able to take what comes—a real source of inspiration."

While the conventions of place have kept her mother's "streak of individuality" and her father's rebellious nature in

check, they have become something altogether different for Mason, the fuel for a spirited, defiant artistic vision. Ironically, it belongs to a painfully quiet woman, a detached observer of life who comes to companionship uncertain, wary. But those who are privileged to share Bobbie Ann Mason's tentative exploration of the surface of her own life find an artist with a clarity of vision and purpose that gleams from the depths.

Mary Terstegge Meagher

By Barbara W. Beard

"The butterfly chose me," reflected Mary Meagher Plant, an unassuming, strikingly beautiful, caring wife and mother who still holds two world records in swimming for the 100-meter and 200-meter butterfly, considered by many to be the most difficult stroke in competitive swimming. Born Mary Terstegge Meagher, the tenth of eleven children, Mary T. followed her active Louisville family into the pool at age five and started a winning streak that would last for twelve years.

The stop watch became her constant companion, and her family provided the cheerleading and support required on a daily basis. Soon she settled into a "do it all" schedule that started at 5:15 every morning but Sunday, followed by school, additional swimming practice and weight training, and finally dinner, homework and sleep.

Weight training was a fairly novel activity for women in the 70s, but Mary T.'s mastery of the butterfly required enormous shoulder strength to allow her to lift her body out of the water. The butterfly stroke is flashy, demanding, and physically aggressive, but she always made it look so easy.

Such training discipline paid off in the classroom as well, and she used her time in the water to practice math, hone her ability to concentrate, and even daydream about boys. A smart girl with lots of friends, Mary T.'s incentive for continuing the grueling schedule required for national and international competition was one factor—every time she dove into the water she won!

In 1979, at the age of fifteen, Meagher set a world record in the 200-meter butterfly, and in 1980 she set a world record in the 100-meter butterfly. Unfortunately, the U.S. boycott of the Moscow Olympics spoiled her chance to compete, so she had to watch East German women swimmers win medals with times slower that her own.

After graduating high school a year early, Mary T. broke world records in 100-meter and 200-meter butterfly in August, 1981. These records still stand today. It is no wonder that *Sports Illustrated* rated her 100-meter mark of 57.93 seconds as the "fifth-greatest, single event record of all time in any sport."

Traditionally there was little interest in scholarships for female swimmers, who took off their braces and hung up their swimsuits almost simultaneously, but Mary T. had an array of offers and she chose to work towards a degree in child development at the University of California at Berkeley. It was the summer before college that she experienced her first loss, at the World Games. Later, trying to balance college academics and social life with NCAA competition brought pressure to quit—and to eat. Away from the family training table, she had to learn how to eat sensibly and cope with losing. She conquered both and won all her NCAA

championships. Physically and mentally fit for the 1984 Olympics in Los Angeles, Mary T.'s new name became "Madame Butterfly" when she won three gold medals and set Olympic records.

She says that all the records, trophies, accolades, and national attention "just happened" to her. She credits God for "giving me the ability, the nerdiness to go to class, the discipline to practice, the concentration; parents who could afford the time, investment, and support; and excellent coaches" to help her touch the wall before everyone else.

Today, her nickname has changed from "Madame Butterfly" to "Mommy." Her life's chapter in swimming is over and the new role with her own family takes its place, but she plays the new family role with the same enthusiasm, self-discipline, and record setting style. Mary Meagher Plant knows how to win.

Timetable of Winnings

1979   Set world record in 200-meter at Pan Am Games, San Juan, Puerto Rico

1980   Set world record in 100-meter at Austin, Texas; Reset world record in 200-meter butterfly at Irvine, CA
(Both records still stand today)

1984   Three gold medals at Olympic Games, Los Angeles, CA in 100-meter butterfly, 200-meter butterfly and medley relay

1986   Gold medal 200-meter butterfly at World Championships, Madrid, Spain

1987   Winner of Broderick Cup as nation's outstanding collegiate woman athlete

1988   Bronze medal in 200-meter butterfly and silver medal in medley relay at Olympic games, Seoul, Korea; 4-time winner, NCAA 200-meter butterfly; 3-time finalist of Sullivan Award for outstanding USA amateur athlete

1991   Inducted into International Swimming Hall of Fame, Fort Lauderdale, FL

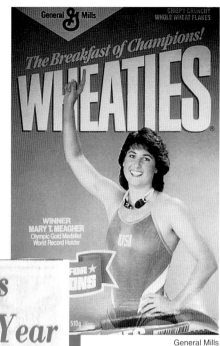

General Mills

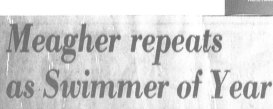

Meagher repeats as Swimmer of Year

Special to The Courier-Journal

SNOWBIRD, Utah — Louisvillian Mary T. Meagher, who has broken her world record in both the 100- and 200-meter butterfly this year, yesterday was named Swimmer of the Year for the second consecutive season by United States Swimming, the national governing body for the sport.

Meagher, 16, who swims for Lakeside Swim Club in Louisville, broke her own world standards in both butterfly events during the USS Long-Course Championships held in August in Milwaukee. She lowered her record in the 200 'fly

record of 59.26 seconds with a 57.93 clocking.

Meagher, who has won 10 national butterfly titles in the past three years, now has the seven fastest 200-meter butterfly times in history, and her world record in that event is three seconds faster than that of any other woman swimmer. Her standard in the 100 betters the second-fastest all-time clocking by 1.53 seconds.

As the USS' Swimmer of the Year, Meagher becomes that body's nominee for the Sullivan Award, which is annually presented in January to the nation's premier amateur athlete. Meagher

The Courier-Journal

115

Ilse Lichtenstein Meyer

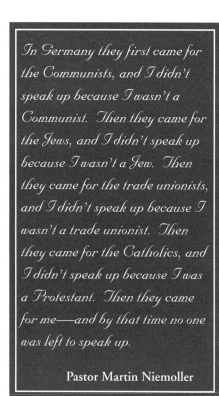

"Survivor" is an inadequate word to describe Ilse Lichtenstein Meyer. She is a healthy, purposeful, caring, and gentle adult who as a child was uprooted, exposed to brutal conditions, separated from a nurturing, once prosperous family, and unceremoniously deposited on foreign soil. Ilse Meyer reminds us that her childhood was a nightmare of despair, but she uses it as a living message of hope and action through example.

Like other German Jews in the 1930s, she could not deny that the world as she knew it was crumbling around her. Once she enjoyed a "very nice normal life" as a member of one of 25 Jewish families in Volkmarsen, Germany, a town where her father's family had lived since 1780. A decorated World War I soldier and owner of a thriving business, her father led Jewish religious services because his town was too small to have a rabbi.

Typical of that time and place, Ilse Lichtenstein attended a Roman Catholic school. Catholic and Protestant friends "used to come over for holidays and be given cakes and cookies or matzo. But after Adolf Hitler came in, it was a different story." These children were required to join Hitler Youth Groups where "they were indoctrinated not to talk to Jews."

"It got worse, every day," she remembers. "The kids would spit at me. They would throw stones at me." Her teacher ordered her to "sit in the back row because otherwise you would contaminate the Gentiles."

Her home life was irrevocably altered by hatred against Jews. Three months after Hitler came to power, she recalls "two SS men in uniforms standing in front of our house with a sign, 'This Is A Jewish House—Don't Buy From Them.'" Worse followed.

Among the horrors that compose her childhood memories is knowing that SS agents tied her 17 year-old cousin behind a horse and dragged him through the cobblestone streets of Kassel. She courageously visited the village of Kassel to check on the safety of the women and children. Within 24 hours of the visit, her parents and younger sister were arrested and briefly jailed. From his jail cell, her father was forced to watch Hitler's agents burn prayer books and sacred objects from the room used as a Jewish house of worship. "His hair, believe me, turned snow white," she says.

One evening the Nazi Party "arrested all the men and the women and they made them march through town to the square and sing 'I Have To Leave My Little Town Now.' I have never, never heard anything like it in my life and never will again." Later the men of Volkmarsen, including her father, were sent for a time to Buchenwald, a concentration camp.

Most of the Lichtenstein's belongings were demolished. "They destroyed every picture, every book. They stole my violin. They took axes to the furniture. They smashed every plate, every cup. They took the feather beds and cut them

Little remains of her family's possessions.

open." Supplies used in her father's business were thrown out windows. Cherished items in her trousseau were missing. The intervention of the police chief, a close friend of Ilse's father, resulted in a coffee pot being saved and the house itself. "If it hadn't been for him, (the house) would have gone up in flames."

When Ilse's mother suffered a heart attack, "the doctor wouldn't come. At midnight I called one of the neighbors. And she came over and we sat and soaked my mother's hands in vinegar because it is all we had—all we could do."

On January 4, 1939, when Ilse Lichtenstein was fifteen, she was sent by train to Holland. As she was the oldest of 120 children on board, she became their informal leader. Lichtenstein left Holland on the last berth of a ship bound for the United States of America. She moved in with her brother in Wisconsin, and for a time her parents were able to write to her. Today their letters are among her most precious possessions. Despite her escape Ilse Meyer has never gotten over the fear or sense of abandonment.

Her parents and sister were sent to a concentration camp, and her last contact was in 1943 when the Red Cross forwarded a message from her father. Ilse Meyer has been unable to document when or where they died. Emotion catches in her throat as she describes the experience of seeing the cattle cars at the Holocaust Museum in Washington, D.C. "I'd forgotten how really small they were. My mother must have had a terrible time," she says as her voice trails off.

She married a man from Kassel. They never speak German. She is an exile who has the supreme confidence to say, "I am an American. I do not long for my homeland," she explains proudly. Most of all she wants all young people to "understand that hatred is wrong—hatred for anyone is wrong." Ilse Lichtenstein Meyer thinks one reason her life was spared in the Holocaust was so that she can talk to children, "so I can tell them what happened and not to ever, ever follow anyone blindly." She is generous with her time and memories, in part, because the 15-year-old in her wants to heal old wounds and pacify hate. She does this in Kentucky schools on a regular basis and now in her 70s seems as determined as ever to convey that message to young people.

Young Ilse with her family in Volkmarsen, Germany.

"Kaethe" is quilted by Penny Sisto in honor of Ilse's mother.

Unfinished cutwork made by her mother, Kaethe Lichtenstein, given to a Christian neighbor before she was transported to a concentration camp, May, 1942. Returned to Ilse Meyer in May, 1996.

Mary Garretson Miller

As you enter the Portland Museum in downtown Louisville, you are greeted by the wooden figure of a woman standing at the wheel of a boat. "Howdy folks, I'm Captain Mary Miller. Welcome aboard the *Saline*, one of the finest little working steams on the Western Waters," says the audiotape. "We usually work the bayou country of Louisiana—around the Red River," she continues, "but right now we're on a special trip home to Portland at the Falls of the Ohio in Kentucky."

Mary Millicent Garretson Miller was born in 1846 to a steamboat engineer and his wife who lived in Portland, near Louisville. Not much is known of her childhood, though no doubt she was familiar with the early nineteenth-century world of steamboats. Opulent, romantic, and beautiful, these white "wedding cakes on water," as one writer described them, attracted young men seeking an exciting and adventurous occupation. But they also brought with them the dangers of river snags, low water, bursting boilers, and collisions.[1]

Steamboat captains, with their extensive knowledge of the river and its ways, were admired and revered in this manliest of professions. Thus, it is not surprising that when Mary Miller applied for her captain's license in 1883, the local U.S. Inspectors of Steam Vessels at the New Orleans office refused her request until they could clear it with the Secretary

Harper's Magazine, 1865

"When I married George Miller, I married the river. And the river's been good to us."

of the Treasury. One story has it that Mary and her husband, Capt. George Miller, were making a run on the Red River and a rival company accused George of operating as both captain and pilot, which was illegal. (Another story suggests that George had developed vision problems, and Mary stepped in to take the exam for him.) No matter the reason, Mary took the exam and passed. The Secretary of the Treasury wired back "that Mrs. Miller be granted a license if fit to perform the duties required, in spite of sex." He also added that such a license may socially degrade any woman to whom it was issued.[2]

Though the Millers operated their steamboat trade out of New Orleans, they continued to maintain their Kentucky residence at 3816 Bank Street in Louisville. George was already a captain when Mary met him, but for four years after they married he worked as a carpenter at a Jeffersonville, Indiana shipyard. Learning the trade as she went, Mary helped him build their 179-foot side-wheeler, the *Saline*. She used an adze to plane long ribbons of shavings from the deckings and with a caulking iron in one hand and a hammer in the other drove oakum into the hull's seams. "Why, not many people are lucky enough to live like me—free and doing what I like best," the museum figure tells us. "When I married George Miller, I married the river. And the river's been good to us."[3]

"She was not a captain only in name

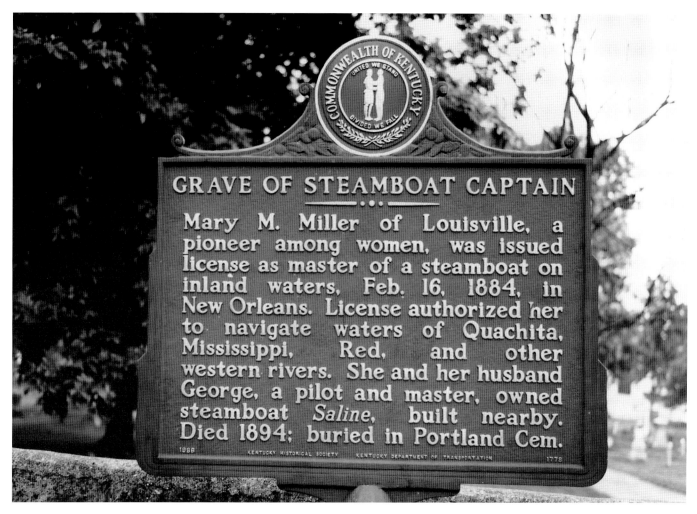

GRAVE OF STEAMBOAT CAPTAIN

Mary M. Miller of Louisville, a pioneer among women, was issued license as master of a steamboat on inland waters, Feb. 16, 1884, in New Orleans. License authorized her to navigate waters of Quachita, Mississippi, Red, and other western rivers. She and her husband George, a pilot and master, owned steamboat *Saline*, built nearby. Died 1894; buried in Portland Cem.

1986   KENTUCKY HISTORICAL SOCIETY   KENTUCKY DEPARTMENT OF TRANSPORTATION   1778

and she managed the boat, did the buying, collecting, etc." wrote a reporter for the New Orleans *Daily Picayune* in September, 1891. The "lady steamboatman," as the article's title called her, was a "pleasant-faced businesslike lady...who combined a natural trading ability with a women's shrewd tact." *The Louisville Commercial* in 1892 described her as "erect of carriage, with muscles of iron, determination depicted on every feature. Her dark brown hair is streaked with gray and is gathered in a careless knot at the back of her head." To insure the reader that she was *still* a woman, he added, "an occasional look of tenderness creeps over her face as she watches her little grandchildren playing..."

Mary Miller continued to serve as captain until 1891, when she and her husband had to sell their boat because of declining business. By then, Captain Miller had seen the importance of steamboats diminished. "Steamboating is not what it used to be. Modern progress has driven steamboat passenger traffic to the wall. People do not want to lose a week of their busy time going to St. Louis by water when they can get there in less

CAPT. MARY M. MILLER DEAD.

She Was the First Woman Granted License As a Steamboat Master.

Stood the Examination In 1883 and Was In Command of the Saline Four Years.

Capt. Mary M. Miller, the first woman to be granted license as a steamboat master, died at 4:30 o'clock yesterday morning at her home on Bank street, between Thirty-ninth and Fortieth.

Mrs. Miller's illness dates back to two years ago, when she returned with her husband, Capt. George Miller, from a trip to the Gulf of Mexico in a small sailboat. Drs. Montgomery and Mayer attended her, and for a while she seemed to get better. About a year ago she lost the use of her lower limbs, and gradually sank until last Friday, when it was thought that she would die. She rallied, however, and was able to talk to her children and other relatives some time before she died.

The manner in which Mrs. Miller became a steamboat captain and the causes which led to it are these: Capt. George Miller, her husband, is an old steamboatman. He is alive and is eighty-six years of age. In March, 1883, he built the steamer Saline, a small boat. He built the boat at the sawmills on the Point. He and his wife started South, Capt. Miller acting as pilot and his wife officiating as clerk. Capt. Miller placed his boat in the Red river trade, running from New Orleans to Bayou Mason. In this trade were several other boats of like capacity, among them the Erie No. 10, of the Blanks line. The owners of this steamer complained to the Board of Steamboat Inspectors at New Orleans

(Above) Marker at entrance to Portland Cemetery, Louisville.

than one-seventh the time by rail," she observed.[4]

When Miller was forty-five and her husband eighty-three, she applied for a position as a lighthouse keeper at East Pascagoula, Mississippi. These plans ended when she contracted an illness that resulted in paralysis, and she died in 1894. Captain Mary Miller's museum statue ends its taped message by telling us that "spirits linger near the places they love...If you listen carefully when you're near this beautiful Ohio River, you may hear the voices of people like me who loved these waters and shores."

Nancy Moore

By Sally Ann Strickler

The Western Reserve Historical Society, Cleveland, Ohio

Nancy Moore was brought into the Shaker colony at South Union in Logan County in 1811 when both she and the colony were four years old. She was a remarkable woman, a shrewd and sensible leader and she lived the remainder of her 82 years at South Union, serving as Eldress or spiritual leader for a nine year period which encompassed the Civil War.

Among the tenets of Shakers were celibacy, pacifism, equality of sexes, and communal ownership of possessions. The religious sect was brought to this country from England by Mother Ann Lee whom they viewed as the maternal component of a Mother-Father God, embodying God's spirit in female form. Although Mother Ann died in 1784, she continued to serve as a role model for women who joined the Shakers. A number of early Shaker women became charismatic national leaders and locally a ministry composed of two elders and two eldresses selected for life guided each community.

Nancy Moore served as an Eldress at South Union from October 1864 until August 1873. Her detailed daily diary, written neatly from approximately 1861-1864 provides an exciting and graphic account of the terrors and tensions of the turbulent days of the Civil War in South Central Kentucky where neighbors and families had divided views on the War Between the States, and where both

North and South required assistance from the Shakers.

Her diary describes persistent appeals by Shaker elders to military authorities, the Kentucky General Assembly and President Abraham Lincoln, for official recognition of the Shakers' pacifism. "Shakertown Revisited," a play by the late Dr. Russell H. Miller, includes an eloquent plea to President Lincoln from Eldress Nancy Moore:

The armies of the South like a great prairie fire swept over this part of Kentucky...We were humbled before their power and for many months remained the quiet subjects of the Confederate Government: Obeying at its behest save one which nobly and generously, they permitted us to disregard: and that was to take up arms in their behalf...Your armies have visited us...Our barns were cheerfully relieved of their contents. Our fences turned into campfires—for these we have been paid by the government. But, gratuitously, have we furnished diets for thousands of your men...We have yet in our Society about 24 young men between the ages of 18 and 45, a majority of whom would be capable of doing some kind of service in the federal army, but whom will not shoulder a musket, nor bear about their persons the weapons of war for they have been taught from infancy to love and not to fight their enemies...if this was respected by the Rebel government, can it be ignored by the best worldly government that ever existed..."

Finally, a telegram from Secretary of

Eldress Nancy Moore's book mark from Shakers at South Union.

State Staunton reached Bowling Green which stated:

If there is any religious community within your district, whose conscientious scruples abjure war, or the payment of commutation fees, you will parole them indefinitely, still holding them subject to any demand from the authority here.
Despite this acknowledgment of their position, three Brethren were drafted though only one served.

Together with another eldress and two elders, Nancy Moore had been chosen to guide her community for life, but physical incapacities made it impossible for her to properly attend to her duties of the Order, and she was released from her high office in August 1873. Some three years later, however, at the age of 69, she was healthy enough to paint the bannisters at the shop and meeting house and to visit Ohio.

When she died, Shaker Elder Harvey Eades prefaced her name in the South Union annual records with the word "good," which he underscored, the only name so treated. A woman of strength, patience, initiative and integrity, Eldress Nancy Moore attained the height of the rigorous Shaker standards and was surely one of the best of the "Believers."

Western Kentucky University Museum

1824 Shaker Dwelling House at South Union.

Carry Nation

By Margaret C. Thomas

orn in Garrard County, Kentucky, on November 25, 1846, Carry Amelia Moore was the daughter of a respected family. She lived in Kentucky until she was nine years old, when her father, an inveterate wanderer, moved the family to Missouri. She remembered her years living in Woodford County as happy times, despite a wild strain of mental illness which plagued her family for generations. Her mother, Mary Campbell Moore, early fancied herself a lady-in-waiting to Queen Victoria, soon promoting herself to queen and over time coming to see members of her own family only by appointment. She was supported in this delusion by her husband, who eventually bought her a regal carriage and presumably watched unperturbed as she came to breakfast robed in purple velvet with a crown of cut glass perched jauntily on her head. Imagining a family life built around the matriarchal figure of a demented, self-styled Queen Victoria gives us a glimpse of the forces which may have led Carry Nation to count on herself

first and foremost, and to maintain the courage of her convictions against all odds.

Unfortunately, Mary Campbell Moore gave her subjects one piece of advice which went unheeded: she warned both her husband and her daughter repeatedly against Carry's allegiance with one Dr. Charles Gloyd. Mrs. Moore considered the young physician, who became a boarder in the family's Missouri household, "common, below peerage rank, emphatically not of the noblesse."[1] Not long after their marriage on November 21, 1867, Carry realized that her new husband was uncommonly fond of rum, a taste which plunged her early unsettled life into even more troubled water. After bearing him one daughter, Charlieu, Carry left her

new husband, taking the child with her. He died of alcoholism within six months. Her frantic efforts—to collect on debts

Nation's birthplace near Lancaster, Kentucky.

owed him, and to sell his surgical instruments and medical textbooks in order to support herself and her young child—hardened Carry's resolve to do everything in her power to eradicate alcohol as a destroyer of lives.

Carry Nation settled in Medicine Lodge, Kansas, with her second husband David Nation, a minister/lawyer nineteen years her senior. Theirs was a tempestuous mismatch which eventually ended in divorce. With the move to Kansas, a dry state, Carry seized the opportunity to take on alcohol head to head. Her own life had been marred by the drunkenness of Gloyd; in the sparsely populated state of Kansas, Carry again saw the decimation of women's lives by breadwinners who drank their paychecks, leaving wife and children desperate.

She was arrested over 30 times for assault, abandoning paper wrapped rocks in favor of axes as her weapon of choice. In spite of becoming something of a caricature of herself in later years, Carry Nation was someone whom Robert Lewis Taylor wrote, "A great many literate persons found Carry Nation charming. In exchanges of wit, her retorts were quick and clear. Her tongue, in fact, was sharper than her hatchet."[2] The sight of Carry Nation, at almost six feet tall and 175 pounds, heading into a bar led more than one bartender to flee by a back door. She was driven by an almost maniacal fervor, on the cutting edge of a flurry of movements to empower women to chart the course for their own lives and free themselves from the tyranny of centuries of male domination.

Carry Nation traveled the United States with a frenetic schedule until her death in 1911. She collapsed from a stroke on January 13, 1911, during a speech in Eureka Springs, Missouri, and died five months later. After her death it was suggested that she suffered from congenital syphilis, a condition which may account for their strain of insanity which decimated her family, including her only child, Charlieu.[3] She was buried next to her mother in Belton, Missouri, and her grave went unmarked until 1923. The granite shaft at her grave is inscribed:

Carry A. Nation - Faithful to the Cause of Prohibition - She Hath Done What She Could

War Between Rum and Religion.
The Bible the Saloon Keeper's Shield & Shelter.

"Lay on McDuff, and damned be him who first cries 'Hold enough.' "—Shakespeare.

"This army of the Home Defenders declares its intent in its name. We are the fathers and mothers who, as God's host, have come to the help of the Lord against the mighty and we are here to withstand all the 'fiery darts of the wicked' with the shield of faith. We demand defense and will have it. No whisky, no tobacco or profanity shall defile our hearthstones. No man or woman who uses any of these defilements shall have or need ask to serve us. We will be your brother to help you to cleanse yourself from the filthiness of the flesh, but you need our assistance. We cannot use you in our business until you clean up. We are going to place before the people men and women who must be examples of virtue and strength, who shall serve us to reward good and punish evil. 'Happy is that people whose God is the Lord, yea, happy is that people in such a case. Kansas shall be free and we will set her on a hill that her light may go to every dark corner of the earth. Come with us and we will do the good, for the Lord hath spoken good concerning such a people."—Carrie Nation."

"A great many literate persons found Carry Nation charming. In exchanges of wit, her retorts were quick and clear. Her tongue, in fact, was sharper than her hatchet."

Patricia Neal

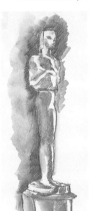

"My life is only a tiny grain of sand upon this fabulous earth," began Patricia Neal in a speech before the convention of the Kentucky Council for Exceptional Children, held in Louisville in 1985. "I was born in a coal-mining town called Packard, Kentucky, which no longer exists. The woods where we lived have been taken over by rats and raccoons, and by the forest itself."[1]

Neal's father, William Blaine Neal, was nicknamed "Coot," and he was the bookkeeper for the Mahan & Ellison Coal Company. Her mother was the daughter of the camp doctor. Packard was a coal company town, and when the coal mines shut down, so did Packard.

"I remember a dirt road and a single-track railway, a little group of wooden shacks surrounding a general store. I remember my father's office and behind it the pit head.

I remember the Baptist Church, the center of our lives, and how we all wore white shoes Easter Sunday," she says.[2] The Neals came home almost monthly to keep up with her grandparents in Williamsburg, so she always stayed in touch with old friends and family.

It all began when she heard someone give a monologue in a Knoxville, Tennessee, church. From that day forth she knew she wanted to be an actress. Her parents gave her a Christmas present, acting lessons from the local drama coach, Emily Faust. Then Neal went on to major in theater at Northwestern University, but like many young dramatists she couldn't wait to get a college degree. Instead, at nineteen, she headed for the bright lights of New York City. Patricia Neal understudied for several actresses in the Broadway play, "The Voice of the Turtle" and when Vivian Vance had a nervous breakdown, she stood in for Vance to give her first professional performance that lasted eight weeks.

Other roles in plays and parts in films

(Above) Neal discusses with students at Walden Theater in Louisville their production of "Packard."

quickly followed. She starred in "The Fountainhead" with Gary Cooper and appeared in "The Hasty Heart" with Ronald Reagan. In 1963 Patricia Neal won the Academy Award for Best Actress as the drab but tantalizing western ranch housekeeper in "Hud." And she was "surprised that it has won me so much because it was a part with no high moments."[3]

It might seem like a long road from Packard to Hollywood, but no one in Packard has ever forgotten their famous resident. Dr. Joanne Sexton and her family bought the Neal's house and although "Patsy" Neal and her family left Packard when she was three years old, many residents of Packard began keeping scrapbooks as her famous life developed. Dr. Sexton shared the pages of one scrapbook that lovingly chronicles every movie in which Neal starred and numerous newspaper accounts of visits to Williamsburg where Neal still had family.

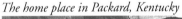
The home place in Packard, Kentucky

On one page is a local theater production program which she signed with a message for her Aunt Josephine: "Here's to eating peas on a knife." Indicative of the times, too, is a lengthy description of the tea given for Patsy Neal in Williamsburg, complete with pictures of her wearing an elaborate corsage and all the ladies, except Neal, in hats. But she poured tea and ate Aunt Maude's famous pecan pie. This was 1969 and she had just made her comeback movie, "The Subject Was Rose." She was almost fully recovered from her stroke.

Neal's life was threatened by a near-fatal stroke in 1965. "My right side was completely paralyzed and I had been left with maddening double vision," she wrote in her autobiography. "I had no power of speech and my mind just didn't work."[4] Her recovery was a slow and painful process, and Neal battled anger and depression. But her husband, British writer Roald Dahl, would accept nothing less than her total recovery. In 1967, he agreed without her consent that she would give a debut speech in New York City at a charity dinner for brain-injured children. She soon found herself standing behind the podium in the Grand Ballroom at the Waldorf Astoria Hotel. "Before I realized it, I had finished the speech. People stood and wept and cheered. I knew then that my life had been given back to me for something more than I had imagined."[5]

Back on the home front in 1979, Neal was treated to a performance of "Packard," a play that tells about the inhabitants of that extinct mining town where she was born. Presented by the drama students at Walden Theater in Louisville, she told them, "Misfortunes come in life, and we have to make the best of them."[6]

Not only did she make the best of them, but the woman with the memorably rich, resonant voice began a journal while she was on a retreat in a Benedictine Abbey. After five years of writing, the result was her autobiography, *Patricia Neal: As I Am*. With characteristic strength born of adversity, she wrote in the epilogue, "I have my life back."

Neal and her husband, Roald Dahl, visited Williamsburg to visit her aunt, Mrs. Will Mahan (center).

SERVING THREE
GREAT COUNTIES
WHITLEY — KNOX — LAUREL

THE CORBI

VOLUME 73   NUMBER 75   ASSOCIATED PRESS LEASED WIRE   CORNER

Patricia Neal

Academy Winner Is Whitley Co. Native

WILLIAMSBURG, Ky. (AP) — It's too bad Packard, Ky., is not around to celebrate the success of its most famous daughter — Patricia Neal, named winner Monday night of an Academy Award as the best actress of the year.

The old Whitley County coal-mining camp, about 18 miles east of Williamsburg, went the way of the car of the same name Packard is less than a ghost town, with just a pair of deserted buildings and a few burned out shells of homes to mark where a busy town flourished when Miss Neal was born 38 years ago.

Her father was a bookkeeper with the Southern Coal and Coke Co., her mother the daughter of the camp doctor. Miss Neal, who kept her given name when she became an actress, lived in Packard until she was 3. Her family then moved to Knoxville, Tenn.

Residents

The town, which she visited on a return trip here a few years ago, did not have the second chance which Miss Neal received. The last residents left about 15 years ago after the mines closed.

Miss Neal, however, made a comeback. When Hollywood producers decided she didn't have enough sex appeal, they ended her career of playing comediennes and sophisticated heroines. So, Miss Neal turned to straight dramatic roles—capped by her performance as a ranch housekeeper in "Hud," which earned the Oscar.

Miss Neal, who is married to British author Ronald Dahl, was not able to attend the ceremony in Hollywood because she is

eight months pregnant. She was in London, England, when the award announcement was made.

Watching

Many of her relatives and friends were watching the award show on television in Whitley County Monday night, said Mrs. Josephine Peavley.

"We've been really excited about it," said Mrs. Peavley. "All of us have kept up with her career and this is all we've talked about," her nominful that Mrs. P

Mahan, they wen to see M Mahan is

"She is such an Mrs. Tea

"From to school sity) she actress when the Loves M burg. She of other

proud that she was born here, and we're very proud of her."

Unhappiness

Miss Neal has had a great deal of personal unhappiness. She had an ill-fated romance in Hollywood, a child whose brain was damaged in an accident and her first-born daughter died.

She studied two years at Northwestern University, then went to Broadway. She won the Antionette Perry Award and the

Neal is honored at a tea given for her in Williamsburg, Kentucky.

Linda Neville

by Nancy Disher Baird

Linda Neville's contemporaries called her the "Angel of the Blind." The daughter of a classical language professor, Linda Neville graduated from Bryn Mawr College in 1895 and acquired a teaching position in Lexington. While

Linda Neville, at left, c. 1914.

or were led by others.

What's the trouble with your eyes?" Neville would ask.

"Oh, I've had sore eyes for quite a spell. They gits mighty nigh well at times and then they busts out worst than ever."

"T'warn't nothin' much, only jest sore eyes which gits powerful weak at times."

"How long has the condition existed?"

The condition was trachoma, a highly contagious form of conjunctivitis that causes a granular condition on the underside of the eyelid, scars the cornea, impairs vision and in many cases results in blindness. Spread by lack of personal cleanliness, trachoma is relatively simple to treat in its early stages. Unfortunately, basic health care was unavailable in the Kentucky mountains, and because folk remedies proved ineffective, highlanders accepted their approaching blindness as the Lord's judgment.

On her return to Lexington, Neville learned all she could visiting Katherine Pettit at the Hindman Settlement School in the summer of 1908, Neville noticed that an unusually large percentage of area residents suffered with eye problems. Some children did not attend school because they could not see the printed pages; mothers with weepy eyes dripped on their babies as they nursed at the breast; and many highlanders of every age, their eyes covered with rags, groped their ways about this disease and then declared war against trachoma. She attended the 1910 meeting of the Kentucky Medical Association and bombarded physicians with information about trachoma. They saw a photograph exhibit which Neville had prepared; they received brochures written and printed by Neville; and they heard a speech by the head of the Russell Sage Foundation about efforts elsewhere to eradicate trachoma. Horrified, the

KMA financed a State Board of Health investigation into the sanitation and health conditions of one eastern Kentucky county, and the study was made in Linda Neville's name.

Neville also encouraged eye specialists to go to Appalachia and provide free care for those in need. She organized, planned and publicized eye care clinics and supplied medical teams with anesthesia, medications and other necessities. She engaged physicians and set clinic dates to correspond with an event that attracted isolated residents to the county seat. Arriving a few days before the scheduled clinics, Neville learned which children were known cases and rode by mule to their homes to urge that the entire family attend the eye clinic.

Neville worked closely with Joseph McCormack, the head of the State Board of Health. Between 1914 and 1920 the effective duo convinced the state legisla-

Wagon load of nurses crossing swollen river coming from Trachoma Clinic at Hindman, 1912.

ture to approve laws requiring that all babies with diseased eyes be reported to the board of health; that physicians and midwives treat the eyes of newborns with silver nitrate drops; that caution labels be required on receptacles of denatured alcohol; and that couples planning to marry be tested for venereal disease.

For a half-century, Linda Neville spent most of her time and money crusading for the eradication of trachoma and other causes of blindness. Her two adopted children, both blind since birth, called her "Mama Linda." But to most Kentuckians, she was the "Angel of the Blind."

All photos from University of Kentucky Library

U.S. Public Health Trachoma Hospital at Hindman, 1912.

Marsha Norman

by Gary S. Chapman for The Courier-Journal

I was just a storyteller. To come into this land of the greatest storytellers and be accepted is a thrill I can't even describe to you."

Marsha Norman's talent broke wide at Actors Theatre's Humana Festival of New American Plays in 1981. She was an unknown playwright living in Louisville, Kentucky, home of Actors and the world renowned festival.

The Humana Festival, which once had trouble drawing critics from Chicago, was now a great success. By the time Norman's "Getting Out' premiered, the Festival hosted a coterie of New York City drama critics. If you made it there, you had made it.

The theatre's Producing Director, Jon Jory, knew early on there was something extraordinary about Marsha Norman's writing talent.

She had a skill level she simply didn't deserve given her level of experience and that sort of took me aback.

Marsha Norman recalls the night she became famous.

My life changed in one moment. I was at the bar at Actors Theatre when the show came down. The doors opened and this crowd surged through the door. Elated.

Ecstatic. These people—it was as though you'd sort of let the lions loose and there was this piece of steak—ME—on the other side of the room. They couldn't get to me fast enough. They couldn't say enough wonderful things...we all knew that night that our lives would never be the same. All kinds of doors opened except the one to the past which slammed shut. Never again would I be a completely private person with a secret dream.

An overnight success? There is no such thing. Norman devoted her life to writing.

"...writing is work. Like any other kind of work you have to stay in shape. You have to keep doing it."

Like many people who become the best at what they do, Marsha Norman had a sense of purpose about her writing—a mission. "I write about what bugs me," she said.

One of the things that bugged her was a story her grandfather told her repeatedly about a coyote. He was a considerable influence on her life and a master storyteller himself. Norman grew up listening to his tales of the old west. She heard the coyote story so many times as a child that she referred to it as her "Red Riding Hood" story. The being bugged, however, came in her adult life.

I came to just the devastating understanding that the story was about running away. That was where my sadness about grandaddy came from—he's running away all his life. What am I gonna do about that? What I do is go back and tell grandaddy's story where he's escaped from this coyote on the road out in this nowhere what field...I write grandaddy a revised ending...the rest of that night means that he doesn't ever have to run away anymore. I write him something that would have helped.

Though she rewrote his history in her play "The Holdup," she would not have had him any

other way. She attributes much to this man who cared about her and knew her as a child.

When the play drew attention from small theatres around the country, people sent grandaddy photographs of the set which, of course, were scenes right out of his life. He was quite ill and this play made him happy. And I think he finally knew that I owed him my life.

"'night, Mother," opened on Broadway in December, 1982 and it was a great critical success for Norman, not to mention a Pulitzer Prize winner. No stranger to fame at this point in her career, she did her best to take it in stride.

We have this common wisdom in the world of dramatists that the play after the Pulitzer is a play you should have somebody else write. And have them go down for it because you are going to get killed for this play no matter what it is.

Fame, criticism, and expectations. All the things that drive and terrify a playwright and all central themes in Norman's writing life. She learned that even a compliment could be difficult to take.

Marsha Norman was born in Louisville and received degrees from Agnes Scott College and the University of Louisville. She wrote for The Louisville Times, taught at the Brown School, and worked with disturbed children at Central State Hospital. Her first play, "Getting Out," was produced in 1977, followed by "Third and Oak." She won the Pulitzer Prize for drama in 1983.

One of the problems of me responding to "Getting Out" now is that it's as though people come up to me and say, "Oh, boy, did your hair look good four years ago." That's nice but there's nothing to do with that information...

Marsha Norman has built a lifetime career in writing plays, motion picture scripts, books, and even a musical libretto. She discovered that work in such a collaborative medium carried with it a great many demands. Nevertheless, when opportunity presents itself she chooses to share herself and her time with writing students at colleges around the country.

I think (being a role model) comes with the territory. I'm glad that I'm able to say to people, "get to work"...I know the value, too, of people who pass along their insights and their passion for what they do. I was very fortunate to have people like that in my life who came along at critical moments and said, "You have talent, you should work, and you should work hard"...passionate people communicate best to each other...I'm not going to be writing forever and I certainly want to have wonderful plays to go see when I'm in the nursing home and obviously some of these people I'll speak to will probably write them.

Opening night of "'night, Mother" with novelist Kurt Vonnegut and Courier-Journal *theater critic, Bill Mootz.*

Eliza Calvert Obenchain

Western Kentucky University Library

*H*iding behind a savvy, ornery veil of an 80-year-old spinster named Aunt Jane, the author Eliza Calvert Obenchain spins stories that offer insights into Kentucky women during the late 1800s: illegitimacy, sorrow, religion, gardens, and quilts. She cuts through some of the traditional duties of hearth and home at a time when women's domestic lives were being pitted against the exciting urban opportunities of the Industrial Revolution.

Choosing not to be the official spokeswoman for her values and beliefs, Eliza Calvert Obenchain wrote under a nom de plume, Eliza Calvert Hall. She uses the character, Sally Ann, to be the actual voice for exposing the flagrant hypocrisy of male-dominated households and patriarchal churches during the Victorian Era. In one of her most famous short stories, "Aunt Sally's Experience," she fingers nearly every man in the church congregation with a different accusation of male dominance and insensitivity. Husband Jacob won't give Sally Ann money to visit her dying daughter; Job

Taylor takes his wife's money to buy her some new parlor furniture but comes back empty handed.

The author grew up in Bowling Green and the family's tranquility shattered in the mid-1870s when Eliza Calvert's father was accused of banking irregularities and left town in the middle of the night, one jump ahead of the sheriff and an angry mob. To support her four children, Mrs. Calvert took in washing and depended upon Eliza Obenchain's meager teacher salary as well as the largess of her brothers.

Obenchain gave up this job because in 1885, no proper married woman worked outside the home. But the union was not a happy one, for it joined a rigid man whose favorite hobby was discipline with an independent, high-tempered woman who became an active, often radical, spokesperson for the women's movement.

To supplement family income, Eliza Calvert Hall wrote essays for national periodicals—sometimes witty, often angry, in which she explained that by the marriage ceremony women lost all property rights. But it was hard to get such opinions and observations published. Eight New York publishers told her that "short stories in dialect would never sell," but one company took a chance and by 1910, *Aunt Jane* had sold 80,000 copies. Even President Theodore Roosevelt recommended it as a "charming little book written by one of your clever Kentucky women."

In 1888, Kentucky was the only state in which a married woman could not make a will. Eliza Calvert Hall reminds us that by law everything a woman owned

belonged to her husband. If husbands did not hide behind that law, they might hide behind the Bible by quoting specific scripture. But the author renders a shrewd outcome when she reminds the men that "you'll have to stand before a Judge that cares might little for Kentucky law..." With mocking humor she suggests that women living in turn-of-the-century Kentucky may have been solid and steady, but they didn't have the rights due them with regard to owning property. As a president of the Kentucky Equal Rights Association, Eliza Obenchain furthered her interests in women's issues by action *and* words.

In 1907, women were not usually vocal about deceit and patriarchal exclusivity that was doled out in the name of justice and religion. But Aunt Jane continues to address the relationship of women to the

church in "Welcome, Sweet Day o' Rest," a hymn obviously intended for men only. Some of the lyrics say:

"Men can stop plowin' and plantin' on Sunday, but they don't stop eatin' and as long as men have to eat on Sunday, women'll have to work."

Almost every woman identifies with Aunt Jane wondering, tongue-in-cheek, how all the fried chicken, biscuits, corn bread, vegetables and desserts ever got cooked and on the groaning dining room table on that glorious "day of rest?" Whose day of rest?

In her Forward to the 1995 reprint, *Aunt Jane of Kentucky*, Bonnie Jean Cox points out that Eliza Calvert Hall's writing promotes women's ways of seeing and being, and it opposes the Calvinistic notion of salvation by grace rather than by good works. *Aunt Jane* gives us a female-centered community whose social system is practical and merciful rather than artificially imposed by a a patriarchal system of justice. Obenchain is a Kentucky author whose humor and wit remind us that most fantasies are bound by a thread of reality.

"You're one o' the men that makes me think it's better to be a Kentucky horse than a Kentucky woman"

Audrey Whitlock Peterson

by Peggy Stanaland

No other game captured the interest of girls or roused the enthusiasm of spectators as did the game of basketball during the first decades of the twentieth century. Girls had shown little interest in football or baseball, but when basketball was invented in 1892, they were clearly intrigued. Turn back the pages of time and focus attention on the successful coaching career of one woman and the influence her strong attributes had on Kentucky girls' and women's sports.

Born in Frye, Kentucky, Audrey Whitlock grew up in Campbellsville and played basketball at Russell Creek Academy High School. Then she played for two years at Cumberland College. In 1924, she married and went to Woodburn, a rural community of 350 people, to launch a teaching and coaching career. From 1926 to 1929, Peterson's teams lost only five games, and in 1932 they won the state championship, the last state tournament for girls for the next 43 years. *During her entire coaching career, all her opposing coaches were men.*

The decade of the twenties represented a zenith in basketball for Kentucky females, particularly at the high school level. The Kentucky High School Athletic Association (KHSAA) sponsored girls' district and state tournaments, but the KHSAA abandoned the girls' state tournament in 1932. The board bowed to the prevailing philosophy among women educators that intramural programs would better serve girl participants. The real reason seemed to be that

men coaches simply did not want to coach girls' teams any longer. The nadir for girls' basketball in Kentucky was during the thirties, when the prevailing attitude seemed to be that girls' health could be harmed while playing by boys' rules.

Audrey Peterson coached her team, trained them, and made all decisions on strategy and substitutions. According to Dorothy Chaney Pearson, an all-state Woodburn player three years in a row, "one male coach said women didn't have any business coaching girls—or any other basketball team—because they didn't

Warren County High School

Championship trophies charred from fire at Woodburn High School

know how to make them train. But that simply wasn't true," she observed. "We lived for basketball from one year to the next," she said. Pearson remembers that they "always prayed before games, but at one game the team wasn't winning and during half-time Coach said: 'You can't leave all this to the Lord—you get in there and play like heck!'" Peterson's amazing teams consistently played more experienced teams from much larger schools and followed rules that were the

same for boys: full court and unlimited dribble. Scoring 60 to 75 points was not unusual. Dorothy Chaney Pearson commented that there was no telling what their game would have been like if played at the speed girls play in the 90s.

The winning combination of girls' basketball and Audrey Peterson helped create a school and community spirit that Woodburn had never known. The winning ways and intense desire to be champions rubbed off on the whole town. Player Pearson quipped that when they played out of town "there were not enough people left in Woodburn to put out a fire. And remember, we didn't even have heaters in our cars during those days."

The coach's remarkable record had a bittersweet ending in 1932, when the KHSAA voted to eliminate the state tournament. The qualities that Coach Peterson stood for in the 1920s (training, academics, discipline, skill, and confidence) were the same qualities upheld by women leaders of sports activities throughout the ensuing three decades. The missing ingredient was intense competition, the smoldering embers which burst into flame once again in the 1970s when the governing body of the KHSAA was mandated by Kentucky legislative action to reinstate the state tournament for girls. Had there been more Audrey Petersons around perhaps "intense competition" would not have been perceived as such an evil.

HERALD **Sports** ■ Racing ■ Financial   Section

Tuesday, March 14, 1

, Woodburn Were Girls Basketball Powers of Another Er

John McGill, retired sports editor of The Herald, was a sports writer in Kentucky for forty years. He previously authored a novel.

McGill

The story is largely that of the amazing Ashland High School Kittens, Ashland's "girls who played like boys" won 232 games while losing only 18. They annexed five state championships in the 12 years, finishing second once.

There were, however, some startling interruptions in Ashland's victory parade--notably by girls representing

Georgetown, Hazard, Paintsville, and Woodburn.

It was Ashland vs. everybody from the start. The reasons were simple. The Kittens won the first two state tournaments. They won their first 46 games. Then after a two-defeat season, they came back for their third state crown in four years. This is what made Ashland the favorite in practically every game it played in 13 years. And it inspired a statewide ambition--to beat the Kittens.

But in the middle of Ashland's era, a little school situated between Bowling Green and the Tennessee border — Woodburn — was beginning an era of its own. And when the end came for girls basketball in the state it was Woodburn's team that reigned supreme. Representing a community of less than 300 persons, the Woodburn girls won the last two state tournaments and their story is a fascinating, inspiring one.

Ashland was guided by a coaching genius, W.B. Jackson, and was blessed with a superstar from the very start. She was Glenna Woods, who averaged 22 points a game in that first season and went past 30 four times. Meanwhile, only one Ashland opponent scored as many as 16 points.

Miss Moore was back for the 1922 season, in which the Kittens outscored their foes 776 to 146 and topped Sardis 39-7 for the state title. "The greatest player in Kentucky," was the title given her by John W. Head, a Louisville official who was given the task of selecting the All-State team.

Ashland tripped Louisa 100-1 and won 26-2 in 1923 but was upset by Crescent Springs in the state meet.

The year 1924 was another cham-

pionship season for Ashland but it also hailed the appearance of one of the most remarkable teams in the history of state basketball.

Mary Ward, Lillie and Nettie Biddle, Margaret Sabel and Elizabeth Sharp formed the nucleus for Georgetown's Wonder Team. Beulah Wallace joined them in a star role the following year, and in those two campaigns the G-town record was 48-1.

Miss Sabel proved to be another superstar of the era. She scored 306 points in the two seasons and in 1924 was called for only one personal foul.

Georgetown's 1924 defense was remarkable. After outpointing three regional foes 49-18, the team turned back its first four state tournament rivals by a composite 98-25. In regular season play, G-town had held eight foes under four points.

The championship game was "the

match of the century" for 1 girls basketball, Georgetown Ashland (16-1). But to Geo dismay, Miss Sabel was disc have a case of the mumps still a tense, exciting battle Kittens prevailed 13-11.

Even stronger in 1925, Go gained the state meet with record, overnsboro and Springs bowed and again stood in the path of the B Their revenge was sweet, even then the Wonder Team exhausted its supply of firew

Won Finale 40-0

In one of the most amazing of tournament play anywhere time, Georgetown won championship game by blan dyville Memorial 40-0.

(Turn to Ashla

133

1868-1936

Katherine Pettit

Katherine Pettit

F irst-time visitors to Pine Mountain Settlement School are always struck by the way light filters through the rustic setting and instills a sense of aesthetic beauty which Katherine Pettit assumed students would take home. If we cluster Katherine Pettit around enriching metaphors referencing

Architectural rendering of Pine Mountain by architect Mary Rockwell (Hook),1913.

light, we see her as the educational lamplighter in an area of eastern Kentucky where there was little opportunity for boys to get jobs and education was considered superfluous for girls, who often married at thirteen. Her educational light had the magical effect of opening windows on their young minds.

September 20, 1916
Letter from Miss Edith Storer
(teacher)

...delicious bracing air, glorious views remind me of Switzerland... these people are considered 250 years behind present civilization. Most of the children have never even heard of the ocean, President Wilson, etc. A great squirrel roast for the laying of the cornerstone... Oh I am frozen, but just look at the mountains! It is beautiful beyond words, the valleys flooded in golden light, and the mountains standing out in sharp relief....

Born on a large, prosperous farm in the Bluegrass region of Kentucky, Katherine Pettit attended the Female Institute of Sayre School for two years (1885-87) but did not graduate. She was a member of the Women's Christian Temperance Union and Federation of Women's Clubs, but she left the ranks of club women and turned from her upbringing, steeped in Protestant values and Republicanism, to her life work as a creative progressive educator. After starting Hindman Settlement School in Knott County with

Students haul firewood to the school c. 1914

May Stone in 1902, Katherine Pettit moved to Pine Mountain with Ethel de Long and opened another settlement school (PMSS) in 1913.

August 14, 1913
From Pettit's Notes

...it was a picturesque sight to see the eight yoke of oxen coming up the narrow, rough, short-curved road to the school grounds with the boiler...I saw a group of drunken men in the laurel thicket and four women electioneering, one of them had a bunch of $1 bills in her hand...Out of the 83 votes cast I can say with a clear conscience that 65-70 were drinking or simply dog drunk...only makes me feel that if we can educate the younger ones that they will have a regard for the laws of our country...

Much class time was given over to the study of local problems with careful, trusting discussions that weighed the community's social and economic issues. Pettit was humble enough to know she couldn't solve all the problems of the children on this side of the mountain, but she demanded students wrestle with their problems and find their own solutions.

Women's Christian Temperance Union Summer Camps, 1899-1901.

...same sore throat is all up and down Poor Fork and many children are dying...

...need for clean living and bathing and the sore eyes...wrote the Surgeon General for help...One night I was sitting on the porch of the log house, about nine o'clock, Dr. McMullen came and said, "Well, you have stirred up a great racket here, and Dr. Blue sent me down from Ellis Island to see about it." (The doctor was still there 15 years later where $25,000 was spent on the eradication of trachoma).

The people said I went around the world to see if it was round or not and when I came back and said it was, they said I was a pure "infidel." One cold, bleak November morning at seven o'clock a man sent for me to come downstairs....said that he had already come seven miles to have me tell him

about the round world. After asking many questions he went away saying he was coming back to talk about it again. He met someone on the road who asked him if Miss Pettit had convinced him... "No, indeed, but she took so much peace and satisfaction in thinking it was round that I didn't like to disabuse her mind."

For women, PMSS is particularly interesting because it was designed by a young female architect, Mary Rockwell (Hook), from Kansas City, Missouri, who donated her services. She became one of the long lasting gifts to PMSS. Hook chose an architectural career at a time when it was not considered ladylike to be an architect. Because there was no such degree for women in America, she went to the L'Ecole des Beaux Arts in Paris, which was not an inviting place either. When she completed final exams in 1905, the male students hurled buckets of water at her as she fled through the courtyard.

Arrived at Hazard in the afternoon and was met by a small boy who gave me a horse for the 30 miles to Hindman where I watched graduation with Ethel de Long and then set out the next day for the 50 mile ride to Pine Mountain....On the way, we passed two wagons, loaded with furniture for the new home. There was no road at all. The wheels were going up over boulders as high as a horse, the horses splashing through water, slipping on stones....The woman who took us in for the night, took up her position in front of the fireplace in our bedroom, with her pipe, so we had to go ahead with our preparations for the night. "Law sakes,

Women's Christian Temperance Union Summer Camps, 1899-1901.

do you all strip yourselves off naked at night?" I said, "What do you do?" She said, "Why I jess kick my shoes off and lay down."

Ahead of her time, Katherine Pettit was keenly interested in which wild plants could make food for the school children. She grew 23 kinds of salad greens and planted wildflower beds terraced on steep hillsides outside her log house to show children what could be done on a piece of seemingly useless land. Weeds are an appropriate metaphor for things that got in the way of this gardener's philosophy, like capitalism and the railroad. And she was savvy enough to view education as a bridge to the encroaching capitalism without losing her students' cultural heritage.

Amidst an intentionally idealized environment she developed a school overlaid with anti-materialism, interwoven with Christian and patriotic values, and armed with practical skills for children to meet their changing world. Light came to PMSS in the shape of Katherine Pettit, and she forever enlightened people on that side of the mountain with a particular simplicity and sincerity that caused the community to regard her as one of them. Publicity was a necessary evil, reporters infuriating, but Pettit received the Sullivan Medal for distinguished service to her state and died gallantly, having written a friend, "This has been a glorious world to work in. I am eager to see what the next will be."

b. 1958

Susan Pfeiffer

Susan Pfeiffer is an artist.
Susan Pfeiffer sold her wood designs
and won many awards.
Susan Pfeiffer spent the money on a
state-of-the-art woodworking shop.
The bottom fell out of the art
market.
Susan Pfeiffer began to
teach art in middle school.
Susan Pfeiffer is a part-
time artist today.

This is not an unusual
chronicle in the life of any
artist, but it does underscore
the vulnerability and the joyous
rewards which come with the
profession. Susan Pfeiffer's
works in wood are unique
because a deep respect for
nature is the source of her
creativity and has become ingrained in
her furniture. "We have to preserve our
environment as we do human life,"
Pfeiffer says. "The two are interrelated.
Like the threads in a weaving, if one is
broken, the whole starts to come apart.
My idea is to change attitudes."

Growing up in Hardin County, she
started drawing with pencils when she
was four or five years old. "If it wasn't
perfect I messed it up," she remembers.
Horses were Pfeiffer's favorite subject and,
because she couldn't own a horse, she
fantasized by drawing them over and over
again. They were usually idealized, like
Pegasus or a unicorn. Out of her world
of fantasy she also built Greek and
Roman chariots and furniture for Barbie
dolls all made out of cardboard.

As a child with dyslexia "I could see an
object from every side. Jigsaw puzzles
were no challenge, but reading was an
awful experience because I couldn't read

in a straight line, so I was tutored. I took
a tape recorder to college and had to
develop a really good memory."

Susan Pfeiffer's father used to buy
wrecked automobiles and beat them into
shape. Sometimes she helped him mold
cars anew, and today she is molding wood
into boxes, tables, cabinets, and non-
functional decorative pieces. She loved to

go fishing and hunting with her father,
and such roots in nature are incorporated
into the basic philosophy and design
elements of her work.

No one ever told her she had artistic
talent until John Lovins, the art teacher at
North Hardin High School, did. He
inspired her to "create reality on paper,"
she says, "like wood grain of a house, the
crack in a window, or the self-portrait in a
door knob. I knew nothing about value
range or perspective, and he taught me all
of that." Along the way he also instilled
a sense of self-confidence and suddenly,
Susan Pfeiffer was proud to be an artist.
Instead of a wannabee cheerleader she
was somebody different, and her school-
mates envied her talent.

Off to Murray State University where
she was no longer unique but in direct
competition with lots of other young
artists. Paul Sasso, a well-known
woodworker, came to Murray her last
year and Pfeiffer became a first-class
woodworker under his tutelage.

Pfeiffer's first taste of real adventure
came in 1988, when she went to Arizona
State University to study for a Masters in
Fine Arts degree. It was her first year and
she entered a competition sponsored by
Harmann & Reimer, a German company
which has long supported the arts. For
two months she worked night and day on
"More Space Required," a wood and
metal sculpture that is actually a
social commentary on overpopu-
lation and the need to explore
new places. She captured first
place, and the early taste of
success was never so good.

Susan began asking herself,
"Why does it have to look like
what it is?" Of course it doesn't,
so the artist broke the paradigm
of using exotic woods in their
natural state. She took wenge, a
naturally black wood, and
bleached it. The pronounced
grain became blonde. With a
background in metalsmithing,
she began weaving gold, silver,
and even copper into furniture. Pfeiffer
deepened her social consciousness about
the environment. "Trees Are Falling,"
one of her favorite creations, is a cabinet
that denounces wanton destruction of the
forests. The door is decorated with
uprooted trees falling down the front.

Success breeds success. Using more
business sense than the public usually
allows artists, Susan Pfeiffer took her sales
receipts and built a state-of-the-art
woodworking shop and studio. As luck
would have it, the bottom promptly fell
out of the art market, but Pfeiffer still
had to eat, clothe her body, and pay the
utility bills. With more resilience than
most, she began teaching art in the
Radcliffe public schools and today her
hope is that "I will influence students to
buy art from an artist, not from Wal-
Mart." But such teaching is draining,
and Susan Pfeiffer often finds little time
for her part-time job as an artist.

136

From an apex in 1990 to a nadir in 1992, Susan Pfeiffer has experienced the fickle nature of the art world. She remains confident, optimistic, and gifted. Just as she interrelates the environment with human life in her wood pieces, Susan Pfeiffer is learning to weave two professions, teaching and creating art, into her life.

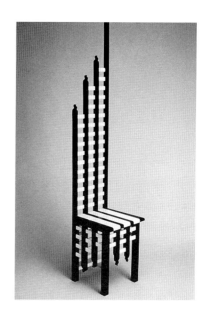

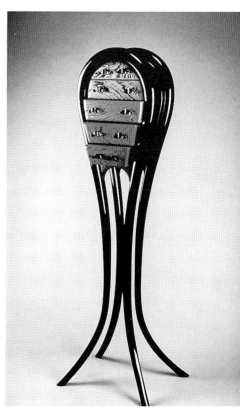

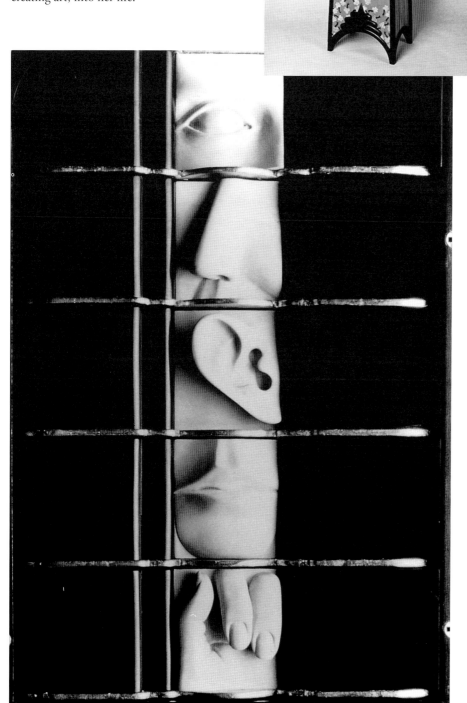

Award-winning "More Space Required."

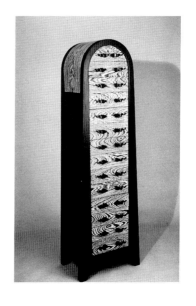

Lena Madesin Phillips

ena Madesin Phillips had no intention of spending her days making jellies, crocheting baby clothes and arranging flowers, and she had no problem finding other diversions. One theme emerges as the patchwork of her life unfolds: "I take it that neither God nor man foreordained or foresaw that the labor of the world was to be performed by one sex."[1] A born leader, she takes a path of incremental steps that prevent her from becoming a "wife of" or "mother of." Instead, her life work becomes the founding and developing of the International Federation of Business and Professional Women. People are just beginning to value the work ethic and lifestyle of single women or married women with no children whose lives and identities are fulfilled by their life work outside the home. Madesin Phillips was ahead of her time.

Born Anna Lena Phillips, at the age of eleven she changed her name to Madesin, after the French word *medecin*, in tribute to her brother who was studying medicine in Paris. Her father was a close companion until his death at the age of 95. Her letters to him are copious, four to five per week every year of her life. He encouraged her to find her true self—they "were of the same stuff, alike in temperament and taste."[2] They camped and fished together, and she broke precedent by riding a bicycle to school, skirt to her ankles and pigtails flying.

"Love of nature, faith in a Supreme Being, faith in myself—these things bestowed upon me in the little town of my birth nourished me through my life,"[3] Madesin Phillips wrote of Nicholasville, Kentucky. But she found the restrictions placed on her because she was a girl maddening. She simply wanted to be herself. Nowhere in Nicholasville "was to be found the belief that all human beings, whatever their nationality or sex, possessed the same desires and needs," she

wrote. "As for women in professions or business...the very word 'woman' was strange and out of place."[4] Madesin listened intently as her father talked politics with his friends, thus sowing the seeds for her own intense interest in political issues.

Phillips was a conspicuous leader at the Jessamine Female Institute, and in 1888, she formed a military company comprised entirely of females. She was chosen the captain of "The Main Avengers," whose members intended to offer their services after graduation to the United States in its fight against Spain.[5]

Phillips went on to Goucher College and then to study at the Peabody Conservatory of Music. Her ambitions to become a concert pianist ended prematurely when she injured her right arm, but this loss for the music world was a gain for the world of politics and social reform.

Without skipping a beat, she turned to the legal profession. In the *Lexington Herald* dated Sunday, December 24, 1916, an article comments on her initial days at the University of Kentucky Law

All photographs, Schlesinger Library, Radcliffe College

School:
Some conservative students disapproved of her entrance in their classes, believing their work would be retarded, but when the semester grades were posted on the bulletin board, their attitude changed: she had made all A's.[6]

She graduated June, 1917 as the first woman honor graduate at the University's 50th commencement.

While practicing law in Lexington Phillips became involved with the local Young Women's Christian Association (YWCA), and she was quickly offered the position of executive secretary for the business and professional women's division of the *national* organization. In this job, she traveled thousands of miles surveying women as to the feasibility of a separate organization for business and professional women. Positive results led to her recommendation that the Business and Professional Women's organization (BPW) be founded. That being accomplished, Madesin Phillips promptly resigned and resumed her practice of law in New York City.

Later, she became the national president of BPW and in her annual address called for supporting organizational policies that were not regional-biased but were for the good of all women. In the 20s her concern was to get women to look beyond their own borders, whether local, state or country, long before the term "global inclusivity" was coined.

Barbecue on grounds of 1898 Nicholasville Centennial.

She was that rare combination of a dreamer *and* a doer. She realized that the BPW was ready to come into contact with the business women of other countries. On August 26, 1930, in Geneva, Madesin Phillips' dream was realized with the establishment of the International Federation of Business and Professional Women. She spent the next twenty-five years of her life dedicated to the Federation.

As one pores over the Lena Madesin Phillips Collection, housed at the Schlesinger Library of Radcliffe College, the meaning of "detail" takes on new dimensions. Inside the boxes are every single note of condolence at her mother's death, meticulous notes for her biography, hand-drawn caricatures, every class program, annual bank books, extensive correspon-

dence, organizational publications, and photographs (personal and business). She kept "Letter Books," blue marbelized ledgers listing and dating every letter she received and answered, beginning in 1932.

Researchers find a letter addressed to President Franklin D. Roosevelt imploring him to include suffragist Susan B. Anthony in the proposed Mount Rushmore Memorial:

To us there seems needless irony in preparing for posterity an enduring memorial of America's liberators and at the same time omitting from it the liberator of one-half of our people.[7]

Instantly one draws a mental picture of a woman who carefully documented her career path that led from being a music teacher in a small Kentucky town to practicing law in New York City and

Pouring tea for brothers and sisters in 1893.

ultimately to founding the International Federation of Business and Professional Women.

She died unexpectedly in 1955, while traveling to the Middle East as part of a Federation study committee. She died being herself, a dreamer *and* a doer.

1899 Graduating class at Jessamine Female Institute.

Ora Porter

Ora Porter was Bowling Green's first registered nurse. Born in Sugar Grove in Butler County, Ora Porter and her family moved to Warren County when she was ten years old. Not much is known about her childhood, except that she was an African American girl growing up in a predominantly white, Victorian society, where racial prejudice and class distinctions were part of the milieu. She would have had few role models for her career choice,

for census records show that at the time jobs for black women were limited to domestic service.

These were the days when river towns were prone to epidemics of cholera and yellow fever, and unsanitary water and inadequate sewage systems contributed to outbreaks of smallpox, typhoid fever, tetanus, and whooping cough. Today these diseases are prevented by childhood inoculations. Infant mortality rates were high, especially for babies born to black women. Perhaps Ora Porter was influenced by what she saw around her when she decided to attend Tuskegee Institute School of Nursing. It had opened in

1892, eleven years after the Atlanta Baptist Female Seminary, established by John D. and Laura Spelman Rockefeller.

The first three nursing schools for white women had been born in 1873 in New York, Connecticut, and Massachusetts. Each assumed the uniforms and military discipline left over from the influence of Florence Nightingale's connection with the Crimean War and her subsequent nursing movement throughout Great Britain.

The modern American hospital with its corps of nurses also evolved in the late nineteenth century. Nursing schools helped create a supply of cheap labor to help run these institutions, but hospitals soon took over the job of training nurses, eclipsing earlier autonomous programs.

The 1894 catalog of the Atlanta Baptist Female Seminary offers telling evidence of the contradictory attitudes of black nursing programs toward their students. "Many of our young women who take the course will never become professional nurses, but take it with a view of being better prepared for the responsibilities of family life." The prevailing Victorian attitude that "proper" women should serve as subordinate, domestic helpmates to men was thus transferred to the medical field. A leader of the Tuskegee Hospital lauded black women as women with virtues of "devotion, endurance, sympathy, tactile delicacy, unselfishness, tact." This underscores the idealized legacy of nurses as the angel of mercy figure, merely honing natural proclivities of females.

Ora Porter on the front porch of her family home in a crisp, white, ankle-length uniform.

When Ora Porter returned to Bowling Green after graduation she was one of two registered nurses to work for St. Joseph's Hospital, which was privately owned by two physicians. People did not go to hospitals as a rule and those who could afford to had private duty nurses. So Porter cared for people in their homes, too. Most of her patients were white since they could afford to pay a private nurse, but Porter also nursed her uncle and other members of the family.

"She had a name for being the best," said one of two nieces interviewed in 1982. "Whenever she went into a house she laid the rules down...everybody had

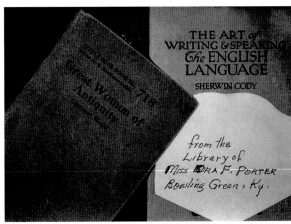

All that is left of Porter's library.

to do what she said do, or else." She liked to clean a house before she felt like things were sanitary enough for the patient to make progress. And in her own home, "everything had to be very clean and everything in place. She had pretty glassware...(and)silver." One of the

nieces dusted with *two* cloths. Her house had large rooms with high ceilings, a piano, and plenty of old pictures, including one of her mother, with whom Porter lived when she returned to Bowling Green after graduation. Porter was also one who "liked society," enjoyed clubs and meetings, and was a faithful member of her church. Sunday after-noons were usually spent on walks from her house to the local florist shop.

Ora Porter died in 1970 at the age of ninety. Unfortunately, books, notes, and other personal things were not kept when the contents of her home were dispersed.

Ora Porter late in life.

Western Kentucky University Library

Letters To The Editor

The correct signatures on communications appearing in this column must be printed in all instances. Letters must be brief, not exceeding 300 words and must avoid defamatory or abusive statements. The Daily News reserves the right to condense any communication considered too lengthy and to limit the number of letters on any one subject. Publication does not imply approval of the Park City Daily News.

Miss Porter First Registered Nurse

Editor, Daily News:
Recently I went to see Miss Ora Porter, the registered nurse now retired and living in her home, 715 College St. We spoke of the death of Mrs. Harry Black, one of Bowling Green's early trained nurses. I asked Miss Porter if she had received her training before Mrs. Black and she said she had a year or two before. She said she herself was graduated from Tuskegee Institute. So Miss Porter was the first registered nurse in Bowling Green.

Miss Ora Porter was born in Sugar Grove, Butler County, and moved here when she was 10 years old.

While she was a student at Tuskegee, she used to go to Florida during vacations as a nurse with some of the wealthy contributors to Tuskegee Institute, among them the family of John D. Rockefeller Jr. She had been recommended by Booker T. Washington and other faculty members of the school.

Following her graduation, she returned to Bowling Green to live with her mother. She was employed by Dr. J. N. McCormack and Dr. Arthur McCormack in their private hospital, the St. Joseph Hospital, 533 E. 12th St. Another registered nurse, Miss Willie Offutt from Louisville, was also employed so that there could always be a registered nurse on duty, one in the daytime and one at night. Each one was assisted by one or two untrained nurses. She also assisted in the State Laboratory under the direction of Dr. Lillian South. The laboratory was located first in St. Joseph Hospital and later was moved to the old Potter College building on Western's campus before being moved to Louisville and finally to Frankfort.

Later she went into private practice here. She has been an active citizen for the improvement of conditions in Bowling Green and has done much to help her race.

She was one of the organizers of the George Washington Carver Community Center, 301 Center St., and is still on the board of directors. She was also one of the organizers of the Interracial Commission in 1949 and was one of the directors during the three years of its existence. She is active in elections and in campaigns for civic improvement.

Before her retirement in 1960, she sometimes substituted for one of the registered nurses at City-County Hospital. She was a greatly beloved nurse and is a highly respected citizen of Bowling Green.

Margie Helm
1133 Chestnut St.

Miss Ora Porter, City's Oldest RN, Dies At 90

2-6-70

Miss Ora Frances Porter, 90, Warren County's oldest registered nurse, died at 5:20 p.m. Wednesday at City-County Hospital.

Miss Porter, of 715 College St., was graduated from the Tuskegee School of Nursing. She received special training at Lincoln Hospital in New York before practicing nursing in Alabama, Florida and Kentucky.

In 1916, she became the first registered nurse in Bowling Green, working with the late Dr. J. N. McCormack who established a hospital here.

The body is at Abel Brothers Funeral Home where it will remain until 11 a.m. Saturday when it will be moved to Taylors Chapel AME Church for funeral services at 2 p.m. Burial will be in Mount Moriah Cemetery.

She is survived by several nieces and nephews.

Death Takes One Of City's Finest

Editor, Daily News:
The death of Miss Ora Porter, 715 College St., took from Bowling Green one of her finest and most beloved women.

She was our first registered nurse. She was active in her church, A.M.E. Church, and in Church Women United until her health failed. She took part in many civic and inter-racial activities and was a director of the George Washington Carver Youth Center. She set an example for many to follow.

Margie Helm
1133 chestnut St.

Susan Sternberg Proskauer

by Harriet W. Fowler

During the years of her Kentucky residence, Susan Proskauer maintained an outstanding thoroughbred breeding operation on a Woodford County property which she owned with her husband, George Proskauer. Buck Pond

UK Art Museum

Farm's graceful, federal-style architecture and acres of lush, fenced pasture, its handsome bloodstock and atmosphere of orderly prosperity met every expectation of a successful, traditional Kentucky horse farm. This was the public impression.

But the first-time visitor to the Proskauer residence quickly discovered a private world of art: a startling, angular George Rickey sculpture by the front door and hundreds of modernist, art glass and folk art works within the house. While the walls of many Kentucky historic homes are lined with ancestral and equine portraiture, the Proskauers' 1783 residence included works by such internationally-famous names as Pablo

Picasso, Jean Dubuffet, Milton Avery, John Marin, Alexander Calder, and Louis Comfort Tiffany. Moreover, Susan Proskauer arranged all her art in an intensely personal way: charming, crude folk art toys marched around chair rails beneath paintings of major artists and sleek kinetic sculpture might be placed on the breakfast bar in the kitchen. For Susan, the dialogue between her and her collection and among the collection works themselves was paramount.

If the walls at Buck Pond Farm held no ante-bellum family portraiture, it was not just the personal taste of the Proskauers that dictated their absence. The German-born Proskauers came to America with little in the way of material histories. Both were fortunate to escape with their lives. Born in Breslau, Susan Sternberg ended her schooling in the eighth grade, she said, because of Hitler. Apprenticed to a dressmaker as a young teenager, she learned skills that would serve her future career as a fashion designer in New York. As the Nazis' campaign against the Jews intensified during the 1930s, Susan's parents grew increasingly concerned for her safety. "They wanted to get me a visa to the U.S., but it was impossible. So, on Easter Sunday in 1938, my father took me to a

Caricature by PEB.

UK Art Museum

nearby slope, kissed me goodbye, and I skied for eight hours until I reached Czechoslovakia."[1] She never saw her parents again—both died in concentration camps.

Eventually, Susan made her way to New York City where she worked as a maid and learned English by going to the movies every day. A casual remark to her doctor during an office visit led to her discovery that George Proskauer, whom she had known in childhood, had endured his own harrowing escape to America and was also in New York City. After resuming their youthful friendship, the Proskauers were married and Susan enjoyed a successful career as a fashion designer (under the name Susan Garber) first in New York and later in Ohio.

After seeing her first horse race at Ascot Park outside Cleveland in 1957, Susan Proskauer became deeply interested in thoroughbreds, studying their pedigrees, and finally making her first purchase of a yearling at Saratoga. The horse business would enthrall her, and turn her attention from fashion design to the racing world. After purchasing a half interest in Buck Pond Farm in 1973, the Proskauers fully acquired the property in 1977.

It was at Buck Pond Farm that Susan Proskauer merged her twin passions for horses and art, commenting once, "We have a need for art. It's like owning a good horse. It gives you a feeling of satisfaction and beauty."[2] Just as the Proskauers bought horses they could live with, they acquired art that participated in a very real sense in their daily lives. Their highly personal, eclectic choices—whether luminous, turn-of-the-century art glass, droll yard sculpture, or modernist masterpieces—reflected their continual engagement with the objects themselves and their attitude that each work of art was part of an important dialogue.

Thanks to the Proskauers' generosity to the Commonwealth, that dialogue continues: the entire collection that once graced Buck Pond Farm was bequeathed to the University of Kentucky Art Museum. Today, all Kentuckians can enjoy the works of art so thoughtfully and lovingly acquired by the remarkable Susan Sternberg Proskauer and be grateful for her vision and generosity.

UK Art Museum

UK Art Museum

The Star *by Alexander Calder, 1960.*

UK Art Museum

Joy *by Nina Winkel, 1905*

Bev Futrell, b.1942   Karen Jones, b.1951   Sue Massek, b. 1948

Reel World String Band

Twenty years ago a group of women from Kentucky joined their talents to celebrate music and to express a woman's point of view. Three of the original members of the Reel World String Band are still jammin', strummin', singin', and hummin' on picket lines, in concert halls, at rallies, square dances and family reunions. Bev Futrell plays mandolin, guitar, and harmonica; Karen Jones, the fiddle and mandolin; Sue Massek, the banjo and guitar. Together, they sing and play a blend of western swing, folk, and traditional Kentucky music. When needed, they add other musicians to fill out the group. Though Kentucky's culture long has been strengthened by female musicians, theirs is the first all-female band since Lily May Ledford and the Coon Creek Girls, whose music was featured on radio in the '40s and '50s.

Although they didn't consciously realize it at the time, they became some of the first women "who took hold of our own entertainment business whether it worked financially or not," they remember. They were part of the feminist arts movement within the women's movement, getting started at a time when women's bookstores, production companies, radio shows, theatre and dance brigades were being developed across the country. Futrell recalls that the first few years they were on the road, they were asked repeatedly , "What do your husbands think? They let you leave home and do this?"

Reel World String Band is a lively blend of music that celebrates women's lives, tells of the impact of strip mining and timber clear cutting on the environment, and recognizes the drama and grace in the everyday lives of working people. Their sensitivity not only to the music and tradition but to the cause and the audience enhances the power and impact of their music. The band uses its full range of talents to remind audiences that if they do not do something about those who control and exploit Kentucky's natural resources and people, the price of personal integrity and a more democratic society may be too late and too steep.

Their repertoire includes renditions of songs by mentors like Lily May Ledford, Sarah Ogan Gunning, Hazel Dickens, and Jean Ritchie. Futrell and Massek write some of the group's selections. Ledford was a special inspiration to Futrell because, like her, "she tried to raise children and play music at the same time." A treasured possession of Massek, who was particularly close to Ledford at the end of her life, is a quilt that incorporates Ledford's favorite performing dress.

Over the past twenty years, the band has crisscrossed the country, beginning when Jones' first job out of law school, a legal services position in Prestonsburg, "bought us credit and we purchased the van and sound equipment." That "credible" job put them, and sometimes Futrell's little girl, on the road. They've restored the spirits of countless demonstrators at strikes and on picket lines. More recently, they played for Jimmy Carter's all-star "Hammering in the Mountains" Habitat for Humanity week in eastern Kentucky. They've used music to raise funds for such organizations as The Urban Appalachia League in Cincinnati and a community center in Irvington, Virginia, and for women's causes that include rape crisis centers and The Women's National Coal Miners Conference in Charleston, West, Virginia. Reel World String Band also has enter-

(Above) Band is pictured left to right Bev Futrell, Sue Massek, Karen Jones.

tained at the Bluegrass Festival in Michigan, outdoor concerts at Lincoln Center in New York City, on a west coast tour with the Osborne Brothers, at schools, parks, and on radio and television. A memorable 1988 tour through Italy, with Lionel Hampton and others, played 23 cities in 14 days. "We played everywhere for the exposure and soon we found out that you could die from overexposure," says Jones. By 1989, well-

Massek on the guitar

(Above) Singing on a flatbed truck in the early years.

loved, successful in many ways, but not always able to pay the bills, they opted to become a part-time operation. "It frees us up," they explain, "because we can pick and choose where we want to go. When we were trying to live off the money, we had to go where people would pay for us.

Bev Futrell's Texas heritage is still in her voice. The group's "historian," she can tell war stories all night long about gigs they've played. She laughs remembering a stage in Virginia that was covered in chicken wire when they arrived because on other weekends it was a wrestling ring. "Lots of people stayed in their cars, like a

drive-up festival," she says. The location "turned out to be an old strip mine site. We got up and sang our anti-strip mining songs and then left."

Karen Jones is the ham of the group, an easy going ad-libber whose witty introductions to pieces delight audiences. She is the offspring of "bourgeois musicians" who provided her with piano and violin lessons. Her introduction to "old-timey" music when she was a student at Berea College has served her well. Today, she is as comfortable playing bohemian fiddle as she is the mandolin for retro Tango Teas. For the past dozen years, Jones and Futrell have spent Sunday nights spinning disks for a radio show at Eastern Kentucky University called "WomenSounds."

Sue Massek, the only full-time musician in the band, hails from Topeka, Kansas. Her grandfather played fiddle and her mother sang her to sleep with Bradley Kincade songs. The Grand Old Opry was the family's television choice of the week. Members of this musical family placed a guitar in Massek's lap when she was nine years old and she's been playing ever since. She is a gentle tree hugger who watches in horror as loggers devastate the landscape harvesting forests in

Clay County for the first time since the 30s. As an official artist-in-residence with the Kentucky Department of Education, she uses music to encourage today's children to protect trees for future generations. Human beings are more important than corporate profits.

Members of Reel World String Band enjoy themselves, their audiences deeply admire their playing, and Kentucky's musical heritage is richer for their contributions.

b.1947

Rosalind Hurley Richards

Kentucky women like Rosalind Richards have always taken the lead in education. Women were pioneer educators in founding Kentucky's settlement schools and private female academies. Historically, women received recognition as outstanding school administrators, county superintendents, national teachers of the year, and state cabinet secretaries for education. But it is the individual classroom teacher like Rosalind Hurley Richards who is the true backbone of Kentucky's education system. Richards is a teacher on the cutting edge of education reform who encourages and celebrates change, one who blends the best of the past with the promise of the future.

What sets Richards apart is that she returned to teaching following an eighteen-year stint in corporate America. "After working many years in a managerial position and visiting schools in third world countries, I am afraid for my students entering the work place and not being able to compete and adapt to changes," she proffers. Her not so subtle statement that "We need to prepare children for *their* future, not *our* past" reveals her belief that education should inspire students "to concentrate on where they are *going*, not where they have been." Based on this philosophy, she

Richards goes to the White House.

To Rosalind Hurley Richards,
Congratulations! Bill Clinton

designed a classroom model for a professional learning and working environment at Squires Elementary School in Lexington, Kentucky. Her vision resulted in her selection as 1996 Elementary Teacher of the Year and the 1997 Kentucky Teacher of the Year, and she was one of four finalists to become National Teacher of the Year. Even more impressive, she was a 1997 recipient of a Milken Family Foundation award, an honor that carries a $25,000 cash reward and recognizes educators who have "an outstanding ability to instill students with sound values and self-confidence."

Another dividend of her recognition was an invitation to serve on the steering committee of *America Goes Back to School in 1997*, a national initiative spearheaded by the U. S. Department of Education. A blue ribbon panel, its members are leaders from business, education, the arts, parent and community groups, political entities, and religious organizations. Richards is one of two teachers who will help the committee develop a plan to support community and family involvement using the theme, "better education is everybody's business." It is a fitting assignment for Richards because her corporate background gives her a keen understanding of the important links between education and business.

Some type of education reform was inevitable when Kentucky's Supreme Court declared the entire system of public schools unconstitutional, putting seasoned and new teachers alike on a path they would find rocky, energizing, controversial, and productive. A futuristic thinker, Rosalind Hurley Richards gives a "thumbs up" to the 1990 Kentucky Education Reform Act

(KERA) which followed the lawsuit. KERA directed the Kentucky Department of Education to design a curriculum framework which would ensure equitable support and access for every child in the Commonwealth. Richards believes in these tenets. Moreover, she knows how to transform them to meet the needs of individual children through work on, for example, mathematics portfolios and integrating the arts into the curriculum. In short, KERA comes to life in Richards' classroom.

How did Richards' youth growing up on a farm in Bourbon County lead her to college, teaching, and becoming a champion of KERA? Higher education degrees were nothing unusual in her family. Her mother, who was a teacher, earned a master's degree in 1959 and her father, who was a mortician and a farmer, returned to college at the age of 63 for a master's degree in business administration from Transylvania College. Like her father before her, Richards believes in lifelong learning. She also learned from him that not all learning comes from books. Her father wanted her to know how to milk cows, pasteurize milk, make home-made cottage cheese, and churn butter—"maybe not more than three times," she says with characteristic good humor. Still, those practical skills and hands-on experiences were the basis for later "how" and "why" questions. Richards remembers carrying pipes out to the pond and later installing them between rows of tobacco plants. She learned not only specific skills and knowledge as she performed these jobs, she also acquired values and attitudes. "One thing about living on a farm," says Richards, "you *have* to get up in the mornings."

Farms are no longer popular classroom units of study. "Today, kids want to learn about dinosaurs," Richards says. She wants students to study farms and in the process they will develop appreciation and pride in an important part of Kentucky's cultural and business history. "It's so easy to teach responsibility and discipline, sequencing and logic as the result of field trips to nearby farms," she says. It is also possible for Richards to instill a passion for discovery, like her childhood memories of making cottage cheese.

Rosalind Hurley Richards' return to the classroom in 1994 was prompted by experiences she had telling stories. Compensatory time earned in her business position allowed her to visit Jenner School in Chicago's tough Cabrini-Green housing project. She delighted young audiences with African American folktales she had first heard from her own family members. Then she began to realize she wanted her own school, her own students, her own classroom. Kentucky has provided all three and she has given much back in exchange, child by child, class by class.

Richards begins each school day with an allegory that illustrates some universal truth and her students write prodigiously in their journals, renaming those truths with personal experience and analogy. Richards spouts Plutarch as easily as the names of the famous painters whose art reproductions fill her classroom walls. She is a renaissance woman who lives out the derivation of the verb "to educate." It comes from the Latin word *educare*: to nurture, to lead, to bring up.

A gifted teacher, firmly committed to KERA, excellence, her students and their futures, she touches each child she teaches. From the Governor's Mansion in Frankfort to The White House on Pennsylvania Avenue, Rosalind Richards represents the *best* of Kentucky's women in education.

Richards wins the Milken Award.

Charlotte Richardson

When Charlotte Richardson was growing up in Greenup County, her Native American heritage was never mentioned. The 1940s were not an era of "finding your roots," she explains. Instead, embarrassment led her family to hide their ancestry. Three generations lived together in a house in the country though her father's job in the steel rolling mill was in in Newport, Kentucky. She remembers her grandmother putting her to bed at night and singing "strange-sounding songs—chants, too." On walks in the woods with her grandfather, the young girl collected paw-paws, nuts, and sassafras. The family used old remedies like turpentine and sulfa to cure ailments.

During World War II the Richardsons moved closer to Newport. At Campbell County High School, Charlotte Richardson became a majorette, was active in the drama club, and worked on the newspaper. She also attended cosmetology school at night in nearby Cincinnati, but soon found she didn't enjoy the work. In 1957 she began working in the trust department of Fifth Third Bank, where she advanced quickly. When they offered to send her to Eastern Kentucky State University she jumped at the chance.

Richardson married during her second year in college and although she did not graduate, a shortage of teachers enabled her to be certified under emergency regulations. She accepted a position teaching at her alma mater, Campbell County High School. Although she enjoyed taking care of three sons and living out the American Dream, something was missing. She began reading about Native Americans and researching her own family history, taking notes with the intention of writing a book. Since Southeastern Native American tribes are matrilineal, tracing descent through the mother's line, she focused on her mother's roots.

A move to Florida gave Richardson the opportunity to attend classes in Native American culture and lore and, beginning in 1980, powwows and other festivals. While helping to build a village on the

site of an old Native American village, she skinned cypress logs and packed the roof with palmetto fronds. Finally she discovered that her mother's family were Creek Indians and her father's family were Cherokee. She applied for tribal identity and received Creek papers. "I had finally found my soul," she says with deep satisfaction.

Charlotte Richardson established a dance group that performed at state parks, wearing traditional clothing and ankle shakers made from shells. In 1992, she was the project coordinator for the Ancient People Culture Project, sponsored by the Seminole Tribe of Florida. Initiated 500 years after Christopher Columbus connected two separate and distinct worlds, the project offered both Indians and others a chance to learn about the contributions of Native Americans.

Richardson eventually brought her expertise back to Kentucky and settled in London, near Lake Cumberland. Her

timbered house is in the woods on a state reserve. She fervently wishes people would learn to listen to the earth and teach their children to do the same. "We live in a frantic world and they need nature," she says.

Charlotte Richardson is a member of Governor Paul Patton's newly formed Native American Heritage Commission, whose task is to promote Native American awareness. The commission seeks funding for a museum in the state to house Native American artifacts that are now scattered across the state at various universities and in private homes. The commission will also work toward getting state laws passed to protect Native American burial grounds and graves.

Richardson wants people to know that "Southeastern Native Americans, unlike those from the west, did not live in tepees and wear buckskin and feathers," said Richardson. She abhors the stereotype of Native Americans that children absorb from popular culture. She tries to convey a more accurate portrait of her forebears through the telling of traditional Native American

myths and legends. She also makes authentic Native clothing, creating designs with applique. Among her many designs are a Cherokee tear dress made from torn fabric and ribbons without the use of scissors and a traditional Creek white lace wedding dress.

As she travels the state educating others about Native American culture, she often hears people brag, "My grandmother traces our relatives back to Pocahontas." Charlotte Richardson knows better. "Pocahontas had one son and no one knows what happened to him. Pocahontas went back to England," is her standard response to such claims. Being part Native American is now fashionable, she observes. "Every woman's grand-mother was a Cherokee princess—like at one time every woman's family came over on the Mayflower." Richardson feels it is critical to de-romanticize the history of her people. Forced removal of Native Americans from their lands and wide-spread mistreatment is seldom mentioned in children's history books. "Children are important conduits to the truth in history," she said, "so start by educating them."

Gaylia Rooks

At the age of sixteen, Gaylia Rooks decided to become a rabbi. Not knowing whether any woman had ever achieved that status, she wrote a letter of inquiry to the

seminary where most American Reform Jewish rabbis study, announcing her attention to apply after finishing high school and college.

Hebrew Union College encouraged the teenager to write directly to Sally Priesand, who would soon be the first woman rabbi. Gaylia Rooks' letter to Priesand mapped out her entire future, including plans for a double major in Judaic Studies and psychology at Brandeis University and a year of study in Israel. Although Rabbi Priesand, who was ordained in 1972, urged the young woman to keep an open mind, Gaylia Rooks made no

detours from the journey she had plotted as a girl. One of only four women accepted to the college, she was the sole representative of her gender at the college's Los Angeles campus.

Although Gaylia Rooks decided to seek the title of rabbi (which means "teacher") at a time when feminist voices were growing in number and strength, her path was not easy. One professor insisted on opening every class with "Good morning lady and gentlemen" while another refused to sign women's ordination certificates in Hebrew as is customary for men's certificates.

It was at a conference of the Women's Rabbinic Network that Gaylia Rooks began to realize that others viewed her as the pioneer she is. At one time, she knew every other woman rabbi, a feat no longer possible since almost 250 women have been ordained as rabbis in America, England, and Israel.

Like other trailblazers, Gaylia Rooks welcomes challenges. The first synagogue she served in St. Louis, Missouri, included numerous people with hearing impairments. Now fluent in American Sign Language, Rabbi Rooks teaches her youngest students in Louisville both the words and signs for several songs.

To the traditional prayer honoring Abraham, Jacob, and Isaac, Rabbi Rooks unfailingly adds recognition of Sarah, Rebecca, Leah, and Rachel, savoring the thought that when her students attend more traditional synagogues, they will be reminded of these vital Biblical women. As she reminds the congregation at the Adath Israel B'rith Shalom (known as "The Temple"):

We need not choose between being shackled like our ancestors or rejecting our heritage completely. We can and must imitate God and create new prayers, new stories, new rituals, and new paths to fulfillment.

She never refers to the Deity by gender, a practice consistent with the fact that both feminine and masculine words are used for God in the Bible. The Temple

congregation still recalls a High Holy Day sermon when Rabbi Rooks described an imaginary conversation between herself and God, who was a woman, and had invited the rabbi to join her in conversation over a cup of tea.

The Jewish obligation of Tikkun Olam, or "healing the world," is one Rabbi Rooks

> *"Modern Judaism has been transformed by the wisdom of women."*

During Rabbinic ordination service.

preaches and practices. She has hung drywall for Habitat for Humanity, fostered an ongoing relationship between the synagogue and a shelter for homeless families, and worked in other ways to promote understanding and support of the disenfranchised. Her desire to extend that sense of connection with her own congregation prompted her to lead two trips to Israel. She came home and created an award-winning web page and virtual reality tour of the Jewish Homeland.

Selfless, compassionate, and creative, Rabbi Gaylia Rooks uses her talents daily to provide opportunities for members of The Temple to renew and deepen their faith, always reminding them of their shared duty to heal the world.

Tears of graduation joy between mother and daughter.

Diane Sawyer

If you want to plot the course of Diane Sawyer's career begin with a list of late-20th century American presidents and the terms they served. Go back as far as Nixon. That's where it all began for her.

Richard Millhouse Nixon took office in January, 1969. By then, Diane Sawyer had earned America's Junior Miss title and a scholarship to Wellesley College, and had returned to her native Louisville. There she was hired on as WLKY television's Weather Maid. It's a story they still love to tell, how Diane Sawyer got her start in the Louisville media world. And it still makes her blush, though the job was short-lived because she moved on to feature reporting for WLKY, then Louisville's CBS affiliate.

1969 was also a year of personal tragedy for Diane's family. Her father, County Judge Executive E. P. "Tom" Sawyer, died in an automobile accident. Even twenty years later, Diane Sawyer still articulated the positive power of his presence in her life. "He was a repository of all our principles and values,"[1] she said in a 1984 interview. Three years later in another interview she said, "While my father was alive he was the reference point, the center of gravity in our family; after he died, he became the unseen eyes."[2] As Nixon moved through his first term, Diane Sawyer helped her mother get their lives back together. Then, in the heat of the summer of 1970, she left Louisville, Kentucky for good.

Her late father's political connections helped her get an interview in the White House Press office and she was hired as a researcher, but in the meteoric rise that would become Sawyer's *modus operandi* she was soon made executive assistant to Presidential Press Secretary Ron Ziegler.

There were trips to Russia and China, the latter marking America's re-entry into China after nearly twenty-five years. Sawyer saw it all, first hand. She was

there when the Vietnam War came to a close. She worked at the heart of foreign policy and the experience stood her in good stead.

Then came Watergate and halfway through Nixon's term during August, 1974, it was over. But Diane Sawyer did something that many would consider career suicide. She stood by the former

Warren Klosterman for *The Courier-Journal*

Sawyer wins title of America's Junior Miss in 1963.

President and boarded the plane with Ziegler, Frank Gannon, and the Nixons. The press trio only planned to stay four weeks, but they stayed four years to help Nixon write his memoirs. By 1978, Diane Sawyer found herself with a head full of Nixon's presidency and no job. As she describes her loyalty in a 1981 interview, "I took part in all the joyful moments, so I felt I had an obligation to—a duty when he needed me."[3]

By now Gerald Ford had finished out Nixon's second term and Jimmy Carter was in The White House, soon to be replaced by Ronald Reagan. Bill Small, former news director at WLKY in Sawyer's Weather Maid days, was now president of CBS News. He took a chance few others would have and hired Sawyer as a reporter. Media journalists immediately registered their clear dissatisfaction. How could Small let someone who had worked for the other side mar the journalistic integrity of CBS News?[4]

As it turns out, her colleagues were asking the wrong question about the wrong woman. In just a couple of years she proved to be one of the best and most devoted reporters on the CBS staff. She came in at 4:00 a.m. and frequently stayed until 7:00 p.m. She was always the expert on the story at hand. Besides, she was the kind of woman so much of America wanted as a role model. She *is* what Americans respect and she *is* what America rewards.

Ironically, all those Nixon years turned out to be useful because the White House was once again Republican, and it was Diane Sawyer who had lots of friends who served as excellent contacts for the young reporter. Her work at the State Department got noticed by CBS and once again, she was on a meteoric rise. She was picked to co-host the network's revamped morning program with Charles Kuralt. "Nobody outworks Diane," Kuralt was soon saying of his co-anchor.[4]

Reagan continued in the Oval Office and Sawyer continued to work diligently. Only now she got to work at 3:00 a.m. so she could write her own copy. A meticulous researcher and voracious reader, she never interviewed anyone without being well prepared and it paid off.

Co-hosts "CBS Morning News" with Charles Kuralt.

As Reagan entered his second term, Diane Sawyer made another barrier-breaking career move. She became the first woman hired as a "60 Minutes" correspondent. Her meteoric rise was complete. Where could one go but to the anchor desk of nightly network news, and even Sawyer knew that was a long time coming. What she hoped for was her own interview program, and that came from ABC, which stepped up to the plate and offered her the co-host position with Sam Donaldson on "Prime Time Live." And there she reigns.

Diane Sawyer is a rare breed. She appears to be a genuinely ambitious woman who holds a rock solid set of old-fashioned values. Ultimately, she is the local girl who made it in the big city. There seem to be only two negative things people find to say about Diane Sawyer. First, that she is too nice; but she is just the right amount of nice and seems to spread it evenly across all levels of humanity. The second, that she's a perfectionist. That's probably true, but it sort of goes with the territory if you're prone to meteoric rises.

Sawyer as the WLKY Weather Maid, Louisville.

Ellen Churchill Semple

by Cynthia Cooke

> *Man has been so noisy about the way he has 'conquered Nature' and Nature has been so silent in her persistent influence over man that the geographic factor of the equation of human development has been overlooked.*

University of Kentucky Library

This was Ellen Semple's point of view molded for the world to see during her thirty years of teaching, lecturing, traveling, writing, and researching. She based the interpretation of economic conditions upon an understanding of the natural factors of the environment. Semple went a step further than her predecessors in defining the influence of geographic conditions upon the development of society, illustrating her findings through colorful and articulate literature and lectures.

How did this environmental determinist begin her career of continuous effort? Born in January, 1863, just months before Morgan's Raid on Louisville, to an old and socially prominent Bluegrass family, Semple grew up and was educated in Louisville. The family lived on Fourth Street on the site of present-day Spalding University. Public and private tutors prepared her for Vassar College, which she entered at age fifteen. She graduated in 1882, still the youngest in her class.

Ellen Semple came back to Louisville and taught at her sister's Semple Collegiate School. Then she returned to Vassar to work toward a Master's Degree in History, and it was during this time that she questioned how much geographic environment influenced human development. Not much worthy literature existed on the subject to quench her curiosity, but the name Fritz Ratzel of Germany was tied to what notable thoughts prevailed.

Semple spent summer of 1911 in a tent in the Catskill Mountains.

In the fall of 1891, she attended Ratzel's class, or rather a closet, for women were not allowed to matriculate at Leipzig University in Germany. She sat with the door ajar in a small room next to the lecture hall filled with five hundred men, Professor Ratzel and the information she came to hear.

Seminar classes were quite a different set of logistics. She actively participated, with the professor giving her "exceptional help and encouragement" in her pursuit of the most exhaustive study of its kind ever made.[1] With the knowledge she gained during the years in Leipzig, she began to travel and write, returning to Ratzel with the finished work in 1895.

Her first published material appeared in the *Journal of School Geography* in 1897 entitled "The Influence of the Appalachian Barrier on Colonial History." Her first book, *American History and Its Geographic Conditions* (1903) was used as a geography text in several universities. But it was "The Anglo-Saxons of the Kentucky Mountains," published by the American Geographical Society in 1910 which began the many debates and disagreements over cultural determinism. Many did not agree that the environment exhibited as much control over the people in Eastern Kentucky as her study found. But the work was in much demand as she presented facts agreeably, lending much color to the subject.

Her writing style was creative, almost entertaining, with a literary flavor lacking in most scientific literature.

1931 Geographic Society of Chicago Medal for distinguished leadership.

University of Kentucky Library

1914 Cullum Medal in recognition for contributions to science.

University of Kentucky Library

She had been developing it for fifteen years as she wrote this to her sister in 1911:

When I begin a book, I eliminate everything else—every activity. For example, I have already ordered my clothes for the two coming years and will only replace such things as can be obtained by telephone...I never read a newspaper in the morning having found it fatal to get interested in any line of thought opposed to the thought I am working with...I allow nothing to interrupt me..I have two hours of exercise every afternoon...follow it six days a week...[2]

Ratzel died in 1904, leaving Ellen Semple an unfinished manuscript on anthropogeography. This prompted her to begin the infamous "Influences of Geographical Environment," an interpretation of his philosophy. She went to the Catskills in New York during the summer of 1911 and worked in an isolated tent "with only the denizens of the forest as company."[3] The work is a monument to environmental determinist thought and it is a good rendition of Ratzel's thoughts, but her own interjections may be confused with the ideals and principles of Ratzel and vice-versa.[4]

She traveled 46,000 miles though Europe, Africa, and Asia, writing and photographing as she went. Her reputation for scholarship made her well received every place she went.

(Left) Helen Culver Medal for outstanding achievements in geography

University of Kentucky Library

After she came back to teach in various American universities and colleges, she was elected president of the Association of American Geographers. Later, she wrote her last book, *Geography of the Mediterranean Region.*

Semple developed a serious heart ailment and thus, we see the end arriving for a dedicated geographer, devoted to the purpose of making clear to others a new geography concerned with the living organisms as affected by their environment.

Today, her philosophy is still pertinent, still appli-cable. She is buried in Cave Hill Cemetery in Louisville. Though perhaps she lies forgotten, she remains a dean of American geographers, author and educator with a style all her own.

Traveling in Java.   University of Kentucky Library

Alice Slone

She was like the woman who came to dinner. She never meant to stay, and in fact, until her dying day intended to leave. "I guess I forgot to leave," she said. Instead she founded the last of Kentucky's settlement schools and the only one still in existence today as a community school.

Born in 1904 at Hollybush in Knott County, Alice Slone inherited the pioneer spirit of her mountain family and community. "Our log house walls were papered by copies of old newspapers and magazines brought into the mountains by missionaries," she writes. "We were tireless readers of these log wall bulletin boards; practicing reading forward, backward, even upside down."

When Slone completed eighth grade, her early love of learning was richly rewarded. She had been a student at a school started in 1916 by Bostonian Alice Lloyd in Hindman, Kentucky. Though today it is a noted college, at the time it provided only eight years of preparatory schooling. Lloyd arranged for 17 *protegées* to further their education with families outside Kentucky in exchange for domestic service. Alice Slone was probably the only one for whom this little discussed, yet questionable, arrangement was a resounding success. After a wagon and train ride, she arrived ready for high school in Cleveland, Ohio, at the home of Ann Anthony Bacon, the niece of Susan B. Anthony, and her three daughters.

From this work-study relationship came opportunities and advantages which enriched and influenced Slone's cultural, political and educational direction. A custodian at the nearby symphony hall observed Slone listening to music performances from the garden. He invited her into the back door of the hall, starting her lifelong devotion to opera, a

love evident today from hundreds of 78 rpm records stacked on the porch of her home.

Slone's deep desire for education enabled her to endure ridicule about her clothing and accent but soon her outstanding school performance received accolades from teachers and students alike. Years later, these students became part of a strategic list of donors living *outside* Kentucky. One former classmate left Slone's school $1 million in 1989 during a particularly lean moment in the school's financial history.

When each school year ended, Ann Anthony Bacon sent Alice Slone with her own daughters to Northway Lodge Camp in Ontario, Canada. As a camper and later a counselor, Slone enjoyed fifteen glorious summers at this girls camp in close communion with Miss Fannie Case, a professor of the Principles of Education at the University of Rochester. Besides living in an idyllic wilderness reminiscent of eastern Kentucky, Slone was imbibing in the principles of education that would become the basic tenets for her school in the Kentucky mountains.

"These were the years of unconscious preparation for the life purpose still unclear in my own mind...not unlike a sprouting seed reaching upward and outward...a life purpose being prepared but not yet manifest. I think of these and some later years as a time of 'the Cloud of Unknowing.'" Besides giving her an introduction to Fannie Case, the camp was the breeding ground for meeting many wealthy young girls who would one day provide critical financial support for Lotts Creek Settlement School, Inc. A tremendous outpouring of

gifts were generated as the result of an article written by newspaper magnate Frank Gannett. He was eternally grateful to Slone for hovering over his daughter who once had been the subject of a kidnapping threat. One reader who first contributed in 1944 left the school $75,000 some forty-five years later.

Although it took her years to work her way through Ohio State University, Lotts Creek was never far from her thoughts. After graduation in 1932, she was soon back home and with the assistance of the community, she built a log cabin which became the nucleus for a school that would eventually grow up the hillside like mountain laurel. Long before public-private partnership became common, Alice Slone was working cooperatively with the state and county education departments. In 1954, with the help of Slone as the consummate fund raiser the community built a no-nonsense concrete block Cordia School, and later, a modern gymnasium. The building is also a community center open for meetings,

When radio came to the mountains.

adult education and "midnight basket-ball." In 1995, Slone's niece, Alice Whitaker broke ground for a new Cordia School. As the anointed torch bearer, she took over for her beloved aunt and keeps the dream alive.

Long before the Kentucky Education Reform Act (KERA) mandated Family Resource Centers, Alice Slone understood that ill-clothed and hungry students cannot learn. To wit, she built a Santa Claus House, which today is still a regional clothes and sundries distribution center.

Sixty years ago, she preached that "every child can learn." Today Cordia School can boast that only 5% of its students drop out, compared to a 70% rate in the area. The beneficiary of an unusual but effective scholarship herself, Slone had an abiding interest in offering stipends and other assistance to students with a passion for higher learning. Some 70% of her school's graduates have gone on to college. An unusually high number of graduates return to live in the area, rewarding the community with genera-tions of well-educated citizens and leaders.

If you listen closely you can hear grown-up grandchildren tell stories of Old Mule who worked at the school for thirty years pulling sleds and tilling crops for the earliest boarding students. You can listen to a tape of Alice Slone tell about the days when rooftop fires were put out by a bucket brigade, or when she opened with nineteen children and three textbooks: *The Bible*, the *Reader's Digest* and the Sears catalog. You can look at hundreds of letters she wrote personally on an old Royal typewriter to former students and future donors. Or browse through the letters she wrote to every

chapter of the Daughters of the American Revolution refusing their donations because they had not allowed the African American Marian Anderson to sing at Liberty Hall. Or you might read newspaper articles about the dark days when Alice Slone took on strip mining with a vengeance. Since the bulldozers were at the property line people looked to Alice Slone to be the official spokesper-son. She responded with intense sense of purpose and advocacy because she believed in conservation of the land *and* the people.

A poet, a naturalist, a hands-on teacher who knew the power of a new vision that plowed the ground with progressive education—Alice Slone was the woman who came back to Kentucky and founded what she described as "a love-centered school where each individual counts, sustained by the old values and centered on new hope."

Summer camp days at Northway Lodge

Effie Waller Smith

by David Deskins

In 1900, educational opportunities were very poor for blacks and whites in most of eastern Kentucky. Black students in Pike County had to leave the mountains to advance their education beyond the eighth grade. The period around the turn of the century was an especially difficult one for blacks. Some refer to the time as a low point for black people in U.S. history after the Civil War.[1] It was a time for self-sufficiency, with emphasis on survival, not the fine arts. Yet, here was a young black woman named Effie Waller writing poems to Bryant and Longfellow and speaking of her "muse for poetry unfired" and naiads and such. An African American woman writing lyrical ballads and other forms of verse in eastern Kentucky, hardly a hotbed for traditional poetry at the turn of the century, was unusual.

Inquiries of Effie Waller Smith at most Kentucky college and university libraries turns up no ready body of knowledge concerning her life, and not one of her books. It was as if Effie Waller Smith had never lived. Despite her efforts and talent, as a black woman writer she had been ignored.

Effie Waller was born in Pike County on January 6, 1879. Both parents were former slaves who provided all of their children a degree of education far beyond the norm of the day. According to her adopted daughter, Ruth Ratcliff:

Her parents read to her, what little they could being (former) slaves

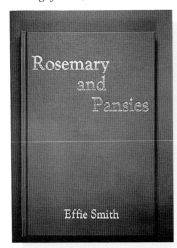

and not having much of a chance. Her parents provided a deeply religious background...She said they did a lot of things together, berry picking...They would gather about the fire and pop corn and her father would tell stories about his slave days. Evidently he had a very good master.[2]

All the children attended local segregated schools and all gained their teaching certificates and further education at the Kentucky State Normal School for Colored Persons.[3] Smith's mother supplied the love and care that protected and insulated the children from harsh realities of the racial situation in the decades prior to 1900. Those days were the happiest and most carefree of Effie Waller's life, and she often alluded to them in her writing. They were a safe haven, in contrast to the realities of racial hatred and discrimination that she found in the world away from home.

"Autumn 1896," a poem in her first book of poetry shows her writing favorably at sixteen. She was extremely well read in classical literature and aware of what other popular writers of her day were doing, but she was also painfully aware of her situation in respect to racial origin and the difficulties that she would encounter because of her race. In 1904, *Songs of the Months* was her first major effort to be recognized as a writer. It is interesting to note that one of the people who likely helped finance her first effort was Mary Elliott Flannery, who was the first woman elected to a Southern state legislature. She penned an ardent introduction to *Songs* imploring readers to give "Miss Effie," as she was known, a chance to impress. Flannery's approval is strengthened by her use of a poem written for Smith by the Rev. Peter Clay, an author of considerable local repute:

Yet God with music touched the singer's heart;
And thoughts in liquid measure
Doth flow out like a treasure,
To charm us with the poet's mystic arts.

As historical documents, some poems depict life on the Cumberland Mountains, circa 1900, and reveal what her own life was like. Some of these include "Berrying Time," "The Corn-husking," "Decoration Day," "The Colored Soldiers of the Spanish-American War." The tension in some of her poetry develops out of "the singing poet of the Cumberlands," a desire to be at one with nature and at the same time a student of school learning. The affinity that Smith felt toward nature cannot be downplayed. One of her former students in Pikeville recalled that she often sang to her class and that "if it was a particularly pretty day she was liable to turn class out early and head for that mountain over there, and spend the rest of the day walking, looking at the birds and the flowers."[4]

One of her most powerful, artistic statements about life, "The Faded Blossoms," appeared in the *Independent*

and ambitions as a creative writer, and yet they remain largely unacknowledged, even by those close to her. Why did she stop writing and publishing at the age of thirty-eight? Probably because of the difficulty black women writers encountered trying to publish their work, let alone achieve literary fame. In 1960 she died in total obscurity.

SUNSET ON THE CUMBERLANDS.
You should have been with us upon
Those "chimneys" and have seen
The golden sun in splendor sink
Behind the hilltops green.

The Bachelor Girl

She's no "old maid," she's not afraid
To let you know she's her own "boss,"
  She's not pleased, she's not diseased,
She is not nervous, is not cross.

She's no desire whatever for
Mrs. to precede her name,
The blessedness of singleness
She all her life will proudly claim.

magazine in 1911, just a few months after her husband, Charles, a deputy sheriff from whom she was separated, was murdered while serving a warrant. The poet only appeared in print one other time and then her work disappeared from public view altogether. In the spring of 1918, Effie Waller Smith was recruited by a group of religious canvassers to join their religious commune in Waukesha, Wisconsin, which she did. Later she became disillusioned and moved to the town of Neenah, Wisconsin. Smith returned to Kentucky only once, to adopt Ruth Ratcliff, the daughter of one of her former friends and students, and take her back to Wisconsin.

Effie Waller Smith left little record of her existence. There are no diaries or journals that might allow one to sift through her thoughts and learn about her. There are only three volumes of verse, three short stories, and a few poems she wrote for exclusive literary magazines, all published during an intense thirteen-year period. They testify to her desires

Poet Smith reminds us what it meant to remain unmarried at the turn of the century.

Mary Levi Smith

by Karen McDaniel

Growing up in Hazelhurst, Mississippi, Mary Levi Smith did not plan to become a university president. She had planned to become a nurse, but the laboratory course work and taking blood forced her to realize that she should seek another field of study. Her second career choice was mathematics,

children born to the Reverend William Levi and Byneter Markham Levi. Her primary role model was her father, who was a Church of God in Christ minister. Dr. Smith said that she and her father "were good buddies." Together, Mary Smith and her father produced a newsletter for the church. Often she traveled

but all of her Jackson State College professors kept telling her that she would make an excellent teacher, and she has never regretted it. In fact, if Mary Smith were not President of Kentucky State University, she would prefer to be a college dean, which she calls "the best of both worlds, teaching and administration."

Dr. Mary Smith was one of seven

with him to different congregations and played the piano. Rev. Levi taught his daughter "to do what you do well or don't do it at all," and "to live according to your word." Through their travels together, Mary Levi learned how to work with people and, like her father, to look for the good in people.

It was her father who had high aspirations for his daughters and pushed them

to stay in school and do well so that they "would not have to depend upon men to accomplish anything." However, Rev. Levi spoiled his own wife, who never worked outside the home. Byneter Levi catered to her husband's every need, cared for the house and children and taught the children proper behavior.

As a student at Jackson State College in Jackson, Mississippi during the civil rights movement, Mary Levi was not allowed to participate in any of the activist initiatives for fear of expulsion from the college. However, she witnessed much of the ongoing civil rights activities in Mississippi. Initially there were some "visible results of the movement at grocery stores, gas stations and restaurants where people were more cautious and afraid that you might get together and boycott." While she could not participate in civil rights activities, she rebelled in other ways.

When Levi was asked by one grocer if she had found what she needed in the store, she replied "Yes." And the grocer asked, "Yes, what?" When she refused to say the expected "Yes, sir" the grocer told her to leave. Whereupon she responded, "You will never get another cent from me." Although she had an account at that particular grocery, she traveled to another store further away as long as she lived in that community. It was only

Certificate of Life Membership

This Certifies that

Mary L. Smith

is a Life Member of the

National Association
for the Advancement of Colored People,

having paid the sum of Five Hundred Dollars into the Treasury of the National Office, testifying forever to our faith in the future of Black Americans in the United States, and in the principles of equality and justice in the American Constitution. In witness whereof the Board of Directors has caused this Certificate to be issued.

September 1995

Rupert Richardson
President

Myrlie Evers-Williams
National Chair

Earl T. Shinhoster
Acting Executive Director

after Smith left Mississippi and returned later was she able to see that major changes had indeed occurred.

Dr. Mary Smith has been recognized by her peers as an outstanding educator and named Outstanding Professor in 1985. As the college President, she has served as a role model and inspiration to many young women in academia who strive to reach the upper administration echelon.

"To laugh often and much; to win the respect of intelligent people and the affection of children; to earn the appreciation of honest critics and endure the betrayal of false friends; to appreciate beauty; to find the best in others; to leave the world a little better place than we found it; whether by a healthy child, a garden patch or a redeemed social condition; to know even one life breathed easier because you lived. This is to have succeeded."

Catherine Spalding

Sisters of Charity at Nazareth Archives

*A*fter Catherine Spalding's father refused to worship in the Anglican Church, he left England in 1657 and ventured to Maryland in the New World. When her father died in 1812, Catherine Spalding's mother brought her to the rugged frontier of Kentucky.

She had designs on becoming a Roman Catholic nun and she joined a community of nuns in Loretto who formed the Sisters of Charity, one of the first purely American orders. Other earlier orders of nuns had originated in Europe. By democratic vote, she was elected the Mother of these pioneer nuns, and at age 19, she led them in the spiritual and corporal works of service and teaching.

"Give us this day our daily bread" became a reality only through hard physical labor in a survival garden, where they raised wheat, oats, carrots, cucumbers, cantaloupes, cabbages, and beans. They had to spin thread to make their own cloth because in those days there was no store or shop to purchase fabric or clothing. When they expanded their good works into Bardstown, they walked two miles each way every morning and evening to church.

Far removed from the Revolutionary War of 1812 that was raging between the British and the American Colonists, the convent did not even hear about the treaty until months later. Yet, they had another victory in store for themselves, designing and adopting new habits to celebrate in an ordination service for their newly-created order. There was much spinning, dyeing, and weaving to make their habits with full-length black wool skirts, sleeves to the wrist, and a black cap, all worn long before the days of air conditioning. But this religious garb became the simple uniform for the Sisters of Charity in Nazareth, Kentucky and subsequently all over the world.

Mother Catherine Spalding went to Louisville in 1831 to open Presentation Academy, a school for young women; in 1832 she opened St. Vincent de Paul as an orphanage for young women. In the many letters still in existence she reassures distraught widowers that she will take over the care of their daughters.

Never one to mince words, Mother Catherine Spalding was outraged when the Mayor of Louisville tried to pay the sisters for nursing cholera victims during the epidemic of 1832. "If we are servants of the poor, the sick, and the orphan, we are voluntarily so. We are *not* hirelings," and promptly returned the $75.00.

Nuns like Mother Catherine Spalding were nothing like St. Therese of Lisieux's description of a "fine bunch of old maids," and she never proved it more visibly than on Bloody Monday, August 5, 1857, when the Know-Nothings attacked and burned Irish and German Catholic homes and businesses in Louisville. The Know-Nothings were a political party who were anti-Roman Catholic and anti-immigrant and their name gives rise to an ugly chapter in Kentucky history. In the 1850 census there were 20,000 Roman Catholics in Louisville and 4 percent of the population was foreign-born. Rioters roamed the streets looking for foreign and Catholic citizens. In the Irish sections, houses were set on fire. As they made their way toward the orphanage, Mother Catherine Spalding stood on the porch facing their shouts, "Let's burn the place down. Kill the Papists." In the presence of such a simple woman in her religious habit, even the hateful, bigoted Know-Nothings could not bring themselves to hurt a nun. After Bloody Monday, many Catholics left Louisville, and the city's reputation for intolerance of religious freedom caused many future immigrants not to settle in the river city. In a letter dated August 25, 1855, Kentucky born Abraham Lincoln wrote to Louisville resident Joshua Speed:

> As a nation we began by declaring that "all men are created equal." We now practically read it "all men are created equal, except Negroes." When the Know-Nothings get control, it will read, "all men are created equal, except Negroes and foreigners and Catholics." When it comes to this, I shall prefer emigrating to some country where they make no pretense of loving liberty, where despotism can be taken pure and without the base alloy of hypocrisy.

"*If we are servants of the poor, the sick, and the orphan, we are voluntarily so. We are not hirelings.*"

Mother Catherine Spalding, for whom Spalding University was named, had the uncanny ability not to dwell on the past but always looked to the future, to the spring of one's life. In an era of living on the rugged Kentucky frontier where everything was built anew, she established a religious order that has inspired strength and loyalty to the well-being and education of women, children and orphans. As one of the founders of the Sisters of Charity at Nazareth, she exemplifies what great things women accomplished in Kentucky's springtime of history.

Jane Stephenson

When Gurney Norman called his friend, Jane B. Stephenson, in the fall of 1986, he posed a troubling question: "How do you help a financially distressed, out-of-work, middle-aged woman find a job if she has no work experience nor traditional job skills?"

Norman, an English professor at the University of Kentucky, described the hard luck case to Stephenson, adding that the woman's problems were compounded by her debilitating lack of confidence. Stephenson soon discovered that there were many more just like her—fallout from an economic, social and cultural upheaval that had rocked Kentucky's Appalachian region.

During the 1980s the collapse of the coal economy and revolutionary social changes shook the social order in the mountains. Men lost their jobs in droves and found themselves unable to rejoin the work force in a different capacity. Women took up the slack, often taking the only job available in a fast food restaurant. Social evolution saw single parenting and divorce gaining acceptability, and the combined result was an increase in the number of families headed by women living in poverty, coupled with a growing feminist awakening in this rural area.

The situation was enough to send Jane Stephenson into action. A long-time activist and wife of Berea College President John Stephenson, she had the drive and the support to make a difference. A grant from California's Education Foundation of America gave her the means. More importantly she had a plan. She had discovered a solution to the problem: rid these women of their sense of worthlessness and their ability to solve other problems will follow.

In order to carry out her simple, inspired mission, Stephenson created the New Opportunity School for Women. Since its inception in 1987, the School has graduated hundreds of women from its three-week, no-cost job training program. The curriculum offers computer basics, resume and creative writing and interviewing techniques. They receive health care and education. Hair cuts, make-overs, and clothes give them a new look. But building self-esteem is the one most important goal of the program.

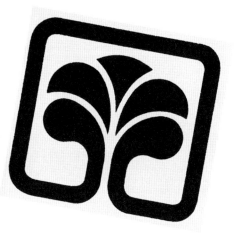

women reach the School they have survived physical, mental, or emotional abuse.

While it is true that the evolution of a spirit takes years, many Appalachian women get a fresh start at Jane Stephenson's New Opportunity School for Women. Were it not for her efforts, they would never enjoy that privilege. But it is their own fortitude that enables them to face the opportunity and conflict that results from their courageous journeys.

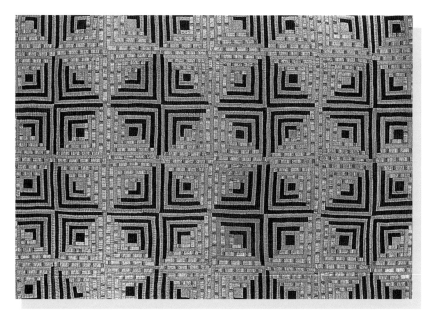

Stephenson understands that without a sense of dignity, unarmed with the ability to care for themselves, her students cannot succeed. By the time many

Here's a true story about what three weeks at the New Opportunity School can mean. There is nothing lavish about this opportunity school. It is a lot of hard work that a determined woman can parlay into a life-changing opportunity. Sometimes it's a confirmation that a woman can find resources to go back to school or that she has the fortitude to divorce an abusive husband. Like Tchaikovsky's "Sixth Symphony," there is a sense of foreboding about Crystal's life as she describes the struggles to reclaim her dignity. Although Crystal's name must remain anonymous, her voice is real and unforgettable as you hear her capturing her strength and self-worth. In her own words . . .

I grew up in a little place, Sand Gap. I have three brothers and six sisters. We grew up rough because both of our parents were alcoholics. I first started looking after the rest of the children when I was eight. At one-thirty my mother would come and pick me up at school and take me home and I would watch the little ones while she went to work. I LOVED school. But in June I got married.

My parents knew that I was dependable. My grandmother had implanted in me that regardless of what my parents did, what they said, how they acted, I was to obey what they said. I can remember so many times going and hiding when he (father) was whipping one of us, or coming out and trying to get him to whip me instead. He wouldn't.

I met Joe when I was 13. He would come by the house and he drank with my mother and daddy. He was nine years older than me. In a very short time I was pregnant. I never went to the doctor until I was nine months pregnant because I didn't know I was supposed to. I can remember the nurses saying to me, "You can't have this baby, you're just a child yourself." I wanted to scream at them that they didn't know what they was talking about—that I had never been a child . . . I had a child when I was 14 and one when I was 15, I had a miscarriage when I was 16. I had another child when I was 17, one when I was 18, and one when I was 19. So there at one time I had four of them in bottles and diapers at one time.

I never felt like a woman because that was something I never wanted to be. To be a woman meant that I was going to act like all these other women that had been in my life—to drink and do the things that they had done. I would never allow myself to be that way. I stayed at home with my

kids. *It wasn't until Penny started high school that I even considered going out of the house and trying to work. I didn't know the first thing about getting a job. I talked to my daughter April and we both decided we'd take a week's training program to be a nurse assistant. We both got jobs.*

Someone showed me this pamphlet about the New Opportunity School for Women at Berea College. I was accepted. I got scared. I've got the kids at home. Joe is at home. I've got to watch after them, and cook for them, and keep house. I've never NOT been there.

Well, I went to the School and I never wanted to go home. My family didn't like it at all. I felt totally comfortable where nobody was but women. The more we talked it seemed like we all had so much in common. The self-esteem classes were excellent. The other women and I just didn't have any self-esteem. I didn't know what the word meant. It was amazing to see the changes in all of us from the day we walked in and three weeks later. These are not the same women.

I'm beginning to like the person I'm becoming and it makes me very sad that my family can't accept this new person. I know my marriage is ending and I can't stop it. They like me going to school but they can't understand why I have to be away from them so much. Here I am at this stage and trying to get through to them: You are young adults and you have to look after yourselves.

I'm scared, but more confident than what I was. I've never had to take care of me. The growing has begun and there's no stopping it.

Pauline Autenreith Tafel

by *Joanne Tafel Oldham*

> "I want to give my children pleasure by writing down the events of my life as well as I can remember them."

With these words, the remarkable Pauline Autenreith Tafel began, at age 75, to write the story of her life. Pauline Tafel was part of the second great wave of German immigrants (Forty-eighters) who came to the United States for political reasons. Her father, Ferdinand Friedrich Autenreith, a bookstore owner in Stuttgart, emigrated to the United States with his wife and ten children after being so advised by good friends. Pauline writes:

> *It was in the eventful year of 1848 that my father became involved in writing articles for the "Fliegende Blaetter" into which he would slip derogatory phrases which referred to a certain well-known personality. (presumably the King of Wurtemburg)*

After a four week trip by sailing vessel, they arrived in New York in 1848 to receive *the terrible news that a cholera epidemic had broken out in Cincinnati, Ohio, our final destination.* Six days later they found out that *the report of the terrible epidemic proved true. Large coal fires were kept burning on every street corner to purify the air. The terrible heat of the summer was intensified . . . Our first task the morning after our arrival was the making of shrouds. During that week, twenty-eight people died in the house where we lived. My little brother Paul, who was only two years old, was one of the twenty-eight.*

Pauline, the eldest daughter, who, in Germany, had been accustomed to a comfortable middle-class life with servants, now *had to do the washing and ironing amongst other chores. Mother could neither help nor instruct me at all since she didn't know how to do this kind of work. I was too proud to ask anybody, and, by and by, I became quite expert at it.*

She continued to show her initiative and resiliency by finding jobs and learning English quickly. Gradually, the family adjusted and, in spite of anti-German prejudice, began to become active members of the community and to develop *a satisfactory social life* within the German community.

In 1850, Carl Tafel, the young man whom Pauline would eventually marry in 1851, arrived at the Autenreith home *to buy a book my father had advertised.* He too had been driven from his homeland.

"My Carl was a trained pharmacist, but insisted on changing his profession to farming..." Many of the "Forty-eighters", highly educated in Germany, wanted to be farmers but they had learned (or thought they had learned) the art of farming from books: These people were called 'Latin

1851 wedding portrait of Pauline and Carl Tafel.

Farmers'. . . They knew Latin, but they frequently did not know how to make a living with their hands. . . Many were complete failures, some actually perished. . .

Immediately after their wedding, Pauline and Carl Tafel traveled in a hired carriage to their first farm *(if you could call it that)* near Sandusky, Ohio. They stayed there eight months enduring muskrat-gnawed floors, rat-eaten clothes, sleeping in a converted chicken coop, getting lost in the dark woods on a freezing night, heavy rain and flooding, deer eating their entire first crop of buckwheat one night, in addition to severe fevers. Carl was so nearsighted he was unable to hunt for food and once mistook a deer for his lost bullock. He plowed the fields in a tailcoat and a stovepipe hat.

In October, 1851, they sold the farm and moved back to Cincinnati where they lived until 1856. Their first three sons were born, and Carl returned to pharmacy and bought his own drugstore. During this time Carl was a *weak man, being nearly always sick.* Most of the pharmacy profits went toward paying a clerk to help out. In May, 1854, Carl inherited *quite a fortune* upon the death of his father. Once again they *were convinced that Carl was destined for farm life, so we sold the pharmacy to the first available buyer and moved to eighty acres of land with a house in the middle near Vienna, Indiana. No other houses were in*

The Carl Tafel Family, 1893—Pauline Autenreith Tafel seated to the right of the portrait.

sight. *Work began. . . Nobody can imagine how much work there is on a farm. The man has to work the land and tend the livestock, while the wife has to churn butter, raise chickens, peel and dry fruit, spin, sew, wash, iron. . . also, I had to swap butter, eggs and chickens. . . for everything you need but can't produce on your own. One didn't get much for one's wares.*

She also, of course, had the children to care for, and they kept coming. Carl was not drafted during the Civil War because he was a pharmacist, but Pauline's brothers fought for the Union, and Pauline herself was vehemently against slavery.

In 1861, Carl began working in Louisville as an assistant pharmacist, coming home every other Sunday. Pauline ran the farm with the help of their older sons (ages 8 and 6) and a young girl whom Carl had brought from the English Orphanage.

Finally in 1864, they sold the farm and moved to Louisville into a small cottage on Chestnut Street. Pauline was happy to be living in a town again. Their seventh son was born in May of 1865: *Our disappointment was great. We wanted so much to have a girl...*

When the Civil war ended, Pauline Tafel became president of a club of German women formed *to erect a monument dedicated to the soldiers killed in action. In the beginning all were willing to contribute as they had remembered the hardships and suffering our soldiers had endured. One had only to look at the returning regiments; the sight of their tattered banners, barefoot soldiers in ragged*

clothes, brought tears to our eyes. But by February, 1866, all they were able to put in place was a foundation stone.

Finally a daughter was born, Paula (Pauline), in 1866. *This was a great joy. At last the seven brothers had a sister.* Then in 1868, another sister and the next year another son, who died at nine months. Each night Pauline sat with her children at bedtime and *taught them to think . . . about how they could have behaved better that day.*

In the years that followed, the children grew, the drugstore on the corner of Preston and Market Streets prospered (it later moved to the corner of Jackson and Market where it remained for the next 100 years). Pauline and Carl Tafel celebrated their silver wedding anniversary. The next year, *we bought a beautiful country estate on Crescent Hill (now 3165 Lexington Road) and being in the country helped us all a great deal.* In the late 1880s, Pauline Tafel recounts:

Our children and our children's children liked to spend their weekends in the country. It was really magnificent when they all came out Saturdays. From afar we could hear them singing! They would stay with their children until Sunday evening. Once we had 28 people with us for Christmas and they stayed for a whole week!

Their first daughter, Paula, died in August, 1889, only ten months after she married. The country house became too lonely and they sold it. Carl had enlarged a son's house on Madison Street and they moved in there. The indomitable Pauline Tafel then turned her energies into establishing a German kindergarten to benefit poor German children. As with the Civil War Memorial, the German women formed a club with Pauline as president:

We worked for and supported the kindergarten in many ways. . .We had between eight and one hundred children, many of whom needed first to be washed and properly clothed...

Throughout her life Pauline had many good friends who helped and supported her as she helped and supported them. Her husband died in 1897, and by 1907, all her closest friends had died. She was *the last surviving member of the old generation.* But, after writing, *Sometimes I wonder why I haven't lost my mind,* she tells her readers that *despite all this sorrow, life goes on. The sun rises and the earth revolves as if nothing had happened. Somehow, we don;t die of grief. Instead, we must remember our duties, we must go on with our lives accepting the inevitable. These reasons gave me the strength to let reason prevail.*

Pauline Tafel has done much more than give pleasure to her children by writing her memoirs. She has given pleasure and a sense of roots to her descendants. She has provided a personal and valuable record of the life of a German girl who became an American woman, a Kentuckian, from 1848-1907. Her memoirs reveal a woman of extraordinary courage and pluck who had a gallant spirit, was able to adapt to changes unimaginable to us in 1997, who, throughout the difficulties and upheavals of her life managed to maintain her sense of humor, her independence and her admirable set of values.

Pauline Tafel's twins, Richard and Hermann—on left is Sally Parker, young girl brought to help on the farm.

Caroline Burnam Taylor

by Nancy Disher Baird

For most 19th century women, few income-producing jobs were available. School teaching was an acceptable position; dressmaking was another one.

Caroline "Carrie" Burnam Taylor was a well-known Kentucky *modiste*, and at the turn of the century her name was synonymous with fine clothing.

Born in 1855, Carrie grew up in Bowling Green, where her paternal grandfather had served as treasurer of the state's Confederate government. In the mid-1870s she and her mother and sister opened a small dressmaking business in their home. Instead of stopping work at the time of her marriage or even at the birth of her children, as was almost the unwritten rule of the 19th century, Carrie added husband Aaron to her work force and they ran a very profitable dressmaking shop.

As business increased, it outgrew the confines of the family home, and in 1903 they paid $3,000 for a lot on which they erected the Mrs. A. H. Taylor Company. At its peak, this company had already served 24,000 customers.

The continued growth of the clientele was due in part to the number of young women who attended Bowling Green's Potter College, which flourished from 1889-1909. Students from all over the South attended Potter College. Many of these young ladies ordered their school dresses from the Taylors, and many returned for party frocks, graduation dresses and trousseaux. They continued to purchase items by mail after they went home, and some of them referred Ms. Taylor's skills to their family and friends. A contemporary Tennessee resident remembers her grandfather's declaration that the only reason grandmother sent "Bessie" to Dr. Potter's College was so she could make frequent trips to Mrs. Taylor's shop in Bowling Green.

Kentucky Museum, Western Kentucky University

Many of the fabrics used in Carrie Taylor's dresses came from Louisville and Nashville. But she also made frequent buying trips to New York and Europe. In 1893, for example, she enjoyed a 24-hour shopping spree in New York City and bought materials valued at over $100,000. In 1895 she made the first of several buying trips to Europe, purchasing tweeds and woolens in London and Edinburgh. In Paris she attended fashion exhibits where she sketched—perhaps pirated—designs and bought silk,

velvets, and laces. In Germany she purchased buttons and trimmings.

Taylor was not only a skilled designer, but she also knew how to advertise her talents. She used engraved cards to announce season styles, and she usually mailed these announcements to customers while she was on buying trips to New York or Europe. In the fall of 1896 one such card declared, "I am again in New York, gleaning ideas which I hope to carry out in your behalf. I have purchased a beautiful line of high priced, medium, and inexpensive materials which will be made up according to the latest and most approved designs."

An account book from the Mrs. A. H. Taylor Company survives and reveals some interesting facts. From September to December, 1905, the average number of employees was 206, which was about two percent of all the women employed in Kentucky. Government records indicate the dressmaking firm was the state's largest employer of women.

Taylor employees worked six days a week and ten hours a day, for wages that varied from as low as $3 for a 60-hour week to about $12, with the

Exclusive Designing and Ladies' Tailoring Establishment

Mrs. A. H. Tayl

824-826 State Street

Trousseau Orders a Specialty

Fine underwear made to order. Suits, Waists, Fancy Gowns, Tea-Gowns, Tea-Jackets made to order. Gloves and Fans and such articles the bride-to-be wants purchased if desired.

Personal attention given to all purchases as well as to garments made in the establishment.

Mrs. A. H. TAYLOR
824-826 State Street, Bowling Green, Kentucky

average weekly wage being $5.78.(The national average was $9.90 for all industries.)

A photograph of the sewing room reveals minimum space for the employees to work and move about, and the lighting appears to be inadequate by modern standards. One can only speculate about heat and ventilation or think about bathroom and lunchroom facilities. It afforded employment for women, mostly widows and spinsters, in a small town where job opportunities were limited, and for women almost non-existent. Most Bowling Green businessmen refused to employ women because they "didn't have the strength and stamina of men, were not as smart as men, got pregnant and left the work force."

In 1917 Carrie Taylor left a successful business and an estate valued at over $250,000. The company did not survive long after her demise. Without her business acumen and sense of fashion and style, the quality on which the Taylor Company based its success began to dwindle. Changes in society also affected the business. Improved travel in the post-World War II years provided greater accessibility to big city shopping, and graduates of Potter College, by the 1920s middle-aged matrons, found new designers and new shopping areas. The Mrs. A. H. Taylor Company closed its doors in 1927, ending a half-century of service to fashion-minded women across the nation.

Wedding dress designed and executed by Taylor, 1882.

9a

MRS. A. H. TAYLOR,

BOWLING GREEN, KY.

Answer Every Question.   Measure Carefully.

Measure of..

Town.. State..

Be particular to measure tight, except bust measure, which should be taken MODERATELY tight over fullest part of bust.   Give age..

Height .... Complexion .... Color of Eyes..

Color of Hair .... Size of Glove................ Size of Shoe ....

1- 1—Around the Neck..
   Side of Neck to 8 – Length of Shoulder ....
1- 2—From Neck to Waist..
2- 2—Around Waist..
3- 3—Around entire Bust and Back under Arms..
4- 5—Across the Bust..
7- 7—Under Arm to Waist..
4- 6—Length of Sleeve Inside..
8-10—Entire Length of Sleeve Outside, Arm Bent ....
8- 9—Length of Sleeve from Shoulder to Elbow..
11-11—Around Arm above Elbow..
12-12—Around Arm Below Elbow..
A- B—Across Back..
C- D—Length of Back to Waist..
E- E—Around Hips..
Skirt Length in front from Waist to desired Length..
Skirt Length in back from Waist to desired Length..

Julia Ann Hieronymous Tevis

by Lynn S. Renau

The school Julia Tevis founded and directed for more than half a century today houses Wakefield-Scearce Antique Gallery, Science Hill Inn and a host of pleasant shops in Shelbyville, Kentucky. Had Julia H. Tevis been a man, she would be remembered for what she was—one of America's great educators.

Science Hill Female Academy opened in 1825. "A good Protestant school was much needed," her husband wrote in a memoir prior to his death in 1861. "Young ladies of Protestant family, educated in Romanish institutions of learning, returned to their parents thoroughly imbued with Romanism." The Reverend John Tevis's remarks served as an introduction to his wife's 489-page autobiography, *Sixty Years In a Schoolroom.*

Julia Ann Hieronymus, a Virginian by birth, married John Tevis, an orphaned Methodist minister, in 1824. The girls' school they operated, initially with support from the Methodist Church, was unlike any other in Kentucky. Rachel Varble, Tevis's biographer, tells us that chemistry did not give way to embroidery; mathematics did not yield to the making of reticules and antimacassars. Tevis herself remembered her early efforts as producing a "perfect flint-mill."[1] Six hours a day devoted to the work of teaching, she eventually concluded, was as much as either teacher or pupil could bear.

In the 1830s, hard times and a cholera epidemic nearly closed the school. In the spring of 1839, when Tevis published the

first Science Hill Female Academy catalogue, she did not know if the school would reopen. By 1857 the school boasted 230 students. John Tevis died months before the Civil War broke out. His widow shocked her supporters by refusing to pray for the Southern cause to prosper, or for God to strengthen "gallant, misled, erring General Lee."[2] Much to the horror of Shelbyvillians, she sheltered Union troops at her school. "The state must hold together," she told those who condemned her. "The Negroes must be freed."[3]

In 1879 she sold the school to Dr. Wiley Taut Poynter. The Poynter family ran Science Hill Female Academy until it closed in 1929, always espousing its founder's creed: "Woman's mind is limitless. Help it to grow."[4]

Julia Tevis with students on porch of Science Hill Female Academy.

In her autobiography, *Sixty years in a School-Room* (1878), Julia Tevis describes the rituals of ballroom dancing school:

I was dressed in a full robe of white muslin, which, being a little too long, was festooned with wild flowers and garden honeysuckle, until short enough to display my 'clocked' stockings and sharp-toed shoes of red morocco...our attentive dancing-master, who was dressed in the full costume of the politest circles of the day—neatly fitting small clothes, with silk stockings fastened at the knees, bows of ribbon and bright silver buckles—corresponding bows and buckles adorning his dancing-pumps. . . we danced cotillions, Virginia reels, minuets, and shaw dances, to the intense delight of the ladies who were seated around the room like wall flowers, while the gentlemen stood about in groups.

Dinnie Thompson

*M*ost white people in Kentucky did not own slaves, not out of any noble moral imperative but because they could not afford to own slaves. In 1790 slaves constituted 16.2 percent of Kentucky's population; in 1830 it was 24 percent; by 1860 it was

The Filson Club

Dressed for the convention of her lodge, The Daughters of the Mysterious Ten.

19.5 percent. Although Kentucky had no huge sugar or cotton plantations like states further east and south, Kentucky participated in a large slave trade until the importation for exclusively commercial use was repealed in 1849.

The Emancipation Proclamation of January 1, 1863, did not set Dinnie Thompson or any other Kentucky slaves free because their state was not "in rebellion" at the time. Freedom did not come for young Dinnie Thompson until the Civil War ended. Thanks to a social

worker from Neighborhood House and a china-head doll, part of Dinnie Thompson's story survives. Researchers are working diligently to uncover additional information about her and more than 50 other slaves associated with Farmington Historic Home, the Jefferson County residence of Judge John Speed and Lucy Fry Speed built in 1810.

Considered "chattel" by law, slaves owned by John Speed at his death in 1840 were assigned a monetary value and divided among his eleven heirs. Diana Thompson, who had been a house slave for Lucy Fry Speed, was given to John Speed's oldest child, Mary L. Speed. Mary Speed's mother had died when Mary was about seven years old. Perhaps the loss of her mother awakened Mary Speed to the grief and anxiety that slave families inevitably experienced when owners separated them. Unlike many other slave owners, Mary Speed allowed Diana *and* her two children to move with her to downtown Louisville. In 1857, a daughter named Dinnie was born to Diana Thompson.

At some point before 1865, Miss Speed gave Dinnie Thompson a dark-haired china-head doll, now on display at Farmington. It is a "Jenny Lind" doll, presumably purchased when the famous singer came to Louisville to give a performance. Young Dinnie carried the doll with her in 1865 when she and her mother traveled to Indianapolis to see President Abraham Lincoln's funeral train as it made its way from Springfield, Illinois to Washington, D.C.

The deeply felt innate desire of all human beings for personal freedom

prompted Diana Thompson and her daughter, Dinnie, to run away twice, being found and returned both times. Although Mary Speed chose not to release the Thompsons from bondage until she had no choice, she did provide a two-room cottage and furnishings to Diana and Dinnie Thompson when the war ended. From tax records, we know the cottage on Rose Lane in Louisville was Dinnie Thompson's house until her death.

As a young woman, Dinnie Thompson found work as an upstairs housekeeper at Neighborhood House, where she was well respected by its director, Elizabeth Wilson and four other social workers on staff. Wilson, whose memories of Dinnie Thompson have been tape recorded as oral history in the 1970s, recalls the woman as "unforgettable...and though short in stature, tall in character, very proud of herself."

Wilson once urged Dinnie Thompson to talk about slavery but she "shut up like a clam." Perhaps it was too painful to call up personal memories of those difficult days, but she also "clammed up" upon learning that Wilson's middle name was Ardenbrun. A slave pen owned by a man with the same name was used for slaves who were captured after attempting to cross the Ohio River to reach an Underground Railroad site in Indiana. Many were tricked into paying a silver dollar for

Farmington Historic Home

the ride, presumably including Dinnie and her mother. Because of an arrangement between slave owners and the boatman, the trip resulted in slaves being returned to their original owners, but only after the humiliation of being placed in the Ardenbrun pen.

Dinnie Thompson must have forgiven Wilson for having such an unfortunate middle name because she gave her the doll and Elizabeth Wilson later presented it to Farmington Historic Home.

When the indomitable Dinnie Thompson died in 1939, the five social workers from Neighborhood House honored her memory with a headstone on her grave in Eastern Cemetery. Sadly, vandals have since desecrated the site.

Little else is known about Dinnie Thompson, but her place in history continues because her doll is safely ensconced at Farmington Historic Home. An awareness and appreciation for the contributions of slaves and former slaves is just one way Kentuckians today can honor Dinnie Thompson and others like her who, against formidable odds, did not let bondage quell their spirits.

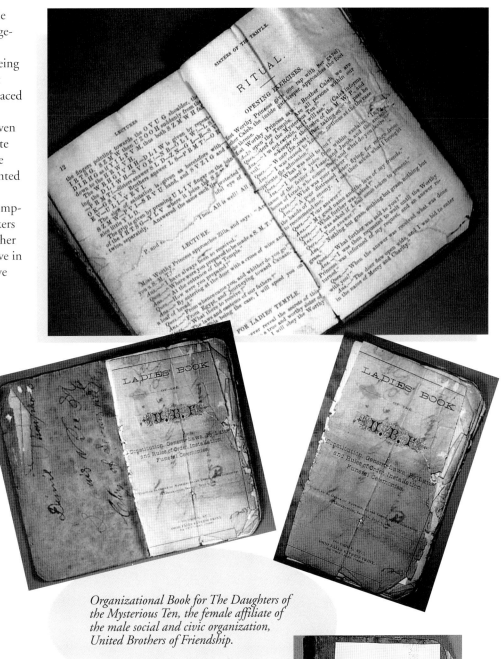

Organizational Book for The Daughters of the Mysterious Ten, the female affiliate of the male social and civic organization, United Brothers of Friendship.

All materials from The Filson Club.

b. 1944

Deanna Shobe Tinsley

alls and fences keep people inside or outside. *Invisible* walls and fences can do the same. When Deanna Shobe grew up, her neighborhood was bound by 28th Street on the west, 13th Street on the east, Broadway on the south, and Market Street on the north. "That was my world. Growing up in Louisville, Kentucky, that was how segregated we were from everything else," she said. The story of her life has been a continuous series of events—some of which she initiated—that kept enlarging those boundaries, not just for herself but for other African Americans, too.

That section of western Louisville enclosed by invisible boundaries might have been an acceptable area of operation for her parents' generation, but for Deanna Shobe and her tightly-knit clique of close friends it was too isolated and too stifling. The generation of young African Americans living in Kentucky in the 50s and 60s watched television, read daily newspapers, and talked endlessly on the telephone. They had different expectations and they wanted the choice to participate in a larger world.

When she was only fourteen years old, Deanna Shobe and her young friends began protests that awakened Louisville and put it on a new path. Never again would the color of a person's skin define her personal freedom and choices. Slowly but surely, the disenfranchised became enfranchised and Deanna Shobe was one of the young leaders whose vision and determination contributed to the change.

Walnut Street (now Muhammad Ali Boulevard) was a "hustle and bustle for black entrepreneurs and shoppers," she remembers. "Before urban renewal this was where our doctors had offices. There were two corner grocery stores and a store called James Department Store, which is still there today. We had three movie theaters—The Grand, The Lyric, and

The Palace—for blacks only." Like most teenagers they were interested in clothes and in elementary school shopping wasn't a problem. But later, "we wanted to go to Kaufman's, Selman's, Byck's and, of course, Stewart's—all the stores where women bought really nice clothes." Gaining access to these stores took ingenuity and courage, but Deanna Shobe and her group met the challenge.

"Segregation made you have to find places to meet, and we got together at the Hi-Y Club, Jack & Jill, or in Chickasaw Park, the only park open to African Americans," Tinsley remembered. "Raoul Cunningham was a born leader and he helped organize the first sit-in. In 1959, there was never any

question that our target would be Stewart's Department Store because it had the worst reputation among blacks. At Stewart's the clerks just stood around and watched us. We couldn't try on *anything*, not just hats. You could go into Stewart's and *buy*, but we also could not sit down and eat in their Tea Room in the basement." Naturally, Stewart's Tea Room was the site of their first protest. Having watched sit-ins around the South on television, "we knew not to be violent, not to be confrontational," yet the presence of these brave youth in the whites-only area soon brought law enforcement officers to the scene.

When the police arrived so did Arthur Smith, an African American alderman, and Frank Stanley, Jr., the son of the editor of *The Louisville Defender*, a weekly newspaper devoted to issues of particular interest to the city's black population. The protesters were dispersed and their parents called. "For us," said Tinsley, "it was just the beginning. It was a triumph in our opinion because we brought attention to the problem and we got involved."

174

And they stayed involved, too. Their initial sit-in was a significant step in the development of Louisville's civil rights movement. Some authority figures supported the young people who staged daily demonstrations. Deanna Tinsley recalls that the voice of the Central High School principal over the public address system excused students early who had plans to join that day's protest. Bright, aggressive students at Central also were inspired by demanding but caring teachers like the legendary Lyman Johnson and Thelma Lauderdale, whose mentoring and sustenance encouraged young people to stand up and be counted. Off they went, usually to Quinn Chapel, which became "command central" because the church had room for large groups. After taking an oath of non-violence, followed by singing, which Deanna Tinsley remembers as "motivational and fun," they picked up placards and headed for Fourth Street. It was the focus of many efforts because of all the theaters, restaurants, and department stores. "Remember," she pointed out, "we still had white and colored water fountains and segregated bathrooms." The kids were arrested many times, but there were never any dogs or water hoses like they'd seen on television. "Yes, we received verbal threats and abuse and we were scared sometimes, but we had fearless optimism. We believed in the cause . . . that we could change things . . . that people really weren't bad."

Back home in the area bounded by those invisible fences, mixed reactions greeted the teen's activities. Her father, a much-respected lawyer and later circuit judge, was naturally frightened for his daughter because clearly she was breaking the law. Her mother, on the other hand, was pleased and urged her participation. In fact, one of Tinsley's favorite memories is the day her mother and some friends dressed up in their Sunday best clothes and hats and entered the Blue Boar Restaurant for lunch.

"Because they were all so light-skinned they looked white and the servers never suspected they were black women. But as the women were leaving they said, 'You have now served colored people and never even knew it,' and left triumphantly."

What does a former civil rights worker do with the rest of her life? After college, Deanna Shobe married and settled down in Louisville to teach school. Inspired by Dr. Martin Luther King, Jr., who came to Louisville during open housing demonstrations, Deanna Tinsley became involved in testing realty advertisements for discriminatory practices. "Eventually," she said, "the time came when the size of the wallet mattered more than the color of an applicant's skin."

In the Jefferson County School System, she moved up the ranks quickly and was principal of Dunn Elementary School for many years. Tinsley has been a particularly outstanding administrator because she brought with her a belief that a young person's opinion *counts*, that one young person *can* make a difference. What better role model can children have?

Deanna Tinsley has come full circle with the school system. No longer part of a segregated student body, today she serves as Director of the Office of Elementary Student Assignment. Her job is to ensure that the county's youngest students participate in a learning environment which has a 15:50 ratio of African Americans to whites.

It is her ability to work with people in an atmosphere of calm, her sense of justice, the desire to eliminate barriers to freedom, and her vigilant support of the underdog that sets her apart. She is a woman who understands fully the isolation minorities may endure. Literally and figuratively she has thrown open the gates of the invisible boundaries of her childhood. Now she can say with quiet dignity and the voice of experience, "Not everything's significant but anything's important."

Marie Roberts Turner

*J*anus was a Roman god, the custodian of the universe, who was represented by two opposite faces. Marie Roberts Turner was a Janus figure. She may have had a smaller sphere of influence in terms of geography, but for decades her power reached into virtually every aspect of life in Breathitt County. She exercised ever-increasing authority over fortunes and lives as a key player in the Democratic party (a Turner family tradition) and in the Breathitt County school system. Today, Janus has also come to symbolize the chaos created in the wake of polar opposites.

As a novice teacher during 1917 in a school that had no running water and was heated by a potbellied stove, she outwitted and earned the respect of bullies who had driven away every previous instructor. As school superintendent in 1931, she rode horseback up and down the hollows visiting 108 one-room schools. Intent on ridding the county of its infamous descriptor, "Bloody Breathitt," she urged students to follow the Golden Rule and turn around their history of violent feuds.

It took an optimistic woman to champion and value education in a region where it didn't offer much hope: minimal job opportunities, unemployment at the state's highest, high school drop-out rate over 50%. Undoubtedly it was more than optimism that motivated her to seek the position of school superintendent for 38 years. Mixing political power with education was natural for Turner, and she once observed that "It's wonderful how many doors a good politician can open."[1] Kentucky's rural history reminds people that in addition to the county judge, the

The Courier-Journal

county school superintendent was the most powerful person because she controlled more jobs, more contracts, and more purchasing power than anyone else. The Turner family had ruled the Democratic party in Breathitt County for half a century and she was elected the party chairperson several times. Election primaries were often won or lost on Turner's backing alone.

The same one-room school doors she once opened on visits, she now closed. Following a consolidation model used successfully in Detroit, she built schools in city centers. Probably appropriate for urban centers, but can you take an urban blueprint and overlay it successfully on a rural model? Marie Turner brooked no opposition. When parents protested closing the Barwick School, county power brokers threatened to cut off their welfare checks. Marie Turner won another battle.

Marie Turner understood that "schools and the (War on) poverty programs went

hand-in-hand, because if children don't have something to eat and something to wear, they don't do much good in school."[2] Yet, she placed every possible barrier in front of the Appalachian Volunteers who wanted to serve free lunches. Marie Turner said that the volunteers "came in here . . . to change the power structure.[3] For their part, the volunteers explained that they had been charged with organizing communities to let the *people* decide what was in their best interest. But matriarch Marie Turner already knew what her people needed better than they did themselves. She didn't like all those young volunteers asking questions. One volunteer professed that when he arrived he "had never heard of people having so much savage political power."[4]

Eventually songwriter Michael Kilne summed up Turner's style this way:

**Now Mrs. Turner is a fine ole dame.
She treats all the poor people
about the same.**

**If you vote for me, I'll treat you right.
If you think for yourself,
your future won't be bright.**

**Now it's hard times in the country
Down on Turner's farm.**

By 1960 the House Investigating Committee on Education issued a report condemning Kentucky's education system as one "riddled with politics, waste and incompetency." Its officials were governed by "greed, inefficiency, nepotism," and "teachers were hired, fired and transferred according to their support of the local superintendents, misuse of school buildings and vehicles, and the granting of contracts to political favorites."[5]

Like Janus, the legendary Marie Turner sometimes seemed at odds with herself. She made sure no child went without a coat, brought bookmobiles into the county, and saw to it that state funds were appropriated for modern schools like The LBJ School (named for President Lyndon Baines Johnson). Yet, this is the same woman who installed new carpeting in The LBJ School and inspired a requirement that students wear only bedroom slippers to classes. Chaos often results from polar opposites of Janus figures. This is the matriarch who worked inordinately long days, always with a smile on her face and with the same sincere question on her lips, "But will this be best for the children?"[6]

Elizabeth Cox Underwood

by Nancy Disher Baird

Much of what we know about the past has been gleaned from the letters and diaries of those who lived long ago. Because she wrote often and to an intimate, the letters of Elizabeth Underwood are particularly revealing about the thoughts, feelings and daily activities of a busy, mid-nineteenth century housewife.

A native of the District of Columbia, Underwood came to Warren County, Kentucky in 1839 as the twenty-two year-old bride of forty-eight year-old Congressman Joseph Underwood, a widower and father of four children, the eldest of whom was six months her senior.

During his first two terms in the House and first two years in the Senate, Elizabeth and the children accompanied Joseph to Washington and visited with her family. However, when he journeyed eastward in November 1849, they remained at home. Economics probably dictated the separation.

In the thirty months they lived apart, Elizabeth Underwood wrote lengthy letters to her spouse several times a week. She told him of family and community happenings; of pregnancies, miscarriages, childbirth and infant mortality; of procuring sufficient meat, vegetables and wood for the winter; of preparing a family of slaves for their journey to Liberia; and of operating their home and 1500 acre farm. Written with a poetic flair, the letters address everything from rendering lard and fighting rats to Jenny Lind's visit to Mammoth Cave and contemporary politics. Selected excerpts from her letters provide a peek at life in mid-19th century Kentucky:

I have been as busy as possible lately pickling & preserving. Blackberries are very abundant this year. I have also gone two or three times today to look at the men at work in the meadow, & the folks say I am a better farmer than you. Mr. Lucas says that the front meadow has produced double as heavy a crop as he has ever seen and several say it is the finest piece of timothy any where. . .

*

I shall send another bag of corn shortly. A few Yankees here would make this country what it ought to be. I hope we will get the Railroad and then we will have a more enterprising population pouring in.

*

Just before this cold weather set in, I was fortunate enough to have completed all my soap making for the year. . . So, if we can only procure plenty of the other necessary attribute, water, we shall be amply provided with purifying materials as an antidote to cholera.

*

Servants are hiring this year at the most unheard of prices. It looks more like buying them. Cooks without children and possessing of good character have gone at $85 and clothes, and none below $60. Young house girls of 16 years of age bring $50 and $55. The boy Wash we had on the farm last year and all about his age have been hired at $75. . . . Grown farm hands hire readily at $125 and those who have a trade at $250 and upwards. . . . I had a little girl sent to me a day or two since about Johnny's age (10) with the price of $30 and I would not take her.

*

We were all entertained at your account of dining at the White House . . . if the Swedish minister does pick his teeth at the table, I say it is not a nice custom . . .

*

Quantum sufficient is my cry (to Joseph's suggestion that the way to keep a wife happy is to have a baby in her arms and another under her apron). . .But as to any more of the same sort, I beg to be excused . . .

Western Kentucky University Library

The family home, Ironwood.

*

(one-year-old) Edith is decidedly our ugliest child at present. She is broken out in boils on her face & head which disfigures her greatly but I have acquired the experience that they are beneficial to her health when teething . . . .

*

I begin already to experience that our children are a source of mental trouble. It costs me more to mend their manners than their torn clothing and I know that these cares will be increased with each succeeding year. This makes me wish only the more for your presence at home, to aid your weaker half in bearing the parental burden. . . .

*

. . . I guess you think I am encroaching on your sphere (in criticizing his speech before Congress) and better return to my former theme of housewifely duties. But recollect families make up states and as I contribute my quota I claim a right to be heard, at least by my husband . . .

"My preference would be for a rural building with wide verandas to serve as a place for exercise in rainy weather and the ornaments to consist of twining vines from Nature's cheap storehouse (sort of a Love in a Cottage edifice. . .) where you would be Adam & I Eve, and we could enjoy arcadian feasts of strawberries & cream . . ."

Elizabeth's correspondence ended when her husband completed his Senate duties in 1853, and little is known about her thereafter. John became a civil engineer and served as mayor of Bowling Green; in 1875 he was elected lieutenant governor of Kentucky. The home of Elizabeth's dreams was completed in 1857. On the National Register, it is one of the county's finest structures.

Elizabeth Underwood outlived her husband by a decade, succumbing to Brights Disease in 1886. The Underwoods are buried in Bowling Green's Fair View Cemetery, but only he has a tombstone!

Mary Wheeler

"t was something I wanted to do," was Mary Wheeler's simple answer to the question of why a young woman would leave Cincinnati, where she was studying and teaching music, to spend a year in the remote mountains of eastern Kentucky.

Mary Wheeler was born in Paducah in a house overlooking the Ohio River. Growing up in the early part of the 20th century, genteel girls were supposed to sing and play the piano as part of their training in the social graces. However, Wheeler's choice to pursue a more ambitious *career* in music was apparently supported and encouraged by her mother, Mary Kirkpatrick Guthrie Wheeler. Her mother had also been a very fine musician, and maybe she encouraged her daughter to follow a career which she had not pursued herself. Her father, Charles K. Wheeler, was a lawyer and served in the U. S. House of Representatives. The family's six years spent in Washington, D.C. certainly exposed her to a range of cultural opportunities.

After high school, Wheeler studied voice in New York City and then moved to Chicago to continue voice training. She became a minor celebrity singing in elegant cabarets and salons. But World War I interrupted this career and Mary Wheeler applied for overseas duty with the American Red Cross. She was assigned to a branch called Hospital Hut Service, which was designed to provide entertainment for wounded and convalescing soldiers. She brought music and singing first to soldiers in London and later in the land of Joan of Arc, the Province of Lorraine. At the end of the war, Wheeler continued Red Cross work in Washington, D.C. and resumed her singing career there.

Her new interest in teaching became paramount but required more education. In 1925, she began the first of twelve summers studying at the Cincinnati Conservatory of Music, earning a degree in voice in 1933, and a graduate degree in musicology in 1937. Her master's dissertation was entitled "Ohio River Folk Songs of the Packet-boat Era." She also gave recitals and taught, both privately

and in various schools in Kentucky and surrounding states.

In the fall of 1926, she took a leave of absence to teach music at the rural Hindman Settlement School, which provided educational opportunities for mountain students. From its beginning in 1902, Hindman has served as a center for those interested in Kentucky's traditional folk music.

Encouraged by professors, Mary Wheeler became a pioneer music collector and documentarian. She trekked up and down Troublesome Creek in eastern Kentucky in a wagon or on mule back to remote cabins, carefully writing down the words and music (pre-tape recorder days) to the untouched, unspoiled songs of the people she befriended. Usually she brought the women small gifts, such as a package of needles or a dress pattern, and her genuine interest helped them overcome their shyness.

Mary Wheeler was trying to record and preserve distinctively Kentucky songs, and she often found the same song in different versions in surrounding counties. One of the songs, "Down in the Valley," was a favorite, and it is a particularly interesting example because Wheeler was able to follow generational changes. While women rocked babies or spun thread, Wheeler listened to ancient English, Scottish, and Kentucky

ballads of unrequited love, jealous lovers, or violent murders. She would play and sing her written versions back, and when she'd finally gotten it correct the women would conclude, "That speaks so plain." The small dulcimer she used had been constructed by a local dulcimer maker; it had three strings and twelve frets and was played with a tiny stick and piece of goose quill.

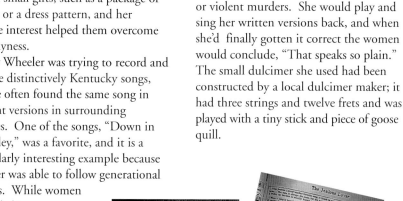

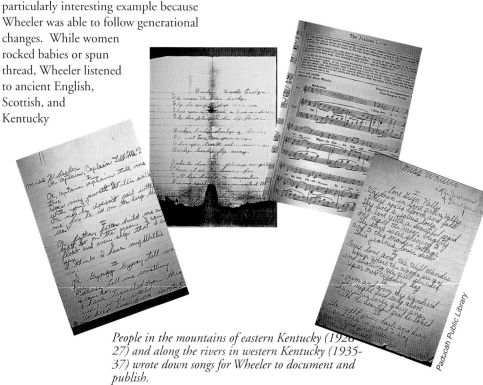

People in the mountains of eastern Kentucky (1926-27) and along the rivers in western Kentucky (1935-37) wrote down songs for Wheeler to document and publish.

Wheeler, second from right, is with the Red Cross group in France, 1918.

No one quite understands why *Kentucky Mountain Folk-Songs* were not published until 1937 because Mary Wheeler had collected them in 1926-27. In the meticulous *Mary Wheeler Papers*, housed at the Paducah Public Library, researchers find scraps of notebook paper documenting the verses mountain people wrote down for her. They represent a rare pioneer effort at preserving authentic traditional Kentucky music.

Wheeler's next recording and preserving effort, which most likely began in 1935 while she was teaching at Paducah Junior College, focused on the songs of the Ohio River packet boat era. Growing up she had watched these boats pass her house, and now she was able to go up and down the river visiting elderly men who had worked as steamboat hands in their youths. During the packet boat heyday, when men loaded and unloaded freight, they coined songs about memorable cruises, sad love affairs, boat races and wrecks, bullies, heroes, hangings, and funerals. In the preface to *Steamboatin' Days* Mary Wheeler writes:

Folk songs more nearly reveal the heart and soul of a people than does any other form of expression. One of the great periods of this nation is associated with the river packet era. The search for songs of the packet boat days leads away from broad city streets . . . into cabins along the river bank or on a hill with the broad stream below . . . They do not understand my interest in steamboat songs and are puzzled at my insistence that they try to remember half-forgotten lines and tunes.

In the Packet Boat days, wherever great rivers met, there grew up important centers for taking on passengers and freight. To the busy wharves and levees the "rousters" would bring songs fathered all along the river highways . . . As the steamboat was leaving port, all rousters were required to line up on the lower deck. When the vessel was loosened from the levee a song was 'raised.' This was always a hymn or spiritual.

Wheeler wanted to record the romance of old time river days. Today it is hard to appreciate the domination of rivers before the automobile. Paducah's golden era of river transportation probably dates from the 1870s when it was first struggling with the railroads. In days when people depended upon the river, boats for passengers and freight were plentiful. Wharves, landings, timber floating on rafts, smoking steamboats, tobacco warehouses all conjure up memories of watery days gone by. To perpetuate that glorious era in song, Mary Wheeler conducted painstaking research to find the songs about the river that gave life to so many Kentucky ports of call.

How serendipitous that Mary Wheeler grew up at river's edge and mastered the musical training that ensured her ability to search out and record what might otherwise have been a lost chapter in American music lore. With quiet perseverance, Mary Wheeler's research efforts into mountain and river music have forever preserved an important piece of Kentucky's musical heritage.

Corinne Ramey Whitehead

*O*n March 1, 1997, Corinne Whitehead stood before the United States House Subcommittee on Water Resources and the Environment. A former resident, home owner, and land owner in the Land Between the Lakes region of Lyon County across from Kuttawa, Kentucky, Whitehead was there that day to testify at a hearing being held in western Kentucky on the Tennessee Valley Authority (TVA) and the Land Between the Lakes (LBL). Whitehead represented herself and former residents as well as the Coalition for Health Concern, the grassroots organization she organized in 1985 in response to the high cancer rates in the Calvert City area. Whitehead and this organization were recognized by the Citizens Clearinghouse for Hazardous Waste in Washington, D.C.:

Your leadership skills, dedication, and courage have inspired many and have helped to advance the work of the grassroots movement for environmental justice.

Whitehead traveled to Washington, D.C. many times in the 60s to represent the landowners of the tri-county LBL area. They wanted Congress to designate the National Park Service to manage and develop LBL rather than TVA. Yet here she was again, thirty-four years later, urging the committee and Congress "to *immediately* transfer by statute the LBL Recreation Area to the National Park Service." This was advocacy born of personal experience, for Whitehead's beloved property, Mockingbird Hill, had been one parcel of land condemned by TVA and, sadly, the house was eventually destroyed by vandals. It is hard *not* to listen when Whitehead tells you that "TVA has squandered U.S. tax monies and has not provided proper maintenance, security and services for LBL. There has been overharvesting and

The Courier-Journal

clearcutting of timber from Kentucky Woodlands, a National Wildlife Refuge that is home to nesting bald and golden eagles and other waterfowl." Whitehead urged the General Accounting Office to investigate and audit TVA.

Corinne Whitehead is no stranger to grassroots advocacy efforts. From the LBL reconsideration to earthquake education to debate over Calvert City's industrial complex, she has spearheaded citizen activism and commitment to make Kentucky's land, air, and water safe and secure. It is her unflinching commitment and unrelenting persistence that is the hallmark of her life's work. It is this work that The Kentucky Environmental Quality Commission recognized in presenting Whitehead one of its 1996 Earth Day awards:

The Coalition for Health Concern was successful in getting the state to conduct a multimedia study of Calvert City's air, water, soil and ground water. She has been active in addressing health risks from the LWD hazardous waste incinerator and conducted a hunt the dump campaign mapping 251 open dumps. She is currently involved in a national effort to eliminate dioxin from the environment and in environmental justice efforts.

What are the roots for such intense interest in the conservation of land and the stewardship attached to the earth? She explains that her "mother's people came to Western Kentucky in the late 1700s and lived on property which traces its title to a Revolutionary War land grant. My father (R. L. Ramey) was from the land between the rivers area, but he went to Idaho as a young man to manage three ranches near the middle fork of the Salmon River." Years after he had returned to Kentucky, Whitehead took a trip with him back to Idaho and remembers that "he fished and I enjoyed the scenery." But the experience left her with an understanding of where his love of land was rooted. Her father could trace his introduction to land stewardship to an uncle who was well-known for how he farmed and raised timber—"a super conservationist," she described. Continuing the same traditions, Ramey taught his daughter all the species of

Whitehead at left meeting with Rosalyn Carter when she was one of "Jimmy Carter's Peanut Brigade."

wildflowers and trees and stressed the need to protect land for future generations to love and enjoy.

As a child, Corinne Whitehead was painfully shy, but the father who became her mentor stressed that "you can do anything you want to do." For a little girl unsure of herself, there was no better way to instill the confidence that stood her in good stead when she needed to rise to the occasion. But her mother never supported her activist roles and often turned up on her doorstep reminding Whitehead that she "needed to be nice and quiet and ladylike."

One thing for sure, Whitehead got the public's attention. It's hard not to listen as she describes the burning smells of sulfa and chlorine that made eyes water and people cough; citizens on oxygen who never smoked; clothes ruined just hanging outside on the line; animals dying; brown cars turning white and paint flaking off; and white porches discolored. Such visible reminders are hard to forget.

It is hard not to listen when she takes you on a tour of Calvert City. If ever a movie set designer needed an eerie industrial complex created, this is the model. But it's not a model—it's real. For her passionate agenda against this debacle, she's been called an eco-freak, anti-capitalist, radical environmentalist, and a one-woman disaster lobby. In fact, if you chart the concerns of chemical abuse, Calvert City jumps off the map. It is a designated hot spot because it is a Superfund Site, which means its toxic pollution is so threatening to public health that it warrants federal clean-up. The complex has pitted environmental activists against the Chamber of Commerce, businessmen, and politicians. A television documentary *Frontline* production called "Who's Killing Calvert City?" concluded that there is not enough money to do science that would produce the truth—that would connect industry to the damage. No one really knows what's being discharged into the air. But the *coup de grace* was when Greenpeace came to Calvert City. The documentary records activities of their familiar boat,

"The Beluga," and toxic commandos paddling in rafts playing watchdogs at river's edge where the industries discharge liquids. Living downwind is a cancer cluster, but Chamber of Commerce supporters say the cancer rate hasn't changed. People accept to live there because "jobs are on the other end of smoke." The Liquid Waste Disposal (LWD) plant has produced fears that run deep while it burns plant waste from anywhere. On the other side you hear about the jobs that produce a lifestyle these employees never had before, "provides our children more opportunities than we had."

What price progress? The complex that has provoked descriptions like "cancer city" or "worse than Love Canal" is the object of watchdog Whitehead's greatest campaign. Whitehead has analyzed and scrutinized site management, EPA oversight, EPA rules and regulations, industry standards and testing. Her detractors can barely contain their frustration with a woman whose un-flinching devotion to quality air, water, and land has been non-stop. Before the ink dries on one decision or ruling, Whitehead begins again. She rails against the folly of bureaucratic paperwork and unnecessary litigation that eats up allocations for environmental clean-up and chokes the court system.

Corinne Whitehead has spent a lifetime talking about basic ethical concerns which affect the very air, soil, and water Kentuckians value. Future generations should be grateful she's been at the forefront of unpopular issues, and her detractors should be praying that she's wrong.

LAND
BETWEEN
THE
RIVERS

Esther Whitley

The Whitley House is probably the only piece of Esther Whitley's life that stands out clearly. There is no picture, no drawing, and little historical reference to her, but what *is* left is an important reminder of Kentucky's early pioneer women. In Kentucky history books, readers are barraged with Daniel Boone and his feats of amazing proportion, but the contributions of early women are as curiously mislaid as the signature bricks at Sportsman's Hill, the Whitley's house. William Whitley's initials are carved into the brick over the *front* door and Esther Whitley's initials are carved into the brick over the *back* door.

Probably built closer to 1794 rather than the legendary 1791, it is the first brick residence built in Kentucky and west of the Allegheny Mountains. Inside there are thirteen steps, each carved with an eagle carrying an olive branch in its beak and each representing one of the original thirteen colonies. Legend hath decreed that the windows are high enough off the ground to prevent Native Americans from shooting people inside the house. Apparently the glass came by wagons through the Cumberland Gap. One of the unusual architectural features of Sportsman's Hill, located in Crab Orchard, is that the bricks are laid in modified Flemish bond, which refers to a type of brick design: one brick laid lengthwise, the next end-on-end, and so forth. The headers in the gable ends are glazed slightly darker so that a diamond pattern takes shape, clearly outlining the two sets of initials.

What *is* known is that unfortunately William Whitley was marching with a Kentucky soldiers unit called "Forlorn Hope," and he was killed. Unsubstantiated evidence that Colonel William Whitley killed the great Native American Chief Tecumseh at this time is the subject of scholarly research that further clouds one's ability to see through the Whitley's personal history with real clear vision.

What leads researchers to pose Esther Whitley as a pioneer heroine is the claim that she was a crack shot and occasionally competed against the men. There is a rifle on display in the house today that does have both Esther and Williams Whitley's initials engraved on it. Important only in that the feats of Kentucky's

Both Esther and William Whitley's initials are engraved on this rifle.

Whitley Historic Site.

white male hunter-gatherers are so well-documented that young women of today need to know there was an Annie Oakley alive and well living in Kentucky.

The invisibility of Kentucky pioneer women leads women to re-examine and re-evaluate women's roles in these early communities. Thinking about the daily life of a woman like Esther Whitley reminds us that women's lives have long been complicated and certainly more inconvenient. If we take a peek inside Esther's life we know it was not easy, especially as the mother of eleven children: it was pure grit and survival. What did the good ol' days mean for women like Esther Whitley? She was 17 years-old at the birth of her first child and she was 37 years-old at the birth of her last child. Women did the laundry on wash boards, there was no electricity or plumbing, and all the beautiful, elaborately-carved wood meant much polish and elbow grease. Long suffering may be noble, but it has its limits!

Although the male Whitleys spent most of their time protecting the property (which included the women at this point in Kentucky history) with life and limb, they were not without sport and leisure. One of the earliest race tracks in America was built on the grounds of the Whitleys' 2800 acres, oval in shape and formed of clay, not turf. In another defiance of British racing tradition, the horses raced counter clockwise at Sportsman's Hill. One reads of lavish breakfasts after the races, which adds a certain throw-your-ringlets-to-the-wind attitude to an otherwise serious lifestyle during the earliest days of Kentucky. From all reports the Whitleys were a colorful couple. Stories are in abundant supply, like the one that Colonel Whitley became an oxymoronic "white chief" of the Kentucky frontier and many Native American leaders came to call at Sportsman's Hill. On one such occasion, Esther Whitley competed in target shooting and won. When asked how she came to be such an excellent sharpshooter, her supposed reply was that she'd learned in order to kill Indians and could do so if conditions should again make it necessary.

Another story goes that in 1784, a certain Mrs. McClure and her four children, who were deserted by a cowardly husband, were left to be taken captive by Native Americans. Three children were killed by Native Americans and they took Mrs. McClure with her infant back to camp. Upon hearing the news, Mrs. Whitley sent a message to the Colonel. He and a rescue company reclaimed Mrs. McClure and her infant baby. We know rather astounding,

intimate details about the famous knife fight—that the knife "was short . . . the savage fury with which the Indian gave an exulting cry, etc." But not the McClures' first names.

Although Kentucky history gives women like Esther Whitley much less play than the men, she suffers from the same unbalanced presentation as the relationship between white pioneers and Native Americans. While Kentucky history may view the plights of pioneer families like the Whitleys and McClures as "rightfully defending their properties," the view from Native Americans would be quite different. The Whitleys and the McClures were invading lands belonging to the *first* Americans and the pioneers continued across the American West until they completely destroyed the traditional Native American way of life. Kentuckians deserve a balanced view of the story of the early pioneers and the Native Americans. Until then, historians do a disservice in presenting a biased rendition of the truth.

Hidden heroines killed in self-defense, learned to shoot with proficiency, and carved out a way of life through hard work and sheer survival. Esther Whitley is one of Kentucky's invisible heroines who sheds light on what it means to be a Kentucky pioneer woman.

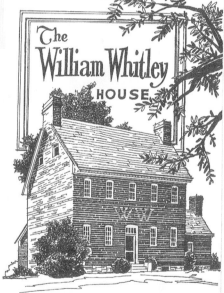

WILLIAM WHITLEY HOUSE STATE HISTORIC SITE
Off U. S. Highway 150
Between Stanford & Crab Orchard, Ky.

Evelyn Williams

*K*entucky needs more citizens like Evelyn Williams who speak out for countless other people whose histories have been affected by inequality and injustice. For Evelyn Williams there is no romanticizing the past and often she uses symbols to articulate her history. She uses symbols of history that validate personal experiences of powerlessness and desecration of land. Evelyn Williams believes that moral standards create a good and just America, so when her land was threatened by an oil and gas company, she just naturally stood her ground. "You **can** if you think you can" has always been her motto.

Evelyn Williams' grandfather was a slave who was in the Union Army. He always believed that you "take care of the land. As long as you have land, you have something." At one time in American history, owning property was legislated and segregated by race and gender. Slaves couldn't own property and when her grandfather became a landowner, he cherished the land because it was a symbol of justice and freedom.

It would be hard to believe that Evelyn Williams ever considered herself powerless, but in 1992 she took on Equitable Resources and Exploration, Inc. (EREX) in its attempt to service an oil and gas well on her property. Although by Kentucky law the company had the right to service the well, Williams knew that her water had turned red from the well's pollution and that there was visible evidence of erosion tumbling down the hillside. Williams chose the route of peaceful demonstration to block the truck's entry, and she sat down in the middle of the road and read a book. Members of the grassroots environmental organization, Kentuckians for the Commonwealth, joined in her protest that surface property owners have some rights, too. For this action, Evelyn Williams received an Earth Day award from the Environmental Quality Com-

by Nyoka Hawkins

mission. For this action, Appalshop Productions made a video about Evelyn Williams. While she was in Frankfort accepting the Earth Day award, EREX moved in its equipment to reactivate the well.

"I sat down in front of the bulldozer because of her," said Evelyn Williams, pointing to the picture of her grandmother shown smoking a corn cob pipe. "When she and my grandfather were freed from slavery and after Emancipation, they bought ten acres of land in Tennessee. Grandma liked to sit in front of the fireplace just like in the picture. I remember the state came through with truckloads of dirt for a new highway and dumped it all over her property just splitting it in two. They'd worked so hard on that property and it was their private property. Just like they did me up on my hillside—I guess that's the reason why I couldn't forget it. I told that man from EREX that it reminded me of my grandmother and my people, but he

didn't care about that. There is a tree up there and they were going to cut down a tree because it was in their way." She reminded EREX that "I'm in your way, too." That tree was another symbol for Evelyn Williams. It was the tree where her grandchildren liked to play and picnic, and she couldn't imagine anyone being arrogant enough to cut down a living symbol of nature that brought so much joy to her family, just because "it was in their way."

Although EREX had the legal right to come on her land, Williams believes that moral standards are embedded in the fabric of American democracy. For Williams, the privilege of corporation includes morals for the common good. But the man standing at the edge of her property had no connection to her moral belief system nor ecological concerns. Most of all he didn't appreciate her people's history or the symbols wrapped up in property ownership. Their standoff exemplified the gap that rages between a person who thinks of society in purely quantitative terms and Evelyn Williams, who envisions a more balanced view of society's environment, economy and social justice.

Symbols keep cropping up in Williams' life. She tells the story of the time in 1925 when she saw the Ku Klux Klan march in Harveyton. What remains an indelible mark is the sight of that fiery cross and their Confederate flag. It rained hard that night and drenched the flag and it "just hung there dripping." Every time she passed it she remembered what those drenched remains meant to African Americans like herself—symbols of hate, inequality and injustice. Time passed and she hadn't thought about it again until her son died in Vietnam. One rainy Fourth of July, she visited the cemetery and someone had put small Confederate flags on each grave, and suddenly Evelyn Williams was taken back to the flag and Ku Klux Klan cross on the hillside. It took her breath away. "You know you never know what impact these things have on youngsters." That's a topic close to her heart because Williams believes we are protecting our children too much from the realities of life.

Her husband was a *union* coal miner and it gave them privileges they'd never had before. But she also remembers going into the company store and when they served black customers "they would put a speck of paint on the bottom of the glasses" so they wouldn't get the drinking glasses mixed up with the white customers. Another symbol of racial injustice.

After the mines were mechanized, they moved to Brooklyn, New York so that he could work in the construction boom. Evelyn Williams attended the New School for Social Research on a scholarship and worked with the Community Action Agency. But they always knew they'd come back to their roots in Kentucky. After retirement in 1974, they bought a piece of land and built a retirement home in the Red Fox section of Knott County.

Memories, symbols, and themes, all from a strong-willed, unpretentious woman whose sense of history connects her to today's struggles for women's rights, civil rights, and the environment. She became rooted in the ownership of land and for Williams this plot of ground became sacrosanct because it is filled with the symbols of powerlessness, inequality, privilege and injustice, which she has overcome.

Page 2

Editorial page

IN CHINA

IN KENTUCKY

Legislature shares blame for standoff

Reprinted from the Lexington Herald-Leader

Close your eyes and conjure up images appropriate to a place called Peach Tree Hollow. Concentrate on the sights and sounds and smells such a name evokes. Charming, aren't they?

Well, reality isn't quite that charming for Evelyn Williams.

Reality is being a one-woman army in a long-running war over a dormant oil well on her Peach Tree Hollow property — a well, according to Williams, that pollutes her water and erodes her land.

Reality is having used her 77-year old body to block bulldozers' access to the well in February.

Reality is going to Frankfort last Wednesday to accept an environmental award for her efforts, and having the Tennessee-based Equitable Resources and Exploration Inc. move its equipment in to reactivate the well while she was away.

putting her body in front of the bulldozers again last Thursday — this time joined by supporters who, like Williams, were willing to go to jail for their belief that surface property owners have some rights, too.

Reality is winning a truce in yet another confrontation with the oil company, but knowing that the fight is far from over.

The fight should be over, though. It would be over if the 1992 General Assembly had enacted a proposed bill that would require oil and gas drillers to guarantee reclamation, test water quality and reach an agreement with surface property owners.

But our enlightened legislators turned their backs on the plight of surface owners whose land is damaged by oil and gas drilling. That's not atypical. Many of these legislators have made a career out of ensuring that the rights of special interests take precedence over the rights of individual Kentuckians.

Lexington Herald-Leader

Williams and her mother.

Williams receives Earth Day Award

Louisa Woosley

Louisa M. Woosley was born on March 24, 1862, in Millwood, Kentucky, in Grayson County. Her father served as clerk in the Baptist Church, which he felt preached a "pure gospel" that excluded all others. Louisa herself first felt a calling to "labor in the vineyard of the Lord" when she was just a girl, but since she had never heard of a woman preacher, she tried to persuade herself that it was not a fit profession. "I was uneducated and many obstacles were in the way," she would later write, and "the struggle was a hard one."

In February, 1879, a month before her seventeenth birthday, Louisa married Curtis Woosley of Caneyville, Kentucky. She says she "entered upon the duties of a wife with a light heart," hoping that her husband would support her desire to become a preacher. But this did not happen. Thus, she began to read the Bible from Genesis to Revelation, finally concluding that "God, being no respecter of persons, had not overlooked the women, but that he had great work for them to do."

Despite feeling that her duty was "as clear as a sunbeam," Woosley continued to struggle with self-doubt. She feared that people would not want to listen to her, that she would not get work, that her husband would not be willing to let her go. After her two children were born, "a sweet boy and a bright little girl," she told herself that she could not preach because they needed her.

But then her little girl fell ill, and Woosley feared that God was opening the way for her to follow her calling by taking her child. Stricken, she prayed: "Thy will be done. If thou wilt have me preach thy gospel, give me back my child." The child recovered, but still she found excuses. She was not educated she told herself; she did not speak articulately enough; people would not listen.

Woosley's final test came when she fell seriously ill herself. She was convinced that God was still trying to make her duty clear to her, and once again she prayed, offering herself, her husband, and her children "upon God's altar" as a sacrifice.

When her health improved soon after, she became determined to preach the gospel at the first opportunity. On January 1, 1887, when Woosley was just twenty-five, she was asked by the church session to conduct the services, since the pastor was absent. It was a "precious hour," she wrote. "My light had reached

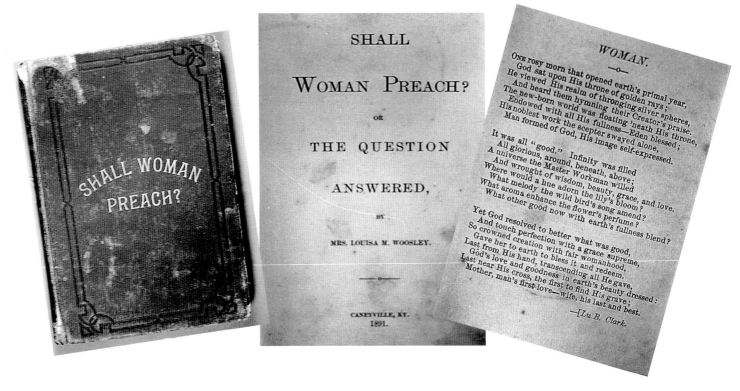

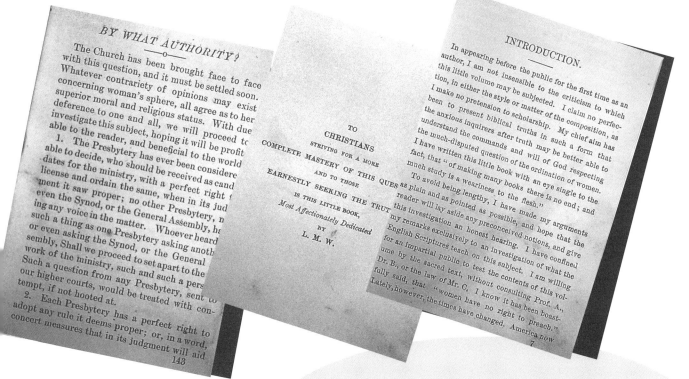

"Who can say he has been harmed by the talk of a good Christian woman?" she asks.

its meridian height, and the light of the Lord in its effulgent fullness shone round about me."

To her distress, however, friends and family did not support her aspirations, but this time Woosley kept her faith and resolve, and in the fall of 1887 entered Nolin Presbytery as a candidate for the ministry. A year later she was licensed to preach and the year after she became an ordained minister. That first summer she preached outside and in schoolhouses. During her first four years of ministry, she preached 912 sermons, for which she wrote, "God has given (her) two souls each."

In 1891, Woosley wrote and published *Shall Woman Preach, or the Question Answered.* She hoped that it would serve as a guide for the general public on the much-disputed question of whether the Bible condoned or condemned the act of preaching for women. Its first chapter counters the two passages (Cor. 14:34 and Tim. 2:12) in which the apostle Paul says women should not speak or teach in church. "Who can say he has been harmed by the talk of a good Christian woman?" she asks.

Her last chapter notes that progress has been made. Since the first woman was ordained in America in 1853, eight hundred more had joined the ministry. She lists the names of many who are "proving themselves men's equals," then ends by both warning and encouraging her female readers.

If we bury our talent, or refuse to consecrate all our powers to the work God has given us, he will take away our talent, and confer upon others the honor of being co-workers with him.

Enid Yandell

by Nancy Disher Baird

Most 19th century women filled the traditional role of wife and mother. Enid Yandell defied tradition and enjoyed a career.

The granddaughter of one of the founders of the University of Louisville School of Medicine, Yandell received her early education in the city's private schools. In 1887 she enrolled in the Cincinnati Academy of Art, where she attended anatomy lessons and dissection demonstrations as well as classes in drawing, painting, sculpture, and wood carving. In some of the school's classes, nudes modeled for the students. Yandell's mother warned her never to mention the models to her Louisville friends, for they would be scandalized at the idea of a *lady* viewing a naked body.

In the summer of 1891, Yandell secured a position on the sculpture staff for the Chicago World's Fair and designed much of the statuary for the buildings and grounds. For her work she earned $5 a day; for the caryatids she designed for the Fair's Women's Building, she received a gold medal.

In Chicago, Yandell also modeled and exhibited a seven-foot tall plaster statue of Daniel Boone. At its unveiling, Louisville attorney and historian Reuben Durrett proclaimed that unlike other facsimiles by portraitists, Yandell's statue of Boone was a "living Boone," an "authentic replica . . . ready to annihilate whatever enemies of civilization are left among mankind." When cast in bronze, Durrett predicted, the statue would endure "as long as the name of Boone shall be known in the land." Tobacco manufacturer C. C. Bickel provided the funds for the bronze, and since 1906, Daniel Boone has stood in Louisville's Cherokee Park. It is perhaps the most widely recognized replica of the frontiersman. In the 1960s a copy was placed on the campus of Eastern Kentucky University, where legend promises that rubbing Boone's toe

Missouri Historical Society

before an exam guarantees a good grade.

During her two years in Chicago, Yandell and her two roommates wrote a book about their experiences as bachelor girls. Entitled *Three Girls in a Flat*, the volume contains a revealing account of Yandell's meeting with Julia Dent Grant, widow of former President Ulysses S. Grant. Horrified to learn that the attractive Kentucky lass earned her living chiseling in marble and clay, Mrs. Grant announced her disapproval and proclaimed that women were meant to care for husbands and children.

"And if one has no husband?" Enid asked.

"Get one," Grant retorted.

"But if every woman were to choose a husband, men would not go around," the young girl pointed out.

"Then let them take care of brothers and fathers," the former first lady answered. Then believing she had won the battle, Mrs. Grant asked, *"Can you make a better housewife for your marble cutting?"*

"Yes," replied Yandell, *"I am developing muscle with which to beat biscuit."*

Enid Yandell turned out a number of noteworthy pieces of public statuary, including a replica of the Louvre's Athena (1897) that served as the focal point for the Tennessee Centennial and "Chief Ninigret," (1914) who overlooks the harbor of Watch Hill, Rhode Island. She filled hundreds of private commissions for busts and small "portrait" figures, many of which belong to Kentucky institutions. A bust of John B. Castleman is housed in the Louisville Free Public Library and a bronze bust of Professor James J. Rucker is on display at Georgetown College. Although her statuary graces public and private collections from Maine to Missouri, the largest collection belongs to Louisville's J. B. Speed Art Museum.

Yandell was in Paris in the summer of 1914 when World War I erupted in Europe. Unable to book passage back to the States she volunteered with the French Red Cross, helped establish soup kitchens for hungry Parisians and cared for hundreds of orphaned children. Upon her return to America, she worked for the American Red Cross in New York City and later confined her professional activities to teaching art and filling private commissions from her studio in Martha's Vineyard.

The sculptor once told a reporter that sculpture was a "lovely occupation for women," but one that required hard work, physical strength and talent. Did she ever regret substituting a career for the more traditional domestic life? At the height of her career Enid Yandell advised a group of Louisville ladies:

"Get married, girls. Success in other lines is hard won. Too hard."

"Athena" Studio Paris
1897

191

ACKNOWLEDGMENTS

It is my pleasure to acknowledge those people who helped bring this book to publication. It would not have been completed without the help of scores of professional and scholarly persons. From the beginning, Kate Black at the University of Kentucky Libraries, Lindsay Campbell at the Kentucky Commission on Women, Sara Jo Hooper, multicultural coordinator for Jefferson County Public Schools, Martha Neal and Graham Cooke at Hawley-Cooke Booksellers routinely fed me with their expertise and enthusiasm. Nancy Disher Baird and Carol Crowe-Carraco at Western Kentucky University were the first two women in academia I visited and one of them quipped, "I don't think you know what you're getting into, but we're really glad you're doing this." They continued to give me support. Seasoned book authors Jan Arnow and Lynn Renau lent their invaluable humor and experience.

I am especially grateful to the thirty-one writers who were willing to contribute their scholarly research and writing. Their essays affirm a personal interest in the value of studying women in Kentucky and provide this book a rich academic resonance.

The following persons provided or located information and materials, spread infectious support, or gave me their time, that most treasured commodity:

Natalie Andrews—Portland Museum
Nancy Atcher-Rowe—Kentucky Craft Marketing Council
Mike Berry
Sharon Bidwell, David Hawpe, Keith Runyon—*The Courier Journal*
Pat Buster—Kentucky Foundation for Women
Lauretta Byars—Minority Affairs, University of Kentucky
Delarna Breetz, Jane Minder, Tim Tingle—Kentucky Libraries & Archives
Jean Calvert—Mason County Historical Society
Nancy Carpenter and Joy Flynn—Kentucky Educational Television
Leslie Cole—KY Environmental Quality Commission
Karen Armstrong Cummings—KY Commodities Growers Council
Anna Catherine Coons, SCN—Library, Nazareth Motherhouse
Lucy Friebert—professor emeritus, University of Louisville
Sue Geiger—Kentucky Center for the Arts
Julie Cooper Gray
Rose Hall—*Daughters of the American Revolution Magazine*
Kelly Hanna and Beverly Ballantine—Farmington Historic House
Gwynn Henderson—University of Kentucky Archeology Department
Tommy Hines—Shakers at South Union
Pat Hodges and Sandy Stabell—Western KY University Library and Museum
Lynn Hollingsworth—Kentucky Historical Society
Janet Holloway—University of Kentucky Business Development Center
Susie Hudgens—Frontier Nursing Service
Vicki Hughes—*Times Leader Newspaper*, Princeton
Judi Jennings—University of Louisville Women's Center
Kathie Johnson and Tom Owen—University of Louisville Archives
Randy Kimbrough—Kentucky Dept. Education, Office of KERA
Mary Jean Kinsman—The Filson Club
Ann Kraft—American Saddlebred Horse Museum Library
Rev. Mary Ann Koffenberger
Ron Langdon—Whitley Historic Site

Anne Lewis and Mimi Pickering—Appalshop Productions

Barbara Lovejoy—University of Kentucky Art Museum

Mildred Mahoney—Pine Mountain Settlement School

Judith McCandless

Claire McCann, Jeffrey Suchanek, Lisa Wood—UK Library Special Collections

Betsy Morelock—CESKAA Archives, Kentucky State University

Dr. Penny Miller—department of political science, University of Kentucky

Mike Mullins—Hindman Settlement School

Elaine Musselman

Cari Norris

John Ed Pearce—*Lexington Herald-Leader*

Pergamon Book Group

Imogene Perrin, SCN—Spalding University Archives

Candace Perry—Kentucky Derby Museum

Irwin Pickett—Kentucky Arts Council

Mary and Ivan Potter—Proud Mary's Bookstore

Laurie Risch—Behringer-Crawford Museum, Covington

Judy Rhoads—Owensboro Community College

Vonnie Shelton—Paducah Public Library Special Collections

Matt Stahl—Maysville *Ledger-Independent*

Rita Steinberg and Debbie Skaggs—Kentucky Arts and Crafts Foundation

Marsha Weinstein

Alice Schofield Whitaker —Lotts Creek Settlement School at Cordia

Contributing Writers

Hannah Baird was born in Stearns but has lived in Boone County for 32 years. She has served on numerous local and state boards and commissions. A graduate of the University of KY, she served under President Jimmy Carter on the Advisory Commission on Economic Opportunity. She is chairperson of the Dinsmore Homestead Foundation.

Nancy Disher Baird, M.A., Ed.S., is a librarian at the Kentucky Library of Western KY State University, Bowling Green. She has written widely on many aspects of Kentucky history. She presents "KY Women Remembered" and "Enid Yandell" for the KY Humanities Council speakers program.

Barbara W. Beard graduated from Vassar College and currently is an executive recruiter specializing in information technology.

James D. Birchfield, Ph.D. is Curator of Rare Books at the University of Kentucky Library.

Victoria Norman Brown is a playwright, dramaturg, and director living in Louisville. In 1996, she wrote and curated the exhibit, "When the Blues Start Talking: Blues/Jazz Traditions in American History" for Actors Theatre of Louisville.

Carol Crowe-Carraco, Ph.D., is a professor of history at Western Kentucky University where she teaches Kentucky History. She is the author of several books, numerous articles and teachers' guides. She is a frequent speaker for the Kentucky Humanities Council when she performs "Mary Breckinridge, the Angel on Horseback."

Cynthia Cooke is a professional cartographer who makes thematic and topographic maps and atlases for the federal government, parks, publications and private interests.

David Deskins is the Clerk of the Circuit Court in Pike County. He is a frequent contributing writer to historical publications.

Aloma Williams Dew, a former adjunct professor of history, holds a B.A. from Murray State College and an M.A. in American History from Louisiana State University. She is working on a biography of Josephine Henry and is the chairperson of the Kentucky Environmental Quality Commission.

Dr. A. G. Dunstan is Associate Professor of History at Eastern Kentucky University, Richmond.

Catherine Fosl is an independent writer, scholar, and activist who is working with Anne Braden on a book about Braden's life. Fosl is a doctoral candidate in American history at Emory University and teaches part-time at Hollins College and Roanoke Colleges in Virginia. She is the author of *Women for All Seasons: Story of Women's International League for Peace & Freedom* (1989).

Harriet W. Fowler is the director of the University of Kentucky Art Museum. She was educated at Smith College and received her Ph.D. from Cornell University. Fowler is the author of many scholarly and professional articles.

Kate Harper is a native Louisvillian who graduated from Georgetown University with a B.A. in art history. Currently, she is a research assistant in Washington, D.C.

Diane Heilenman, a native Kentuckian, graduated from New York University's Institute of Fine Arts. She is the art critic and garden columnist for *The Courier-Journal* newspaper. Heilenman is the author of *Gardening in the Lower Midwest* (1995).

Lynne Hollingsworth is the manuscripts curator and archivist at the Kentucky Historical Society. She holds degrees in history with concentrations in Frontier and Public History. Hollingsworth has worked as an archivist and records officer and has consulted on historic preservation projects.

Claudia Knott received her Ph. D. in history from the University of Kentucky. Her field of research is social history with a special emphasis on issues of race and gender, particularly in the South.

Karen McDaniel graduated from Berea College and received a Masters in Library Science from the University of Kentucky. She is Director of Libraries and associate professor at KY State University.

Joanne T. Oldham is a native Louisvillian. She is interested in writing and family history, particularly the impact of family history on current generations.

Jennifer Pettit, a native of western Kentucky, is finishing her Master's degree in history at the University of Kentucky. She presented her research on Fouse at the Kentucky Women's History Conference, the Bluegrass Symposium, and the Southern Association of Women Historians.

Lynn Scholl Renau is a psychiatric social worker and former museum curator. She is the author of *Racing Around Kentucky*, the first history of Thoroughbred racing written by a woman, and *Jockeys, Belles and Bluegrass Kings*, for which she received the Isaac Murphy Award for her research on African American contributions to racing. *FREEBEE :The Story of a Good-For-Nothing Horse* was published in 1997.

Anne Shelby collects and performs Appalachian folk tales and is the author of poems, essays and children's books. She lives on a farm in Clay County. A long-time friend of Belinda Mason, Shelby has written a play based on Mason's work.

Barbara Hadley Smith, Ph.D. has worked for 25 years in communications and government, starting out as a newspaper reporter. She worked as press secretary for Governor Collins during her administration.

Michal Smith-Mello is an analyst for the Kentucky Long-Term Policy Research Center in Frankfort. She writes articles and monographs on politics, labor law, government, and industrial management relations.

Peggy Stanaland is a retired professor of physical education at Eastern KY University, Richmond. She lectures and writes on the history of women's basketball in Kentucky and Southern women in sports. Stanaland wrote the chapter, "The Early Years of Basketball in Kentucky," for *A Century of Women's Basketball.*.

Sally Ann Strickler, Ph.D., a reference librarian at Western Kentucky University, received degrees from W.K.U. and Vanderbilt University. She is a member of the Board of Directors, the Shaker Museum at South Union.

Margaret Caldwell Thomas is a native Nashvillian who graduated from Vanderbilt University and has been a civic volunteer in Louisville for over 25 years.

Karen W. Tice, Ph.D., is assistant professor in the Department of Educational Policy Studies and Evaluations at the University of Kentucky. She studies gender and sociology. Tice is the author of the book, *Tales of Wayward Girls and Immoral Women: Sociology Case Records in the Construction of Professional Knowledge.*

Sergeant First Class John M. Trowbridge of the Kentucky Army National Guard is a member of the Anna Mac Clarke Memorial Fund Committee.

Dianne Watkins is the former education curator at the Kentucky Museum, Western KY University, Bowling Green. A native Kentuckian now living in Tampa, she edited *Hello, Janice: the Wartime Letters of Henry Giles* (1992). Watkins will publish a biography of Janice Holt Giles in 1998.

Shirley Stamper Williams grew up in Eastern Kentucky and graduated from the Hindman Settlement School and Berea College. She worked for the *Louisville Courier-Journal* from 19661-1995, except for 1973-74, when she was a Professional Journalism Fellow at Stanford University.

Michael Anne Williams, Ph. D., is the coordinator of the program in Folk Studies at Western KY University in Bowling Green. She is conducting research for a book about Sarah Knott.

Notes

Abbreviations used for:

BCL   Berea College Libraries
FCHQ   *Filson Club Quarterly*
KY   Kentucky
KHC   Kentucky Humanities Council
KLA   Kentucky Libraries and Archives
KOHC   Kentucky Oral History Commission
LHL   *Lexington Herald-Leader*
TCJ   Louisville, *The Courier-Journal*
Register   *Register of the Kentucky Historical Society*
UKL   University of Kentucky Libraries Special Collections
ULARC   University of Louisville Archives and Records Center
WKUL   Western Kentucky University Libraries (includes special collections and the KY Museum)

The following notes record sources and suggest further reading.

Introduction

I am grateful for *Women in Kentucky,* by Helen Deiss Irvin, published for the state bicentennial (1979) and *Women Who Made a Difference*, by Carol Crowe-Carraco, published for beginning adult readers (1989). See *Becoming an Outdoors Woman* program, conducted by KY Fish & Wildlife Resources, Frankfort; Betty Darnell and French, *Out of the Shadows: Bullitt County Women* (1996); Patti Rai Smith and Grace Hunt, *Famous KY Women*, (1986); see back issues of *Kentucky Heritage*, magazine of student work by members of the KY Junior Historical Society (Frankfort); Hester Stewart for KY Workforce Cabinet, *Women in KY: Documentary Profile* (1991); Ann Pierce and Harrison, *Women in (KY)State Government, 1940-80*; Bess Ray, *Dictionary of Prominent Women in Louisville and Kentucky* (1940); Mary Florence Taney, *KY Pioneer Women: Poems/Prose* (1893). See also Ruth Ashby and Deborah G. Ohrn, *Herstory: Women Who Changed the World* (1995); Catherine Bateson, *Composing a Life* (1990); Susan Cahill, *Writing Women's Lives* (1994); Cheryl Cline, *Women's Diaries, Journals, Letters: Annotated Bibliography* (1989); Robert Coles, *Doing Documentary Work* (1997); Mary Ann Gentry, *Woman's Touch in Carroll Co.: 200 Years to 1987*; Sherna Gluck and Patai, eds., *Women's Words: Feminist Practice of Oral History* (1991); Carolyn Heilbrun, *Writing a Woman's Life* (1988); *Kentucky Voices: Collection of Contemporary KY Short Stories* (1997); Olga Kenyon, ed., *800 years of Women's Letters* (1992); Ann Lamott, *Bird By Bird: Instructions on Writing & Life* (1994); Priscilla C. Little & Vaughan, eds., *Southern Women's Cultural History from Civil War to Civil Rights* (1989); Judy Mann, *The Difference: Growing Up Female in America* (1994); Nancy K. Miller, *The Heroine's Text* (1980); Phyllis Rose, *Norton Anthology of Women's Lives* (1993); Lynn Sherr and Jurate Kazickas, *Susan B. Anthony Slept Here: Guide to American Women's Landmarks* (1994); F. Kevin Simon, *WPA Guide to Kentucky* (1939/1996).

Web Sites on Women include:

Women's Wire	http://www.women.com/guide
Women's Issues Encyclopedia	http://www.refdesk:com/women.html
Women's Issues Resources	http://www.bmm.com/kit/womens-issues-resources.htm
Women's Web	http://www.womweb.com/
Moms Online	www.momsonline.com

Allen

1 Kathy Flowers, *Poem*, written for retirement scrapbook (25 Feb. 1997).
2 "Elmer Lucille Allen," in-house video produced by Brown-Forman in honor of Allen's retirement.

Picture of Allen credited and used with permission. Taped interview conducted with Allen at The Portland Museum, April 9, 1997. See Dr. E. Lucy Braun, a botanist and conservationist, and Dr. Annette Braun, an entomologist, who spent first part of century studying ecosystems and wildlife in Eastern KY. An exhibit and diorama about the Braun sisters is located at the Salato Wildlife Education Center, near Frankfort. They grew up and spent their lives in the Cincinnati area; see also Gail Austin, comp., *African-Americans in Science and Related Disciplines* (1993); KY Academy of Science, *Kentucky Mentors: Women in Science, Math* (1991); Susan Ambrose, *Journeys of Women in Science and Engineering* (1997); Marilyn B. Ogilvie, *Women and Science: Annotated Bibliography* (1996); Mary Rossiter, *Women Scientists in America Before Affirmative Action* (1995); Nancy Sweezy, *Raised in Clay: Southern Pottery Tradition* (1984).

Anderson

Taped interview with Ann Stewart Anderson conducted at the KY Foundation for Women, January 28, 1997. Photos furnished by Anderson. See *Ladies Lunch: Exploring the Tradition*, exhibit catalog, 1992; Peter Alexander, *Artist's Quilts*; Judy Chicago, *Beyond the Flower* (1996); Sarah Whitaker Peters, *Becoming O'Keefe* (1991); Charlotte Robinson, *The Artist and the Quilt* (1983); Louisville Visual Art Association: *KY Feminist Artists* (4 taped interviews, 1970-90); J.B. Speed Art Museum, Louisville, *Breaking the Rules: Audrey Flack Retrospective 1950 90*, exhibit catalog(1993).

Visit Web site of KY feminist artist, Jacque Parsley: jpcollage@aol.com

Arnow

Photos credited and used with permission. Permission for adapted use by *The Courier-Journal* gratefully acknowledged. See full text of Shirley Williams, "The Maker of 'The Dollmaker,'" *TCJ Magazine* 4 Nov. 1979. See also Haeja K. Chung, ed., *Harriette Arnow: Critical Essays on her Work* (1995); Diane El-Rouaiheb, *The Dollmaker as Agrarian Novel* (Master's Thesis, University of Kentucky,1988); Ruth Fister Hull, *Tentative Proposal for KY in American Letters* (Master's Thesis, University of Kentucky,1984); Al Smith, "Exodus to Promised Land," KY Classics Series," *Lexington Herald-Leader*, 15 Mar 1992; Herb Smith, producer, *Harriette Simpson Arnow*, Appalshop Productions; Robert Higgs, "Harriette Arnow," *Now and Then* (spring 1988), includes letter from author; oral history tape, *KY Author Series*, UKL(1985); Martha Turner, *Harriette Arnow* (Ph.D. disser. UK, 1997); see excerpt from her diary recounting first days on KY farm where she writes *Dollmaker*, in *Now & Then* (summer 1988). For other KY women writers, see William Ward, *Literary History of Kentucky* (1988) and L. Elisabeth Beattie, *Conversations with Kentucky Writers* (1996). See also *Annie Fellows Johnston Papers* at BCL and *Alice Hegan Rice Papers* at WKL; see also Elizabeth Madox Roberts' character, Ellen Chessler, in *Time of Man*. Arnow's works include: *The Dollmaker* (1954), *Flowering of the Cumberland* (1972), *Hunter's Horn* (1949), *Kentucky Trace* (1974), *Mountain Path* (1963), *Old Burnside* (1977), *Seedtime on the Cumberland* (1960), *Weedkiller's Daughter* (1970), *What Berea Meant to Me* (1950).

Atkins

Taped interview with Atkins conducted at office of Melita Farms Warehouse near Winchester, June 17, 1997. Photos credited and used with permission. See also Anne Lewis, *Grassroots Small Farm*, video, Appalshop Productions(1988); KOHC: *Tobacco in KY*(58 hours,1900-1988); Roberta McKenzie, *Farm Women, Self-Concept and Role Performance* (Ph. D. disser. UK, 1988); Akin' Back perennial/herb farm's Web site at http://www.akinback.com.; KY Long-Term Policy Research Center, *The Future of Burley Tobacco* (1994); *Farms, Factories and Free Trade: Rural KY in Global Economy* (1995); *Ag. PROJECT 2000: Comprehensive Master Plan for KY Agricultural Economic Development*; Lorraine Garkovich, *Farm Women and Agricultural Coops in KY* (1987); see also farmer Gale Glenn (Winchester), advocate for reinvigorating the hemp industry in KY.

Barton-Collings

Taped interview conducted with Nelda Barton-Collings at her home in Corbin, April 11, 1997. Photos furnished by Barton-Collings. See also *Black History*, interviews with black and white residents of southeast KY focusing on incidents in Corbin during early 20s when black residents were forced to leave town, located at Sue Bennett College, London; Appalshop video, *Fast Food Women* (1991); Emily Card and Miller, *Business Capital for Women: Essential Guide for Female Entrepreneurs* (1996); Judith Clabes, *By Judy! About Working Moms* (1990); KY Comm. on Women, *Woman's Place in KY: Professional Yellow Pages* (1984); KY Long-Term Policy Research Center, *Exploring Frontier of the Future: How KY Will Live, Learn, and Work* (1996); Elizabeth Perle McKenna, *When Work Doesn't Work Anymore* (1997); Hester Stewart, KY Cabinet for Workforce Dev.,*Women in KY: A Documented Profile* (1991). See other KY business leaders: Myra Ball, CEO, Ball Homes, Inc.(Lexington); Juanita Burks, CEO, Burks Enterprises (Louisville); Kim Burse, CEO, Louisville Community Development Bank; Jeanette Davis, CEO, AdMart (Danville); Virginia Fox, CEO, KY Educational Television (Lexington); Betty Gentry and Sheila Pruitt, owners, Big Meadow Oil Co.(Knob Lick); Lois Gray, CEO, Gray Construction (Glasgow/Lexington); Bonnie Quantrell Jones, owner, Quantrell Cadillac (Lexington); Nancy Lampton, CEO, American Life & Accident Insurance (Louisville); Elaine Musselman of Neace, Musselman & Mayfield Insurance(Louisville); Goldie Payne, owner, Best Little Opry House in KY(Owensboro); Linda Slagel, Pres., Highbridge Spring Water(Wilmore); Mary Ellen Slone, Pres., Meridian Communication (Lexington); JoEtta Wickliffe, Pres/CEO, State Bank & Trust(Harrodsburg).

Baye

Permission for adapted use by *The Courier-Journal* is gratefully acknowledged. For full text, see Betty Winston Baye, "American Dreaming," *TCJ* (14 Feb. 1993). Photographs furnished by Baye. Interview conducted with Baye Sept. 3, 1996. See tape of "Betty Winston Baye Address," Sept. 9, 1992, University of Louisville TV Services, available at University of Louisville Women's Center; see also Maria Braden, *She Said What? Interviews with Women Columnists* (1993); Patrice Gaines, *Moments of Grace* (1997); Charlayne Hunter-Gault, *In My Place* (1992); Leanita McClain, *Foot in Each World* (1986); Roger Streitmatter, *Raising Her Voice: African American Women Journalists Who Changed History;* Arthur Thomas, *Like It Is: Interviews with Leaders on Black America* (1981); see Alice Kinder, former columnist of *Appalachian-New Express*; Annie Poage (1862-1938) staff of *Ashland Daily News;* Merlene Davis, currently a columnist, *Lexington Herald-Leader.*

Bingham, Mary

Clippings, unpublished speeches provided by Eleanor Bingham Miller. Photographs credited and used with permission. Quotes taken from "Mary Bingham in Her own Words,"*TCJ*, 20 April 1995; "Mary Bingham in Search of Truth," *TCJ*, 19 April 1995; Sheldon Shafer, "Mary Bingham Wanted City, State to Reconcile,"*TCJ*, 4 May 1995, used with permission. See Harry Caudill, *Night Comes to the Cumberlands* (1963); *KY River Project* and *KY Conservationists*, oral history tapes, UKL. The KY Libraries and Archives has a collection of photographs on the *WPA Packhorse Librarians*; see also *Eugenia Young Papers*, who was instrumental in establishing the Boyle Co. Public Library, Danville; Lucille Little(Lexington), benefactor supporting libraries throughout KY.

Bingham, Sallie

1 *The Kentucky Foundation for Women* brochure.
2 Sallie Bingham, "Starting the Foundation," unpub. paper. KY Foundation for Women (December, 1991).
3 Ibid.
4 Ibid.
5 Sallie Bingham, *Passion and Prejudice* (1989), 19.
6 Kathy Brown, "Escaping an imprisoning Southern past," *Lexington Herald-Leader* , 10 April 1994, E-4.
Excerpt and quote taken from Bingham, "On Being a Feminist Mother," *The American Voice* (summer 1991), used with permission.

Photograph of Bingham by Julie Dean, credited and used with permission. Cover of book used with permission of Zoland Books. Visit Web site of KY Foundation for Women: www.kfw.org

Sallie Bingham Papers are located at the Perkins LIbrary, Duke University. See KY Foundation for Women *Annual Reports*; see oral history interview with Bingham, UKL; articles by Sallie Bingham in *The American Voice*, literary magazine of the KY Foundation for Women; see also Nina Auerbach, *Communities of Women: Idea in Fiction* (1978); Rebecca Caudill, *High Cost of Writing* (1965); Josephine Donovan, ed., *Feminist Literary Criticism* (1989); Barbara Findlen, *Listen Up: Voices from the Next Feminist Generation* (1995); Adrienne Rich, *Of Women Born* (1976); Ellen Bayuk Rosenman, *Room of One's Own: Women Writers & Politics of Creativity* (1995); Miriam Schneir, ed., *Feminsim: Essential Historical Writings* (1994). Works by Bingham include: *After Such Knowledge* (1960), *Matron of Honor* (1993), *Passion and Prejudice* (1989), *Small Victories* (1992), *Straight Man* (1996), *The Touching Hand, and Six Short Stories* (1967), *Upstate* (1993), *The Way It Is Now* (1972).

Bismarck

Photographs credited and used with permission of The Filson Club. See James Birchfield, *Kentucky Countess: Mona Bismarck in Art and Fashion*, University of Kentucky Art Museum exhibit catalog (1997); Warren Buckler, "Mona Strader Bismarck: Countess from Louisville," *TCJ* , 5 May 1996; Alice Delman, "Louisville's Cinderella Countess," *TCJ Magazine* ,10 Feb. 1963; Bettye Lee Mastin, "Lexington's 'International Beauty' Has Led Colorful, Checkered Life," *LHL*,15 Sept. 1981; Annette Tapert, "Mona, Countess of Bismarck," *Women of Style* (1994), 105-20; Diana Vreeland, *D.V.* , George Plimpton and Christopher Hemphill, eds. (1984); see Bismarck in Annette Tapert and Edkins, *The Power of Style* (1994); see Francois Boucher, *20,000 Years of Fashion* (1987); Christopher Breward, *The Culture of Fashion* (1995); Axel Madsen, *Chanel: Woman of Her Own* (1990); Richard Martin, *The St. James Fashion Encyclopeida* (1997). Mrs. Potter Palmer (Chicago) was from Louisville and The Filson Club has small collection of her correspondence; see also *Margaretta E. du Pont Coleman Papers*, b. Louisville in 1862, a resource for research on upper class Caucasian women's concerns, attitudes, lives, located at Hagley Museum and Library, Greenville, Del.; *Ethel Biedermann du Pont* (Louisville),1896-1980, news clippings at The Filson Club; *Elizabeth Johnson Hulbert Tyler Diaries* (Louisville), 1909-1910 includes politics, marital life, shopping, social life.

Boileau

Taped interview conducted with Linda Boileau at the Kentucky Commission on Women, Frankfort, August 16, 1996. Caricature of the cartoonist drawn for this publication. Cartoons and book cover used with permission of the cartoonist. Boileau's editorial cartoon runs daily in *The State Journal*, Frankfort. See Linda Boileau, *Loaded Pen* (1995) and *Stink Ink* (1990); see editions of *Best Editorial Cartoons of the Year*. See also Amy Brooke Baker, "Female editorial cartoonist is one of a rare breed, *LHL*, 31 Aug.1989.

Booe

Some material taken from Rebecca-Ruth Candies marketing brochures and files; photographs taken from business office collection, all used with permission of Charles Booe, president. See "How Sweet It Is," *Southern Living* (Nov 1993). See also Ruth Hunt Candies (Lexington).

Braden

1 "At least we shall soon learn what evidence is," *TCJ*, 4 October 1954.

2 Anne Braden, interview with Catherine Fosl, 8 March 1989 and June 2-4, 1997, Louisville.

3 Anne Braden, *The Wall Between* (1958), 24-30.

For more on Braden as adviser to women of the 60s, see Sara Evans, *Personal Politics* (1979); see also Braden's restricted oral history tapes at ULARC and see Murray Atkins Walls Series re: open housing under *Walls Family Papers*; Hollinger F. Barnard, ed., *Outside the Magic Circle: Autobiography of Virginia Foster Durr* (1986); Vicki Crawford, ed., *Women in Civil Rights Movement: Trailblazers & Torchbearers, 1941-1965* (1990); Sara Evans, *Personal Politics* (1979); Golden/Shreve,eds., *Skin Deep: Black and White Women Write About Race* (1995); Lillian Smith, *Killers of the Dream* (1949); Morton Sosna, *In Search of the Silent South: Southern Liberals and Race Issue* (1977); see also made-for-television movie, *A Passion for Justice: Life Story of Hazel Brannon Smith*, April, 1994. Cate Fosl is at work on a biography of Anne Braden.

Breckinridge, Madeline

1 *The Breckinridge Papers* , special collections, University of KY Libraries.

2 Lexington *Herald-Leader*, 26 March 1990.

3 Sophonisba Breckinridge, *Madeline McDowell Breckinridge: A Leader in the New South* (University of Chicago, 1921), 176.

Permission for adapted use of Karen Tice, "The Battle for Benevolence: Scientific Disciplinary Control vs. "Indiscriminate Relief," *Journal of Sociology and Social Work* (June 1992): 59-76 was granted by the author. Photographs and memorabilia used with permission of UKL special collections. See also *Madeline Breckinridge Papers*, Library of Congress (1904-06); Sophonisba Preston Breckinridge, *Madeline McDowell Breckinridge* (1921); Melba Porter Hay, "Madeline McDowell Breckinridge: Her Role in Kentucky Woman Suffrage Movement, 1908-1920," *Register* (Oct. 1974); Hay, "Madeline Breckinridge" (Ph.D. diss., UK,1980); Hay, "Suffragist Triumphant...", *Register* (1995); James C. Klotter, *The Breckinridges of Kentucky, 1760-1981* (1986); Lexington Associated Charities, *Annual Report* (1914), UKL special collections; *Henry Watterson Papers* include correspondence and editorials re: his opinions of woman's suffrage, The Filson Club.

Breckinridge, Mary

The Mary Breckinridge Papers are located at UKL. The collection is not large and must be supplemented by *The Records of the Frontier Nursing Service*, also located at UKL. Unfortunately, Mary Breckinridge burned her journals and the majority of her papers when she completed her autobiography. KOHC and UKL have 192 interviews related to the *FNS*. The photographs, as credited, are used with permission of FNS. See back issues of *FNS Quarterly Bulletin*; *Mary Breckinridge, Wide Neighborhoods: A Story of the Frontier Nursing Service* (1952); Carol Crowe-Carraco, "Mary Breckinridge and the Frontier Nursing Service," *The Register* 76 (1978): 179-91; James C. Klotter, "The Last Pioneer," *The Breckinridges of Kentucky,*

1760-1981 (1986), 247-271; see also Anne G. Campbell, "Mary Breckinridge and the American Committee for Devastated France: Foundations for FNS,"*Register* (July 1978); *Frontier Nursing Service*, video, Appalshop (1984). Site visit and interview with public relations director, Susie Hudgens, conducted June 20, 1996. Visitors may stay overnight at Wendover, FNS headquarters, and sleep in Breckinridge's bedroom just as she left it. See also the permanent exhibit of Breckinridge and FNS at the Museum of American History, Smithsonian Institution, Washington, D.C.

Carpenter

See Virginia T. Carpenter, *The Carpenters of Carpenter Station* (Photocopy, 1976). Materials furnished by KY Historical Society, used with permission. *The Carpenter Family Papers* are located at the Kentucky Historical Society Special Collections. See also (relevant time period but urban setting) Margaretta Brown's unpublished, transcribed letters (early 1800s), at Liberty Hall in Frankfort; Brown's letters also in *Draper Manuscripts* at Wisconsin Historical Society and at UKL; Margo Culley, *A Day at a Time: Diary of American Women 1764-1985*; Andrea Ramage, "Love and Honor: Robert Wickliffe Family of Antebellum KY," *Register* (spring 1996); Rebecca Lee Smith, *Mary Austin Holley* (1962), commentary on life in Lexington c.1820s.

Cary

Taped interview conducted with Cary at her office in Louisville, April 10, 1997. Photo and materials furnished by Cary. See James Badham, "A Kentucky Chef's Sunday Supper," *Bon Appetit* (Sept. 1996); Sarah Fritschner, "Bluegrass Takes The Big Apple," *The Courier-Journal*, 31 March 1993; Joshua Greene, "Kentucky Cuisine," *Wine & Spirits* (June 1995); David Lynch, "World Class Whiskey," *Cheers* (Sept. 1996); Susan Hawthorne Nash, "Kentucky Tradition," *Southern Living* ; Julie Stillman, ed., *Great Women Chefs* (1996); see also Martha Barnette, *Ladyfingers and Nun's Tummies: How Foods Got Names* (1997); Jennie Benedict, *The Blue Ribbon Cook Book* (1899/1923); *Best of Best from KY: from Favorite KY Cookbooks* (1988); Letitice Bryan, *The Kentucky Housewife* (1839); The Colonettes, *KY Cooking New & Old* (1958); Sidney Saylor Farr, *More Than Moonshine: Appalachian Recipes and Recollections* (1983); Marion Flexner, *Out of KY Kitchens* (1949/1989); Camille Glenn, *Southern Heritage Cookbook* (1986); *Cissy Gregg's Cookbook* (1953); Nannie Talbot Johnson, *What to Cook and How to Cook It* (1899/1923); *KY Derby Museum Cookbook* (1986); Ronni Lundy, *Festival Table* (1996); Officers' Wives' Club, *Ft. Knox Presents* (1991); *Official KY State Fair Cookbook* (1986); Marty Godbey, *Dining in Historic KY*(1992); *Let's Cook with Scott Co. Homemakers* (1957); *Queen's Daughters Recipes* (1957); Cherry Settle, *Claudia Sanders Dinner House Cookbook* (1979); Lynn Winter,*Women's Ventures* (1997).

Caudill

Taped interview conducted with Caudill at her office in Morehead, June 23, 1997. Photos furnished by Caudill. See Anne Cassidy, "A Tale of Two Sisters," *Bluegrass* (fall 1996); James E. Caston, "Dr. Louise: A KY Pioneer," *Appalachia* (summer 1994); James McConkey, *Rowan's Progress* (1992); Shirley Gish, Morehead State University, "Susie and Me" (one-woman play). See also Dr. Leah Dickstein, "Female Physicians (KY) in the 1980s, *Journal American Medical Women's Assoc.*, Jul-Aug. 1990; Lillian Furst, ed., *Women Healers & Physicians: Climbing A Long Hill* (1997); "Women in Medicine," *Bulletin of Jefferson County Medical Society*, Sept.,1991; see Dr. Artie Ann Bates (Hazard); Dr. Mary E. Britton (1864-74 Berea College); Dr. Sarah Helen Fitzbutler (1892 graduate of Louisville National Medical Center); Dr. Julia Ingram (1852-1933), Louisville; *Dr.Grace James Papers 1942-89*, ULARC; Dr. Ann Johnson (Owensboro); *Dr. Letitia Kimsey Papers and Oral History*, UL Medical Archives; *WPA Kentucky Medical History Project Records* include: Linda Neville, Mary Breckinridge; Doctors Alice Pickett, Lillian South, Julia Ingram; nurse Jennie Casseday, UL Medical Archives.

Cecil-Ramsey

Taped interview conducted at her home in Louisville, June 3, 1997. Photos furnished by Cecil-Ramsey and used with permission. See *KY Requirements for Accessibility in New Construction*, Americans with Disability Act (1994); *The Family and Medical Leave Act of 1993 and Americans with Disabilities Act,* EEOC update, University of Kentucky College of Law (1992); Mark Batshaw, et al, *Children with Disabilities: Medical Primer* (1992); Mary Jo Deegan and Brooks, *Women and Disability: Double Handicap* (1985); Barbara Hillyer, *Feminism and Disability* (1993); John Hockenberry, *Moving Violations: Memoir of War Zones, Wheelchairs, Declaration of Independence* (1995); Nancy Mairs, *Waist-High in the World* (1996); Resources for Rehabilitation, *A Woman's Guide to Coping with Disability* (1994); Marsha Saxton and Howe, *With Wings: Anthology of Literature By and About Women with Disabilities* (1987); Rosemary Garland Thompson, *Extraordinary Bodies: Figuring Physical Disability in American Culture and Literature* (1997); Heidi von Betz, *My Soul Purpose: Living, Learning, Healing* (1996); Heather Whitestone, *Listening with My Heart* (1997); see issues of *Friendly Wheels* magazine.

Clarke

John M. Trowbridge, *Anna Mac Clarke: A Pioneer in Military Leadership*, Kentucky African American Heritage Commission, 1996 (can be ordered from KY Military Museum, Frankfort). Photograph of Clarke furnished and used with permission of the James Family. See also Judith A. Bellafaire,*The Women's Army Corps; A Commemoration of World War II Service*, brochure, U.S. Army Center of Military History Pub 72-15; see Lenwood G. Davis and George Hill, *Blacks in the American Armed Forces, 1775-1993;* Charity Adams Earley, *One Woman's Army: A Black Officer Remembers the WAC* (1989); Leisa Meyer, *Creating GI Jane: Sexuality & Power in Women's Army Corps during WW II* (1996); *Martine Calhoun Thornberry Papers* (1940-57), WKU, first KY female officer in Marines and later, the postmistress at Livermore; *Virginia Towles Papers*, 1918-54, describes Women's Army Auxiliary Corps and Officers Training School, The Filson Club; Mattie Treadwell, *The Women's Army Corps* (1991) and Treadwell,*The Women's Army Corps* (1954).

Clay

1 Paul E. Fuller, *Laura Clay and the Womans' Rights Movement* (1975).

2 Aileen S. Kraditor, *The Ideas of the Woman Suffrage Movement 1890-1920* (1965).

3 Joel Williamson, *A Rage for Order* (1986); Marjorie Spruill Wheeler, *New Women of the New South* (1993);

4 Ross A. Webb,*Kentucky in the Reconstruction Era* (1979); Hambleton Tapp and James C. Klotter, *Kentucky: Decades of Discord 1865-1900* (1977).

5 Fuller, *Laura Clay and the Woman's Rights Movement* (1975), chapter 3; *Statistics of the Population of the United States at the Tenth Census* (1883), 37, 392-393; *Census Reports Volume 1: Twelfth Census of U.S.* (1901), 618.

6 Kentucky Equal Rights Association Reports of Annual Conventions, 1895; *The Leader* (26 Sept. 1895); *Prather's Dictionary of the City of Lexington* (1895).

7 Laura Clay to Ida Husted Harper, *Laura Clay Papers*, Univ. of Kentucky Libraries,Special Collections (April 3, 1902).

8 *Kentucky Equal Rights Association Reports of Annual Conventions, 1901*, Re: female voter turnout in Lexington from 1895 through 1901 has been gleaned from four surviving registration books and the federal census of 1900.

Photos used with permission of UKL. Laura Clay's birthplace, White Hall, is located on route 7 near Richmond and open to the public. See *Laura Clay Papers*, located at UKL; *Laura Clay: Voice of Change*, video by Heather Lyons and Chris Blair (1996); see also Susan B. Anthony, *History of Women's Suffrage* (1902); Nancy Hewitt and Suzanne Lebsock, eds., *Visible Women: New Essays in American Activism* (1993); Hull, Scott, Smith, *All women are white, all blacks are male, but some of us are brave* (1982); KOHC: "A Generation Remembers," *Owensboro Inquirer* interviews re: women's suffrage; KOHC: *Remembering the Vote* (18 hours); *KY League of Women Voters Records, 1920-83*, UK; Marjorie Spruill Wheeler, *New Women of the New South: Leaders of Women's Suffrage Movement in So. States* (1993) and Wheeler, *One Woman-One Vote* (1995); Ross A. Webb, *Kentucky in the Reconstruction Era* (1979).

Cochran

1 Yvonne Eaton, "Kentuckian's quilt returns in all-star show." *The Courier-Journal* ,19 August 1993.

Interview conducted with Cochran at her home in Rabbit Hash, June 6, 1997. Photos furnished by the artist. See Mirra Bank, *Anonymous Was A Woman* (1979); Diane M. Bolz, "No two of a kind in this show of cards," *Smithsonian* (Mar 1995); Hank Burchard, "The Cutting Edge of Quilts," *Washington Post Weekend*, 6 Oct. 1995; Patricia Malarcher, "Jane Burch Cochran," *American Craft* (Feb/Mar 1994); Nobuaki Seto, *88 Leaders in the Quilt World Today* (1995); Robert Shaw, *Quilts: A Living Tradition* (1995).   See also Elizabeth Barret, *Quilting Women*, Appalshop Productions video; Nikki Giovanni, ed., *Grandmothers* (1994); Lilly Golden, ed. *In Praise of Mothers* (1994); Carolyn Heilbrun, *Hamlet's Mother and Other Women* (1990); KET video *Crafting Traditions*; KOHC: Interviews with KY Quilters, 1983-90; Hugh Lauter Levin Associates, *The Art Quilt* (1997) includes Cochran; Penny McMorris and Michael Kline, *Art Quilt* (1986); Charlotte Robinson, *The Artist and the Quilt* (1983); Alice Walker, *In Search of Our Mother's Gardens* (1975); see also art quilter Rebekka Seigel(Owenton).

Collins

Campaign buttons from collection of Mike Berry, used with permission. Cartoon from Boileau's collection, used with permission. Photos credited, used with permission. See also Terry Besser,*Team Toyota: Transplanting Toyota Culture to the Camry Plant in Kentucky* (1996); Maria Braden,*Women Politicians and the Media* (1996); Penny M. Miller and Malcolm E. Jewell, *Political Parties and Primaries in Kentucky* (1990); Frances Smith, *Little Girl Who Grew Up to be Governor* (1991). Large photograph collection of Collins administration located at KY Libraries & Archives; oral history interview, UK.

Comer

Photograph of Comer used with permission of Maysville *Ledger-Independent*. Others furnished by Comer. Taped interview conducted with Comer in Maysville Feb. 28, 1997. See Caroline Bird, *Lives of Our Own: Secrets of Old Salty Women* (1995); Susan J. Douglas, *Where the Girls Are: Growing Up Female with the Mass Media* (1994); Katharine Graham, *A Personal History* (1997); Howard Katz, *Media Circus: Trouble with America's Newspapers* (1993); see also Judith Clabes, former editor of *KY Post* ; Pamela Luecke, current editor, *Lexington Herald-Leader* ; Carol Sutton, first female managing editor of a major newspaper in America, *The Courier-Journal*.

Crabtree

1 Helen Crabtree, "Friendly Advice,"*Saddle and Bridle Magazine* (Jan. 1966).

Taped interview conducted with Crabtree and Lynne Girdler Kelley at Crabtree Farm in Simpsonville, Feb. 11,1997. Photos of her are credited and used with permission of *TCJ*. Other materials furnished by Crabtree. See materials on Crabtree at Kentucky Saddlebred Museum and Library. Crabtree continues to write column for *Saddle and Bridle*. See Helen Crabtree,*Sport's Illustrated Book of Gaited Riding* (1962); *Saddle Seat Equitation* (1970); *Hold Your Horses* (1997). See also Chris Aldridge, "Charles and Helen Crabtree inducted into UPHA," *Shelbybille Sentinel-News* , 17 April 1992; Bill Carrington, Speech at induction ceremony of Crabtrees into the World's Championship Horse Show Hall of Fame (Sept. 18,1989); Peter Chew, "She Raises the Ultimate," n.a., n. d. (Saddlehorse Museum Library files); Al Cross, "Simpsonville stable providing horses for inaugural parade," *TCJ* , 7 Jan. 1981; Gayle Lampe, "Down Memory Lane with Helen Crabtree," *Saddle & Bridle* (Jan. 1997); Joseph Pfeffer, "A Special Day for a Special Couple," *Saddle & Bridle* (Oct. 1989); Billy Reed, "Kentucky's peerless horsewoman," *TCJ Magazine*,18 Aug. 1974.

Dance

Taped interview conducted with Dance at her home in Paducah. Photos furnished by Dance. See also Anne Lewis, *Sarah Bailey: Folk Artist*, Appalshop Videos (1984) and Lewis, *Minnie Black's Gourd Band*.; KOHC, *Interviews with Folk Artists* (8); William Ketchum, *Grandma Moses: American Original* (1996); Joyntyle Theresa Robinson, *Bearing Witness: Contemporary African-American Artists* (1996); see slide-and-cassette programs

Interrogating Identity: Contemporary Artists of Color (1992) and *African-American Art in the 20th Century*, both available from The Walker Art Center (612) 375-7614; see also primitive artist Helen La France, Viola, KY.

Desha

1 Beverly Fortune, "A liberated woman," *The Courier-Journal*, 27 April 1973.

2 Ibid.

3 "Judge Wilson's Address," *Lexington Herald-Leader*, 19 December 1915.

4 "MEMORIAL to MISS MARY DESHA," *American Monthly Magazine* (August 1911): 71.

5 Ibid., 75.

Photos from collection of *DAR Magazine*, used with permission. *The Mary Desha Papers* are located at the National Society Daughters of the American Revolution, Washington, D.C. There is a small collection of *Mary Desha Papers (1850-1911)* located at UKL. See also "Memorial to Miss Mary Desha," *American Monthly Magazine* (August, 1911); Sophonisba P. Breckinridge, "MARY DESHA," *New York State News Sheet* (Oct. 1942); Works Project Administration, Kentucky, "Mary Desha," *A Dictionary of Prominent Women of Louisville and Kentucky*; Beverly Fortune, "A liberated woman," *The Courier-Journal* , 27 Apr.1973; Ann Arnold Hunter, *A Century of Service: The Story of the DAR* (1991) 33-36; various tributes on the death of Mary Desha, *Lexington Herald-Leader*, 19 Dec.1915; Mary Desha, "The True Story of the Origin of the National Society of the Daughters of the American Revolution."

Dinsmore

The original *Dinsmore Family Papers* are housed in the Tucson Branch of the Arizona Historical Society. Photos from Dinsmore Homestead, used with permission. Dinsmore Homestead is open to the public April - Dec. 15. It is located on KY Highway 18, west of Burlington. See Julia Stockton Dinsmore, *Verses and Sonnets* (repub. 1991). *Dinsmore Collection* at the Homestead includes area research and oral histories re: Dinsmore family and Homestead. See KET segment, "Julia Dinsmore," *Women Mean Business Series*; Christen Cheek, "Memoirs of Mrs. E.B. Patterson: Perspective of Danville during Civil War," *Registrar* (autumn 1994); Drew Gilpin Foust, *Mothers of Invention: Women of Slaveholding South in Civil War* (1996); Penelope Franklin, ed., *Private Pages: Diaries of American Women, 1830-70*; *Cora Owens Hume Journal* 1863-66, records Civil War events and school in Louisville, Filson Club; *Rosannah McConnell Diary*, 1897-1901, records daily life on farm near Cobb/Otter Park, The Filson Club; Mary Jane Moffat & Painter,eds., *Revelations: Diaries of Women* (1974); *Betsy Taliaferro Papers*, WKL, includes copy of her 1839 diary documenting travel from Los Angeles to Versailles; Mary E. Wharton and Ellen Williams, eds., *Peach Leather and Rebel Gray: Diary & Letters of KY Confederate Wife* (1986). See also *The Hopkinsville Diaries,* important Civil War diaries of Annie McConnell Starling and Ellen McGaughy Wallace, transcribed at KY Historical Society. The former is a teenager who sees the war simply as an inconvenience (i.e. keeps all the young men away) and the latter is a grandmother, who is the epitome of the female caregiver and the excruciating lack of opportunity to use her educated mind—a picture of Hopskinsville during the Civil War as seen from two different vantage points.

Dunnigan

1 Alice A. Dunnigan, *Alice A. Dunnigan: A Black Woman's Experience* (1974), 382.

2 Ibid., 455-56.

Photographs taken from *Alice A. Dunnigan: A Black Woman's Experience*, used with permission of her son, Robert Dunnigan. This book is no longer in print. See also Alice A. Dunnigan, *Fascinating Story of Black Kentuckians: Their Heritage and Traditions* (1982); Rodger Streitmatter, *Raising Her Voice: African American Women Journalists Who Changed History* (1994); see also Helen Thomas (contemporary dean of White House Press Corps, United Press International reporter), *Dateline: White House* (1975).

Engle

Permission for adapted use of this article by the *Lexington Herald-Leader* is gratefully acknowledged. See original full text: Barbara Ward, "A life flying high," *LHL*, 7 November 1996. Frank Anderson is a *LHL* staff photographer and photo used with permission. Documents used with permission of UK Libraries; airplane photo furnished by family. *The Mary Edith Engle Papers* are located at UKL. It is a very small collection of flight records, maps, training notes, and an oral history tape. See also Dr. Mary E. Walker, who entered service as Acting Ast. Surgeon, U.S. Army, in Louisville, 1861. She worked in the Women's Prison Hospital (Louisville) and later in Civil War battlefields and hospitals. A colorful character and women's rights advocate, she is the only woman ever to receive the Medal of Honor. Her papers and medal are located at Oswego, N.Y. Historical Society; see also D'Ann Campbell, *Women at War With America: Private Lives in Patriotic Era* (1984); Sally Van Wagenen Keil, *Those Wonderful Women in Their Flying Machines* (1979); Anne Noggle, *For God, Country and the Thrill of It: WASPS in WW II* (1922); Teresa Cecilia Sharkey, "Home Front: Women in Lexington During WW II," *FCQ* (Oct., 1994); Liz Strohouse, "The WASPS in World War II," tape, Forum Recordings, Marion, Iowa; Doris Brinker Tanner, "Cornelia Fort: A WASP in WW II," *TN Historical Quarterly* (winter 1981 and spring 82); Marianne Verges, *On Silver Wings: Women Airforce Service Pilots of World War II* (1991).

Fair

Interview conducted with Fair at her home in Radcliffe, June 25, 1997. Fair photos furnished by family, used with permission. In 1995, Kentucky had 11,869 arrests for driving under the influence of alcohol and 287 alcohol-related deaths—See *Rating the States: A Report Card* (1996) and back issues of *MADDADVOCATE*, pub. by MADD National Office, 511 E. John Carpenter Freeway, Irving, TX 75062; Visit MADD's Web site for information and to download brochures: http://www.madd.org
Visit Web site for AL-ANON/ALATEEN: http://www.al-anon.alateen.org/
Visit Web site for Alcoholics Anonymous: http://www.alcoholics-anonymous.org
See also: Caroline Knapp, *Drinking: A Love Story* (1996); *Distillery Industry in KY*(120 hours, 1920-87)KOHC; Dept. Mental Health and

Retardation, *KY Women are Losing Race: Alcoholism and Other Drug Addictions* (1995); Laura Parker, "Nine years after bus tragedy, the healing goes on," *USA Today*, 3 July 1997.

Fields

Taped interview conducted with Fields at Midway College, May 30, 1997. Photos from her collection, used with permission. See also John R. Boles, *Religion in Antebellum Kentucky* (1976); Alethea Helbig and Perkins, *This Land Is Our Land: Guide to Multicultural Literature fo Children and Young Adults* (1994); Paulie Murray, *Song in a Weary Throat: Autobiography of a Black Activist, Feminist, Teacher, Priest* (1987); Jay Pederson and Smith, *African American Breakthroughs: 500 Years of Black Firsts* (1995); Michele Steptoe, *African-American Voices* (1995).

Flanery

1 "First Woman in Legislature," *The Herald-Dispatch* , 16 April 1922.

2 *The Courier-Journal,* n.d. *Flanery Papers*, UKL.

3 *Flanery Papers*, UKL.

Excerpts of letters, telegrams, *United Daughters of the Confederacy* organization booklet, clippings from *Ashland Daily Independent* are from *Flanery Papers*, UKL. Only two KY women have ever served in the U.S. Congress, both Republicans: Catherine Langley, Pikeville (1927-30) and Ann M. Northrup, Louisville (elected 1996). See Florence Shelby Cantrill, first woman from Lexington to serve in Legislature; Emma Guy Cromwell, *Woman in Politics,* first woman elected to statewide office in KY; Anne Firor Scott, *Southern Lady: From Pedestal to Politics, 1830-1930* (1970).

Fouse

1 Lizzie B. Fouse, "The Better Homes Department of the N.A.C.W., *National Notes*, March 1929.

Photo, ledger, letter, memorabilia, et al from the *Fouse Papers*, UKL, used with permission. See also "Proceedings of the Kentucky Negro Education Association, 1877-1913" in the *Fouse Papers*; District House of Ruth #24 annual yearbooks, 1916-30, Center of Excellence for the Study of KY African Americans (CESKAA) at KSU; see Evelyn Brooks Higgenbotham, *Righteous Discontent* (1993); E. Belle Jackson in Lauretta Flynn Byars, *Lexington Colored Orphanage Industrial Home: Building for the Future* (1995); *KY Assoc. of Colored Women's Clubs*, annual yearbooks, 1930-35 and 1938-46, CESKAA at KSU; *Mary Lyle Reynolds Manuscripts* (woman's club leader post Civil War), Behringer-Crawford Museum, Covington; Lucy Harth Smith, *Pictorial History of KY Assoc. of Colored Women* (1945); Janice Theriot, *Tradition of Service: History of KY Federated Women's Clubs* (1994).

Freeman

Taped interview conducted with Freeman at Mt. Folly Farm, Winchester, June 5, 1997. Photos furnished by Freeman. See KET segment, "Laura Freeman," *Women Mean Business Series*; see also Lorraine Garkovich, et al, *Harvest of Hope* (1995); Mary Neth, *Preserving Family Farm: Women...Midwest, 1900-40* (1995); KOHC: *Family Farms Project* (45 hours in 21 counties) and *Cattle Farming in Central KY, 1970s-86*; See bison farm owner Laura Lee Brown (Louisville) and Freeman in Missy Warfield, "Back to the Farm ," *Town & Country* (June 1997); see also Mattie Mack, activist with Kentucky Community Farm Alliance.

Geiger

1 Joe Creason. "Lady of The Lake," *Courier-Journal Magazine*, 26 Sept.1954.

2 The Lady of the Lake, Ruth Geiger," *Russell County News*, 4 Oct.1974.

3 "From a "River Rat" to the "Lady of the Lake," *The Times Journal*, 3 October 1974.

4 "Mrs. Geiger Tells Secret of Success," *The Louisville Times*, 14 April 1960.

5 Finley Willis, "Guided By A Grandmother," *Kentucky Happy Hunting Ground*, Department of Fish & Wildlife, Jan. 1968.

Photographs furnished by Geiger's daughter, Betty Story. See also Sally Bly, "Mrs. Geiger Bags An Outdoor Job," *Courier-Journal*, 13 Nov. 1968; see back editions of Geiger's columns, "Lines from the Lady of the Lake, *Russell County News* at the county library.

Giles

1 Henry and Janice Holt Giles, *A Little Better Than Plumb* (1981), 55.

2 Giles, "My Darling Daughter," unpublished MS, The Kentucky Library, Western Kentucky University, Bowling Green, 229.

3 Janice Holt Giles, *Around Our House* (1971), 143-44.

4 *I bid.*, 144.

5 Ibid., 146.

6 Janice Holt Giles, *The Believers* (1957), viii.

7 Elizabeth Hancock, Letter to Janice Holt Giles, 10 February 1956.

8 Henry Giles, Letter to Janice Moore, 26 October 1943.

Photos credited and used with permission. See James Alan Riley, ed., *Kentucky Voices: Contemporary Short Stories* (1997). Works by Giles include: *40 Acres and No Mule* (1952), *The Believers* (1957), *The Enduring Hills* (1950), *Great Adventure* (1966), *Hannah Fowler* (1956), *Johnny Osage* (1960), *The Kentuckians* (1953).

Gunning

Photographs credited and used with permission. Album cover permission of Folk-Legacy Records. Excerpt from album notes of "Sarah Gunning: Silver Dagger," (Rounder Records), written by Mark Wilson, used with his permission. See also: Mimi Pickering, *Dreadful Memories: Life of Sara Ogan Gunning*, Appalshop Videos (1988); Cassettes and CDs available from Folk-Legacy Records (Sharon, CT) and Rounder Records (Cambridge, Mass).

Hall

1 David Goetz, "Eula Hall: Tribulations don't deter mountain activist," *Courier Journal*, 12 Dec. 1982, E7.

2 "Mud Creek Clinic", video, Appalshop Productions.

3 Oral history tape conducted with Eula Hall by Glenna Graves, June 15, 1988, University of KY, special collections.

4 David Goetz.

Photos furnished by Hall. Taped interview conducted with Eula Hall at Mud Creek Clinic in Grethel, May 14, 1997. See Appalshop Videos: *Five Conversations on Violence* (1983); *Mud Creek Clinic* (1986), and Elizabeth Barrett, *Coal Mining Women* (1982) and Anne Lewis, *Justice in Coalfields* (1995); Candie and Guy Carawan, *Voices of the Mountains* (1996), includes Hall; Stephen Fisher, *Fighting Back in Appalachia* (1993); Betty Friedan, *The Feminine Mystique* (1963); Mary Ann Hinsdale, Helen Lewis, et al, *It Comes from the People: Community Development and Local Theory* (1995); Kathy Kahn, *Hillbilly Women* (1973); Helen Lewis, *My Life and Good Times in the Mountains* (1995); Sally Ward Maggard, *Eastern KY Women on Strike* (PH. D. disser, UK, 1989); Marat Moore, *Women in the Mines* (1996); Randall Norris, *Women of Coal* (1996); KOHC: *Women and Collective Protest in Eastern KY* (115 hours); Michael Winerip, "Kentucky's Godmother to the Poor" (Hall), *People*, Fall 1991; see other activists Gaynell Begley (Blackey); "Widow" Ollie Combs (Knott Co.); Pat Gish (Whitesburg); Granny Hager (Harlan); Florence Reece (Harlan).

Hearn

Photograph of Hearn at Centre College, used with permission. Photo of her credited to *The Courier-Journal*. Other photographs furnished by Hearn. Taped interview conducted with Hearn in Louisville, May 13, 1997. See Margo Adler, *Heretics Heart* (1997); Lady Borton, *After Sorrow: American Among Vietnamese*(1995); Geraldine Gan, *Lives of Notable Asian Americans: Arts, Entertainment, and Sports* (1995); Mary Malone, *Maya Lin: Architect and Artist* (1995); Elizabeth M. Norman, *Women at War: Story of 50 Military Nurses in Vietnam* (1990); Katherine Paterson, *Park's Ques*t (1988); Gary Paulsen, *The Monument* (1991); U.S. Congress, "Vietnam Women's Memorial Report" (1988); Kenneth Wapner, *Teenage Refugees From Vietnam Speak Out* (1994) and others in this series.

Henry

Photograph and materials furnished by Woodford Co. Historical Society. See also "Political Activist v. Southern Belle: Conflicting Views of Suffrage," KHC presentation by Aloma Dew giving divergent views of two women, including Henry. See Elizabeth Cady Stanton, *The Women's Bible* (1895/1993) and Maylynn Salmon, *Women & the Law of Property in Early America* (1986). A small *Josephine Henry Collection* is located at the Woodford County Historical Society, Versailles.

Horlander

Photographs furnished by Horlander. News clip from *The Courier-Journal*, used with permission. Taped interview conducted with Horlander at her home in Louisville, June 16, 1997. See Appalshop Production video by Anne Lewis, *Roving Pickets*; Zickfoose & Mohn, *UMWA 1970: House Divide*d; Christina Looper Baker, *In a Generous Spirit: Biography of Myra Page* (1996); *Foote Family Papers* include letters from Bertha Foote, 1942, describing working in shirt press mill in Ft. Knox, The Filson Club; Marat Moore, "Women's stories from Pittston Strike," *Now & Then* (fall 1990); Appalachian Oral History Project at Alice Lloyd College in which interviewees discuss Mother Jones; see articles on International Women's Year of 1977; *Equal Pay Act of 1963*, which prohibited sex discrimination and *Civil Rights Act, Title VII* (1964), which established U. S. Equal Opportunity Commission.

Howard

Photo of Petticoat Mafia credited and used with permission. Other materials furnished by Howard. News clip from *Lexington Herald-Leader*, used with permission. Taped interview conducted with Howard and Griffey at the Court House in Benham, Feb. 11, 1997; taped speech of Howard, March 1, 1997, KSU. See KOHC oral interviews, *Appalachia: Family and Gender in Coal Communities*; and Glenna Graves, *In the Morning We Had Bulldog Gravy: Women in Coal Camps* (Ph.D. disser., UK,1993); Barbara Angle, *Rinker* (1994); Paula Cizmar, *Death of a Miner* (1982); Barbara Grossman, *Funny Women: Fanny Brice* (1992); Marat Moore, "Hard Labor: Voices of Women from Coal Fields," *Yale Journal of Law and Feminism* (spring 1990); see also Pam Miller, Mayor of Lexington.

Visit Benham Web site: http://www.uky.edu/~rsilver/benham.htm

Humes

Helen Humes Collection of photographs and memorabilia is housed with Ken Clay, KY Center for the Arts, Louisville, and used with his permission. Helen Humes Award is given annually to the person who has contributed the most to jazz in Kentucky. See Donald Clarke, *Wishing on the Moon: Life and Times of Billie Holiday* (1994); Linda Dahl, *Stormy Weather: Music & Lives of a Century of Jazzwomen* (1984); Leslie Gourse, *Sassy: Life of Sarah Vaughan* (1993); Daphne Duval Harrison, *Black Pearls: Blues Queens of the 1920s* (1988); Sally Placksin, *American Women in Jazz: 1900-Present*.

Hutchins

1 Interview conducted with Hutchins by Schlesinger Library Radcliffe College, Cambridge, MASS

2 Ibid.

3 "Three Decades of Family Planning in Appalachia," *Hartwick Review* (spring 1967).

Photos credited and used with permission. See "Louise Gilman Hutchins Papers" as a series of the *Francis Hutchins Papers,* and *The*

Mountain Maternal Health League Records (1936-1981), both located at Berea College Library Special Collections. They are extensive collections. Oral history interview with Hutchins, including impressions of Mary Breckinridge, was conducted by Schlesinger Library, Radcliffe College, Cambridge, MA and used with their permission. A restricted copy has been transcribed and is located at Berea College Special Collections. See also Ann Boes, "Wives of Berea Presidents Have Been Valuable Adjuncts to Success," *Berea Citizen*, 25 Nov. 1970; David Crumm, "Doctor's life guided by social conscience," *Lexington Herald-Leader*, 26 Sept. 1982; "Dr. Louise Frances Gilman Hutchins, Helen B. Fraser Award," n.a., n.d.; Irene Nolan, *The Courier-Journal*, 6 June 1971; Jane Todd Crawford, *KY Pioneer Heroine of Surgery* (1932); Dr. Louise Southgate (1857-1941) in Covington; Ruth Abram, ed.,*Send Us a Lady: Women Doctors in America, 1835-1920* (1985); see "Eleanor Marsh Frost Series" (1886-1950) under *Pres. Wm. Frost Papers*, BCL, includes her *Diaries: 1905-1915*, describing trips on horseback through eastern KY mountains.

Jordan
In the KY Legislature, c.1997, there are 100 members of the state house and 11 are women; there are 38 members of the state senate and 2 are women. Only Alabama has a lower representation of women in its state governing body. Photographs credited and used with permission. Others furnished by Jordan. Taped interview conducted with Jordan at her office in Frankfort, June 18, 1997. See Elizabeth Cox, *Women in Modern American Politics: Bibliography 1900-95* (1997); Diane Dujon and Ann Withorn, eds., *For Crying Out Loud* (1996); Wade Hall, *Passing for Black: Life and Careers of Mae Street Kidd* (1997); Brian Lanker, *I Dream a World: Portraits of Black Women Who Changed America* (1988); Penny Miller, "Striking Their Claim: Impact of KY Women in Political Process," *Kentucky Law Journal* (1995-96); Pippa Norris, ed., *Women, Media and Politics* (1997); John Ed Pearce, *Divide and Dissent: KY Policitics, 1930-63*; Georgia Davis Powers, *I Shared the Dream* (1995); see also the *Pearl Carter Papers* at WKU Library, first female sheriff in KY.

Kizito
Taped interview conducted with Elizabeth Kizito in her Louisville store, May 8, 1997. Photographs furnished by E. Kizito. See Chinua Achebe, *Things Fall Apart* (1959); Gerda Lerner, ed., *Black Women in White America* (1972); Rick Simonson & Walker, *Multicultural Literacy* (1988); Alice Walker, *In Search of our Mother's Gardens* (1967).

Knott
1 *Paul Green Papers*, Southern Historical Collection, Wilson Library, University of North Carolina, Chapel Hill.
2 *Sarah Gertrude Knott Collection*, Folk Life Archives, Western Kentucky University, Bowling Green, KY.
3 Ibid.
4 Ibid.
Photographs of Knott are credited and used with permission. The program covers are from the *Sarah Gertrude Knott Collection*, Western KY University Library Special Collections, Bowling Green, used with permission. See Anne Lewis, et al, *Open Windows: American Festivals of Music, Theater, Dance,* Appalshop video(1991); see also*Thomas Papers*, re: American Folk Song Festival (1930-72) at Jean Thomas Museum & Archives (Ashland).

Lang
Photographs furnished by Lang. Taped interview conducted with Lang by Nancy Gall-Clayton at Crane House. See also Pang-Mei Natasha Chang, *Bound Feet and Western Dress* (1996); Jung Chang, *Wild Swans: Three Daughters of China* (1991).

Ledford
Photographs credited and used with permission of Berea College Library Special Collections Library. Taped interview conducted with Ledford's granddaughter, Cari Norris, in Louisville, May 1, 1997. See also Anne Lewis, *Lily May Ledford*, Appalshop video; Charles Wolfe, *KY Country Folk & Country Music of Kentucky* (1982); Berea College Sound Archives includes Ledford and Coon Creek Girls recordings and oral history interview tapes; KOHC Tapes: *Renfro Valley Barn Dance* (1930-86) and*Vintage Fiddlers* (video and tapes); Northern KY University Archives: *KY Musicians and Their Music;* see also the exhibits at the museum at Renfro Valley, KY; Appalshop video, *Jean Ritchie Story*; Jean Ritchie, *The Singing Family of the Cumberlands* (1988).

Lesch
Permission for adapted use by *The Courier-Journal* gratefully acknowledged. See full text of original article Diane Heilenman, "Stitchery Wizard..." *Courier-Journal*, 5 January 1997. Photograph of Lesch credited and used with permission of *TCJ*. Other material provided by KY Arts & Crafts Foundation during "Lesch Retrospective," 1997. See also Dobree Adams, a sheep-to-shawl award-winning weaver (River Bend Farm, Frankfort); Phyllis Alvey (Lexington), weaver; see *Eleanor Churchill Records* at BCL(founder, Churchill Weavers in Berea); see master weaver Lou Tate's oral history interviews with friends and colleagues at Little Loomhouse, Louisville.

Lovely
Photographs used with permission of Lovely's daughter, Chris Durall. Interview with Florida Slone conducted July 7, 1996, at Hindman Settlement School. Interview with Florida Slone conducted by Lee Smith aired on NPR Nov. 11, 1996. See Anthony Slone and Angelyn DeBord, *Homemade Tales: Songs and Sayings of Florida Slone*, Appalshop Video Productions (1993); Florida Slone sings on *Golden Rocking Chair*, tape cassette. See also Eleanor Arnold, ed., *Voices of American Homemakers* (1985); *Warren County Homemakers*, oral history interviews re: 1930s-86, KOHC.

Lynn
Interview conducted with Bobbi Gothard, director of Coal Mining Museum (includes Loretta Lynn exhibit), Benham, KY, Feb.12, 1997.

Photographs credited and used with permission. Loretta Lynn's house is located at Butcher Hollow and is open to the public. Sissy Spacek won the Academy Award for her portrayl of Lynn in the film "Coal Miner's Daughter." See Kira Megan Cary, "Queen of Country Music," *Kentucky Heritage* (fall 1996); Robert K. Krishef, Loretta Lynn (1978) and Nash, Alanna, *Behind Closed Doors* (1988); see Lynn in Charles Wolfe, *Kentucky Country-Folk & Country Music of KY* (1982); see other famous Kentucky female singers Patsy Cline, Rosemary Clooney, Crystal Gayle, Wynonna and Naomi Judd, Jean Ritchie, and Mary Travers.

Markey

Photos used with permission of KY Derby Museum. Small collection of *Lucille Markey* at KY Derby Museum. See also some Calumet Farm public relations material, a newspaper clipping file, and photographic negatives at Keeneland Association Library(Lexington); Calumet Farm's racing trophies are located in the KY Horse Park Museum(Lexington); see Ann Hagedorn Auerbach, *Wild Ride: Rise & Tragic Fall of Calumet Farm* (1994); Warren Wright, *Calumet Farm* (1943). See also Patsy Yount in Linda Light, *Passions and Prejudice: Secrets of Spindletop* (1996); *Elise Shackelford Papers-1916-1930*, active in breeding race horses, UKL; see also Alice Headley Chandler, Penny Chenery, and Dell Hancock, Kentucky's female members of The Jockey Club; back issues of *Thoroughbred Record* and *Bloodhorse*; Essie Sitgraves and Mildred Bachelor(Louisville), for particular insights into horse race industry; Lynn Renau, *Jockeys, Belles, and Bluegrass Kings* (1996) and Renau, *Racing Around Kentucky* (1995).

Martin

Photographs furnished by Martin. VISTA materials located at Berea College Library Special Collections, *VISTA and Appalachian Volunteers Collections*, used with permission. Taped interview conducted with Martin, July 27, 1997, at the Save the Children Field Office, Berea. See Laurel Shackelford and Bill Weinberg, eds., *Our Appalachia: Oral History* (1977) and the complete *Appalachian Oral History Project, Union Catalog*, published by Alice Lloyd College, et al (1977) ; *The Appalachian Photographs of Doris Ulmann* (1971); see also Stella Marshall (Owsley Co.), Workers of Rural KY; Ina Taylor (Livingston), LEAP; see results of AV evaluations and other observations in Robert Coles, *Migrants, Sharecroppers, Mountaineers: Vol. II Children of Crisis* (1967); see also Judy Sizemore, *Partnership for Change: Save the Children/ACC* (1990); Wendy Ewald, *Appalachian Women: Three Generations* (1980); Appalshop Videos: Elizabeth Barrett, *Long Journey Home* (1987); Wendy Ewald/Garrison, *Portraits & Dreams* (1984); Anne Lewis, *Peace Stories*; Mimi Pickering, *Millstone Sewing Center*; see also Verna Mae Slone, *What My Heart Wants to Tell Me* (1990); *Marie Tyler McGraw* (16 hours) Oral History Tape, re: Appalachian Volunteers and War on Poverty activists, BCL. *The War on Poverty Collection* at BCL includes papers, memorabilia, records and photographs on AVs and VISTA, as well as Robert Coles' research work. *Council of Southern Mountains Collection* also located at BCL; *War on Poverty* oral history tapes conducted by Margaret Brown, located at UKL, includes Martin. See Allen Bateau, *Invention of Appalachia* (1990); Terry Birdwhistell and Susan Emily Allen, "Appalachian Image Re-examined: Oral History View of E. KY," *Register* (summer 1983); John Gaventa, et al. *Conversations Between Paulo Freire and Myles Horton* (1991); John Glenn, *Highlander: No Ordinary School* (1986); John Glenn, "War on Poverty in Appalachia: Preliminary Report," *Register* (winter 1989); Glenn, "Council of So. Mountains and War on Poverty," *Then and Now* (fall, 1988); Doris Ulmann, *Appalachian Photographs of Doris Ulmann*(1934).

Mason, Belinda

1 *Gifts of the Spirit*, a play written by Anne Shelby, et al.
2 "Letter from a president," *Times-News* , Hartford, KY, 19 Sept. 1991.
3 Anne Lewis, *Belinda*, Appalshop Videos, 1988.
See Anne Lewis, *Belinda*, video, Appalshop Productions(1992); HIV Legal Proj. of KY, *Legal Handbook for People Living with HIV Disease in KY*(1993); see also Janice Burns, *Sarah's Song* (1995); Gena Corea, *The Invisible Epidemic: Story of Women and AIDS* (1992); Deborah Cotton and Watts, *Medical Management of AIDS in Women* (1997); Patricia Klosner and Craig, *The Woman's HIV Sourcebook* (1994); Elisabeth Kubler-Ross, *AIDS: The Ultimate Challange* (1987); Ann O'Leary & Jemmott, eds., *Women and AIDS: Coping and Care* (1996); Susan Sontag, *Illness As Metaphor and AIDS and Its Metaphors* (1990); Abraham Verghese, *My Own Country: A Doctor's Story* (1994); Ryan White and Cunningham, *My Own Story* (1992).

Mason, Bobbie Ann

Photographs credited and used with permission. Permission gratefully acknowledged for adapted use of Michal Smith-Mello, "Bobbie Anne Mason, Artist and Rebel," *The Kentucky Review*, (autumn 1988): 56-62. See Bobbie Ann Mason,*Shiloh and Other Stories* (1982); *In Country* (1985), *Spence + Lila* (1988), *Feather Crowns* (1993); see also other contemporary Kentucky women writers: Gwen Davenport, Sue Grafton, Denise Giardina, George Ella Lyon, Barbara Kinsolver, Barbara Taylor McCafferty and under her pen name, Tierney McClellan, Betty Layman Receveur.

Meagher

Uncited quotes taken from interview conducted May 6, 1997 at the home of her parents in Louisville. Photograph of Wheaties box used with permission of General Mills Corp. *Courier-Journal* photo used with permission. Others furnished by Meagher. See also Tori Murden (Louisville) as first woman/first American to ski to South Pole and first woman to climb Mt. Lewis in Antarctic; Paula Gmerek (Shelbyville), Alaskan Iditarod Trail sled dog racer; Tamara McKinney (Lexington), Olympic skier; Marion Miley (Lexington) the #2 USA golf champion when murdered in 1941; see Lois D. O'Neill, *Women's Book of World Records & Achievement* (1979).

Meyer

Taped interview conducted with Meyer at her home in Louisville, March 21, 1997. Photos furnished by Meyer. Meyer's quilt,"Kaethe," was created by Penny Sisto, who furnished photo. See also *Sara Landaur Papers: 1910-86* (first Jewish professor at U of L) ULARC; *Anita Grad Ades Collection* (microfilm, 1946-50), includes thoughts on being Jewish from a small KY community, Cornell University Library; *Holocaust and Yad Vashem*, documentary video(1994); Harry Cargas, *Conversations with Elie Wiesel* (1992); Magda Denes, *Castles Burning: Child's Life in War* (1997);

Rochelle Miller, et al, *New Perspectives on Holocaust: Guide for Teachers* (1996); Carol Rittner and Roth, eds., *Different Voices: Women and Holocaust* (1993); Ruth Schwertfeger, *Women of Theresienstatt* (1989); Audre Stein, *Hidden Children: Forgotten Survivors of Holocaust* (1994); Edgar Stern, *Peppermint Train: Journey to German-Jewish Childhood* (1992); Jeffrey A. Wolin, photographer, *Written in Memory: Portraits of the Holocaust* (1996); see *Daniel*, video produced by Holocaust Museum, Washington, D.C.; and Turner Broadcasting video by Steven Spielberg, *Survivors of the Holocaust* (1995).

Miller

1 Maryann Hamer, "The Captain Was A Lady," *Back Home in Kentucky* (Jan./Feb. 1995).

2 Ibid. and see obituary, "Capt. Mary Miller Dead," *The Courier-Journal*, 31 Oct. 1894.

3 "Timeline" at The Portland Museum.

4 Sandra Rae Miller, "Captain Mary Miller." In Ray Samuel, Huber, and Ogden, eds., *Tales of the Mississippi* (1955).

The Capt. Mary Miller interactive exhibit is located at The Portland Museum, 2308 Portland Ave., Louisville. Photograph of Miller is a woodcut from *Harper's Magazine*, March, 1865. Other materials furnished by Portland Museum. See also "Winifred Green: River Matron," presented by KHC speaker Gail King, which records life on a Henderson Co. farm along Ohio River, circa 1822; Mary Wheeler for documenting songs of riverboat roustabouts; KOHC: *Folk Life of KY River*; Behringer-Crawford Museum (Covington); see also materials on river residents, Anna and Harlan Hubbard, at Behringer-Crawford and in books; see John Ed Pearce and Richard Nugent, *The Ohio River* (1989); *Portland Women's Archives*, Portland Museum, Louisville.

Moore

Photograph of Moore credited and used with permission of Western Reserve Historical Society, Cleveland, OH. Photo of the dwelling and book mark credited and used with permission of Shakers at South Union. Moore's Shaker box credited and used with permission of Western KY University Museum at Bowling Green. *Journal of Eldress Nancy: Aug. 15, 1861-Sept. 4, 1864* is located at WKU Libraries. "Shakertown Revisited" was a drama scripted by the late Dr. Russell H. Miller, Theater professor at Western Kentucky University. It was presented each summer at the South Union Shaker Festival from 1962 until recently. See also Elizabeth Combs, "Brief History of the Shaker Colony at South Union, Kentucky," *The Filson Club Quarterly* (vol. 14, 1940): 154-73; Mary Julia Neal, *By Their Fruits: Story of Shakerism in South Union, Kentucky* (1947); Mary Julia Neal, ed., *The Journal of Eldress Nancy, Kept at the South Union, Kentucky Shaker Colony, August 15, 1861-September 4, 1864* (1963); Mary Julia Neal, *The Kentucky Shakers* (1977). See also PBS Video, *THE SHAKERS: Hands to Work, Hearts to God*, by Ken Burns (1996); Edward D. Andrews, *Gift to be Simple* (1940); Thomas Clark, *Pleasant Hill in Civil War* (1972); Nancy Coman Coveney, *Eleanor Hatfield's Journal* (Pleasant Hill); Flo Morse, *Shakers and World's People*; Diane Sasson, *Shaker Spiritual Narrative* (1983); Jane Cowan and Annie Farmer, *South Union Diary, 1899-1921* records daily events and closing of the community in 1921, located at Shaker Museum, Emma King Library, Old Chatham, NY.

Nation

1 Robert Lewis Taylor, *Vessel of Wrath* (1966).

2 Helen D. Irvin, *Women in Kentucky* (1979).

Cartoon and other materials credited, used with permission. Carry Nation's birthplace is off Fisher Ford Rd. near Pope's Landing on Herrington Lake (south of Lexington)—it is a private residence. The Carry A. Nation House is run as a museum by the WCTU in Medicine Lodge, KS. The KS State Historical Society (Topeka) has collection of Nation memorabilia. See also Vance Randolph, *Carry Nation of Kansas* (1900); Robert Lewis Taylor, *Vessel of Wrath: Life and Times of Carry Nation* (1968); see another temperance figure in *Writing Out of My Heart: Journal of Frances Williard, 1855-96*.

Neal

1 Roger Fristoe, "Patricia Neal: Able Actress," *The Courier-Journal Magazine* (21 July 1985).

2 John Fetterman, "Green Valley of Ghosts," *The Courier-Journal* (1963).

3 "Miss Neal 'Surprised'" (no citation—found in scrapbook).

4 Patricia Neal, *As I Am* (1988).

5 Ibid.

6 Greg Swem, "Patricia Neal sees young players unearth her roots," *The Courier-Journal* (22 Nov. 1979).

Taped interview conducted with Dr. Joanne Sexton, childhood friend of Patricia Neal, at the KY Commission on Women, Frankfort, June 3, 1997. Newspaper clips from Williamsburg paper, c. 1950, found in Sexton scrapbook. Unless credited, photographs taken from Sexton scrapbook, used with her permission. See also *Hud* and other movies available on video; see Warder Harrison, *I Didn't Know That! Kentucky's Ties to Stage and Screen* (1994); see also Callie Khouri, Paducah native, who won 1991 Oscar for the Best Original Screenplay of "Thelma and Louise."

Neville

Photographs are credited and used with permission of UK Libraries. *The Linda Neville Papers* are housed in the Special Collections of the University of Kentucky Library. A large collection of papers, including letters, charts the fight against trachoma and her efforts. See also D. Anthony Smith and Arthur H. Keeney, "Linda Neville: Kentucky Pioneer Against Blindness," *FCQ*, (July 1990) 360-76. See also *Sadie Price Papers* (1894-1963), naturalist and botanist from Bowling Green, at WKUL.

Norman

Photographs credited and used with permission of *TCJ*. Author gratefully acknowledges permissions to use the following: "Marsha Norman" interview, conducted by David Farrell for University of Kentucky, *Kentucky Writers Oral History Project,* August 19,1980; tape recording of

"Marsha Norman," for *Kentucky Voices*, a joint project of Kentucky Center for the Arts (KCA), KY Bicentennial Commission, WFPL (orig. recorded March 1989 as part of KCA Reading Series), used with permission of KCA; "Marsha Norman," produced by Guy Mendes and directed by Nell Cox for *Signature Series*, Kentucky Educational Television, Lexington. *KET Signature Series* , a six-part PBS series, includes KY women writers Bobbie Ann Mason and Barbara Kingsolver, as well as other contemporary Southern writers. Norman's works include: "The Fortune Teller " (1987), "Getting Out" (1987), "The Holdup" (1987), "'night, Mother" (1983), *The Secret Garden: a Musical Book and Lyrics* (1992), "Third and Oak" (1980), *Traveler in the Dark* (1988); see Norman in Michael Dixon and Volansky, eds., *By Southern Playwrights: Plays from Actors Theatre of Louisville* (1996).

Obenchain

Photographs are credited and used with permission of Western KY University Libraries. Bonnie Jean Cox, "Introduction to Eliza Calvert Hall," *Aunt Jane of Kentucky*, University Press of Kentucky (reprinted edition 1995). *Eliza Calvert Obenchain Collection* is located at WKU Manuscript Library. See also: *Life and Work of Lucinda B. Helm* (1898), Micro, KLA; see also *Melville Wortham Briney Papers*, includes diaries, correspondence, scrapbooks, 1912-16, Filson Club; see exhibit at WKU Libraries, "Growing Up Victorian," using the *Diary of Josephine Calvert*, republished 1983, available at WKU Museum Shop.

Peterson

Photographs furnished by Stanaland and Pearson and the high school, used with permission. Taped interview with Peggy Stanaland conducted at her home in Richmond. Taped interview was conducted with Dorothy Chaney Pearson, June 10, 1997 at her home in Woodburn, KY. See also Peggy Stanaland, "The Early Years of Basketball in Kentucky," *A Century of Women's Basketball: From Frailty to Final Four*, Eds. Joan S. Hult and Marianna Trekell (1991); Peggy Stanaland, "Basketball Becomes Viable Sport for Women in Kentucky: 1900-1920, unpub. paper (1990) and "One Southern Sportswoman: A Personification of Basketball," unpublished paper (1990) ; Josephine Richardson, *Hoops* video in production, Appalshop Productions; Kitty Rogers Baird, *Women in Phys. Ed. & Sports at Centre College* (Thesis, Eastern Kentucky University); P.J. Creedon, ed., *Women, Media & Sport* (1991); Allen Guttman, *Women's Sports* (1991); Ann Hall, *Great Women in Sports* (1996); Margaret Ware Parris, *Outstanding KY Women in Sports* (1968).

Pettit

Material, including photographs, furnished and used with permission of Pine Mountain Settlement School, Inc. PMSS archives contain Pettit's papers, correspondence, records, notes, newspaper accounts, school newsletters and other publications, boards of trustees records, photographs, memorabilia, plus letters and memorabilia of students, teachers, and the architect. Visitors may arrange to stay overnight. "Big Log," Miss Pettit's house, is maintained as a guest house and small meeting center. Site visit for research in archives and conversations with acting director, Mildred Mahoney, conducted Feb. 13-14, 1997. See KET production, "Settlement Schools"; Lucy Furman, *Register* (1939): 79 and Quare *Women;* Rhonda England, *Voices from History of Teaching: Pettit, Stone, Watts at Hindaman Settlement School, 1899-1956*, Ph. D. diss., UK(1990); Nancy Forderhase, "The Clear Call of Thoroughbred Women: KY Fed Women's Clubs and Educational Reform, 1903-09," *Register* (winter 1985); James Greene, *Progressives in the KY Mountains: Formative Years of Pine Mountain Settlement School 1914-30* (Dissertation, Ohio State University,1982); Willie Nelms, "Cora Wilson Stewart and Crusade Against Literacy, 1916-20," *Register* (spring 1984); Searles, David, *College for Appalachia: Alice Lloyd* (1995); Doris Ulmann, *In Focus: Appalachian Photographs*(1971); David Whisnant, *All That is Native and Fine* (1983); see also *Katherine Pettit Papers* (1868-1937), which includes interesting diaries from early (1907-09)summer camps at Sassafras, etc and *Pine Mountain Settlement School Papers* , Berea College Special Collections. *The Doris Ulmann Photograph Collection* at Berea College Art Department includes Pettit.

Pfeiffer

Taped interview conducted with Pfeiffer at her home in Radcliffe, June 9, 1997. Photographs from the artist, used with permission. See Michael Owen Jones, *The Handmade Object and Its Maker* (1975); Erice Sloane, *A Reverence for Wood* (1973); Eliot Wigginton, ed. the *Foxfire* books.

Phillips

1 "Woman's Equality with Man—A Myth," *Harper's Magazine* (30 Mar. 1927).
2 Lisa Sergio, *A Measure Filled: Life of Lena Madesin Phillips* (1972).
3 Ibid.
4 Ibid.
5 "Maine Avengers," *New York Post* 11 Sept. 1930, located in the *Lena Madesin Phillips Collection*, Schlesinger Library, Radcliffe College.
6 *Lena Madesin Phillips Collection*, Schlesinger Library, Radcliffe College.
7 Ibid.

Photographs, including copies of telegrams, are from the *Lena Madesin Phillips Collection* , Schlesinger Library, Radcliffe College, used with their permission. Research conducted at Schlesinger Library, Radcliffe College, Cambridge, MASS, May 20, 1997. See also *Records of KY Federation of BPW (1921-91)* at ULARC; see Nancy Ellen Barr, *Profession for Women: Education, Social Service & Feminism in Life of Sophonisba Breckinridge* (1993); *Sallie Brown McCampbell Wagner Papers* include diary of 1856 by Amanda Lindsay recording young girl's thoughts and verse as school friend of Sallie Brown (Nicholasville); see other diaries of Sallie Brown (1757-69) which include descriptions of days at Jessamine Female Institute, religion and Civil War, at The Filson Club.

Porter

Photographs credited and used with permission of KY Libraries, WKU. Quotes taken from oral history tape conducted with Porter's two nieces; tape housed at KY Libraries special collections, WKU. Newspaper column from *Park City News*, used with their permission. See Addie Louise Butler, *The Distinctive Black College* (1977); Sarah Lawrence-Lightfoot, *Balm in Gilead: Journey of a Healer* (1988).

Proskauer

1 Larry Bloom, "Susan the Matchmaker, *Akron Beacon Magazine* ,18 July 1971.

2 "Art for Money," *Lexington Herald-Leader*, 25 Sept. 1979, C-1.

3 This essay is adapted from *A Spectacular Vision: The George and Susan Proskauer Collection*, exhibit catalogue, UK Art Museum, 1994, introduction.

Photographs credited and used with permission of UK Art Museum. See also other KY women benefactors to the arts: Alice Stoll, who bequeathed $50 million to JB Speed Art Museum, Louisville; Jane Morton Norton (Louisville and Danville); Lucille Little (Lexington and statewide).

Reel World String Band

Photographs furnished by band. Taped interview with Sue Massek conducted in Willisburg, April 17, 1997; taped interview with Bev Futrell and Karen Jones conducted in Lexington, June 17, 1997; Tape of Reel World Concert held at Eastern Kentucky University, April 24, 1997. See Reel World's "whatnots," (1996); see also Bufwack & Oermann, *Finding Her Voice: Saga of Women in Country Music* , cassette tape (1993); Carole van Falkenberry, et al, *Wild Women Don't Have the Blues* (1984); Federal Music Project in KY for WPA, *FolkSongs from Eastern KY* (n.d.); Bernice Johnson Reagon, *We Who Believe in Freedom: Sweet Honey in the Rock* (1993); see Richard Rothschild, "Songs of Protest: What's Become of Political Music?", *Chicago Tribune*,10 May 1996; *Sweet Honey in the Rock*, all-female group, Smithsonian Folkways.

Richards

Taped interview conducted with Richards at her home in Lexington, June 19, 1997. Photographs furnished by Richards. See also Jane Coomes, first KY school teacher at Ft. Harrod, c.1775; Delta Kappa Gamma, *Well-spring in Wilderness: KY Women Teachers* (1955); Heather Forest, *Wonder Tales from Around the World* (1995); Madeline R. Grumet, *Bitter Milk: Women and Teaching* (1988); Brenda Stevenson, ed., *Journals of 19th century Charlotte F. Grimke* (1988); Appalshop Video Productions: *Mabel Parker Hardison Smith* (1985); *The Cora Wilson Stewart Papers* (1900-40) are located at UKL. She was first president of KY Educational Association; see "Hairpiece: A Film for Nappy-Headed People," produced by Women Make Movies; see *Multicultural Review* magazine which reviews classroom materials; *Teaching Tolerance* , a magazine for teachers promoting interracial/intercultural understanding in classroom; see also Shirleen Sisney (Louisville), National Teacher of the Year,1984-85.

Richardson

Materials and photographs furnished by Richardson. Taped interview conducted with Richardson at her home at Lake Cumberland, June 28, 1997. See also A. Gwynn Henderson, *Kentuckians Before Boone* (1992); Henderson and other members of the UK archeology department conduct ongoing research and digs at KY Indian sites; see Trail of Tears Park, Hopkinsville, KY; see Bath Brant, ed.,*Gathering of Spirit: Collection of Native American Women* (1988); Michael Caduto and Bruhac, *Keepers of the Earth* (1988); Sara Evans, "The First American Women," *Born for Liberty* (1989); Michael D. Green, *The Creeks: Critical Bibliography* (1979); Karen Harvey, Harjo, and Jackson, *Teaching About Native Americans* (1992); Arlene Hirschfelder, *American Indian Stereotypes in the World of Children: A Reader and Bibliography* (1982); Charles Hudson, *Southeast Indians* (1976); *Indigenous Woman* is a publication devoted to Native women who are activists in their communities (P.O. Box 174, St. Elmo, MN 554042); Richard Mancini, *Indians of the Southeast* (1992); Carolyn Niethammer, *Daughters of the Earth: Lives and Legends of American Indian Women* (1977); A. S. Medearos, *Dancing With The Indians* (1991); Theda Perdue, *The Cherokees* (1989); Milton Melzer, *Columbus and the World Around Him* (1990); Perdue, "Columbus Meets Pocahontas in American South," speech given to Southern Association of Women Historians, Nov. 1992; Perdue, "Southern Indians and Culture of True Womanhood," *Web of Social Relations*; Beverly Slapin and Seale, *Books Without Bias: Through Indian Eyes* (1992); Aletha Wells, *Lady in the Moon* (1996).; see *Trail of Tears: An Inquiry Simulation*, from GSP (602) 744-1911; Oyate is a Native organization that emphasizes books written and illustrated by Native people (Call 510- 848-6700 for information).

Rooks

Photographs furnished by Rooks, used with permission. See Lisa Albrecht and Brewer, *Bridges of Power: Women's Multicultural Alliances* (1990); Melanie Kaye/Kantrowitz and Klepfisz, eds., *Tribe of Dina: A Jewish Women's Anthology* (1989); Morris Norman Kertzer, *What is a Jew?* (1993); James Michener, *The Source* (1965); Milton Steinberg, *Basic Judaism* (1987). See "The Journey of a Lifetime" virtual tour of Jerusalem on Rooks' award-winning web site: http://rj.org/uahc/ky/thetemple

Sawyer

1 Tom Dorsey, "Morning Star," *Courier-Journal Magazine* ,3 June 1984.

2 Michael Shnayerson, "Diane Sawyer: The Glamour and The Mystery," *Vanity Fair* (September 1987) 198.

3 Tom Dorsey, keeps fast-rising Diane Sawyer moving, *The Courier-Journal* , 30 June 1981, E-7.

4 Dorsey, "Morning Star."

Photographs credited and used with permission. See also Shana Alexander, *Happy Days* (1995); David Brinley, *Everyone is Entitled to My Opinion* (1996); Jeff Cohen and Normoan Solomon, *Adventures in Medialand* (1993); Fleur Cowles, *She Made Friends and Kept Them* (1996); Walter Cronkite, *A Reporter's Life* (1996); Jeff Kisseloff, *BOX: Oral History of TV ,1920-1961*; Brooke Kroeger, *Nelly Bly* (1994); Marshall McLuhan, *Understanding Media* (1964); Alanna Nash, *Golden Girl: Story of Jessica Savitch* (1988); see Sawyer in James Fallows, *Breaking the News: How Media Undermines American Democracy* (1997); and in Steven Stark, *Glued to the Set: TV Shows and Events that Made Us Who We Are Today* (1997).

Semple

1 Bertha Trunnell, "Study of the Life of Ellen C. Semple," speech given to the Delta Kappa Gamma Society (1942)

2 *Ellen Churchill Semple Papers*, University of Kentucky Libraries, special collections.

3 Trunnell.

4 Millicent Todd Bingham, "Ellen Churchill Semple, *Vassar Quarterly* (1932).

Photographs credited and used with permission. Photograph of Semple in tent provided by Cynthia Cooke. *Ellen Churchill Semple Collection* is housed at UKL. The original manuscript for *Geography of the Mediterranean Region* is located in the Rare Book Room, Ekstrom Library, University of Louisville. See Millicent Todd Bingham, "Ellen Churchill Semple," *Vassar Quarterly* (July, 1932); see Semple: "The Influence of Appalachian Barrier on Colonial History"(1897) and "Louisville: Study in Economic Geography"(1900), *Journal of School Geography*; *American History and Geographic Conditions* (1903); *The Anglo-Saxons of KY Mountains* (1910); *American History and Its Geographic Conditions* (1903; *Influences of Geographical Environment* (1911); Susan Brooker-Gross, "Ellen Churchill Semple," *American Women Writers*; Bertha Trunnell, "Study of Life of Ellen Semple," speech (1942); Anne Gibson & Fast, *The Women's Atlas of U.S.* (1986); see also Darlene Stille, *Extraordinary Women Scientists* 1995).

Slone

Photographs and materials furnished by Alice S. Whitaker at Lotts Creek Settlement School. Taped interview conducted with Alice Whitaker, at Slone's log house, April 2-3 1997. *The Alice Slone Papers* are located in the offices of Lotts Creek Settlement School, Inc. at Cordia and include all of her business and personal correspondence, photographs, public relations materials. Arrangements can be made to stay in Slone's house. See other women involved in coal and strip mining activities in eastern KY: Gaynell Begley, the Widow (Ollie) Combs, Eula Hall, Lois Scott, Bessie Smith, Edith Easterling; see also Loretta Lynn video, *Coal Miner's Daughter*; the *Appalachian Oral History Project* includes 1,000+ interviews re: settlement schools to Mother Jones to Ku Klux Klan to folk life and it is located at Alice Lloyd College Library, Hindman, KY; see also Diane Gentry, "Renaissance in Lotts Creek, *NRTA Journal* (Nov-Dec 1980); Karen Samples, "New Cordia School builds...", *Lexington Herald-Leader*, 5 May 1995; Alice Slone, unpub paper, Aug.1984; "Cordia receives large donation," *Troublesome Creek Times*, 18 Oct. 1989; Susan White, "Cordia School: where Appalachians learn to succeed," *Lexington Herald-Leader*, 20 May 1990; see Ronald Lewis and Dwight Billings, "Appalachian Culture and Economic Development: A Retrospective View on the Theory and Literature," *Journal of Appalachian Studies* (spring 1997).

Smith, Effie Waller

1 Interview with Prof. Ron Bailey, Director of Afro-American Studies, University of Mississippi, (May,1988).

2 Interview with Ruth Smith, Neenah, Wisconsin, (September 1987).

3 This school is now Kentucky State University.

 4 Around 1900 or 1912. Interview with Amanda Roosevelt Owens Lark, Pikeville, (September 1987).

Materials and photograph furnished by David Deskins. Research indicates there are two extant copies of Waller's first book, *Songs of the Months,* published in 1904; approximately 10 copies of her second book, *Rhymes from the Cumberland*, published in 1909; and only three copies of her third book, *Rosemary and Pansies*, also published in 1909. In 1987, Deskins published these volumes in order to make her work more widely available. The second reprint in *The Schomburg Library of Nineteenth-Century Black Women Writers* should help to spread her writing even further. See also David Deskins, "Effie Waller Smith: An Echo Within the Hills," *The Kentucky Review*, vol. viii, No.3, (Autumn 1988); David Deskins with Jennifer Kovach, "Introduction" to Schomburg reprint; see Margaret Busby, ed., *Daughters of Africa: International Anthology of Words and Writings by Women of African Descent* (1992); Rebecca Carroll, *I Know What the Red Clay Looks Like: Voice & Vision of Black Women Writers*(1994); Nikky Finney, *Rice* (1995); Mary Church Terrell, *Colored Woman in a White World* (1940); *Memphis Diary of Ida B. Wells:1862-1931* (1995); see "Zora," PBS video on Zora Neale Nurston; see Joy Bale Boone (Trigg Co.), appointed KY's Poet Laureate,1997-199.

Smith, Mary

Photographs provided by Smith. See also *Dr. Winona Lee McCloud Papers*, professor of theatre & drama, 1951-1991, CESKAA at KSU; Sarah Gibson Blanding (b.1898), first female dean of women, UK and later president of Vassar College, oral history interviews at Cornell University, Ithaca, N.Y.; Eileen M. Egan, SCN, former president, Spalding University(Louisville); Sister Ruth Gehres, past president, Brescia College(Owensboro); Oscie Sanders, first female president of Sue Bennett College,1944-58(London).

Spalding

Drawing of SCN logo used with permission of the Sisters of Charity at Nazareth, KY. Photo furnished by the same. *Catherine Spalding Papers* are located at Spalding University, Louisville and at the archives of The Sisters of Charity at Nazareth Motherhouse, Nazareth, KY. Material for this essay drawn from: Sister James Maria Spillane, *Kentucky Spring* (1968) and Miriam Corcoran, "Kentucky Biographical Notebook: Catherine Spalding,"*FCQ* (April 1988) and the archives at Spalding University. See also archival records of the community and other SCN nuns; see Fred Hood, *Kentucky: Its History and Heritage* (1978); Sister Mary Ramona Mattingly, *The Catholic Church on the Kentucky Frontier, 1785-1812* (1936); Emmet Mittlebeeler, "Aftermath of Louisville's Bloody Monday Riot of 1855," *FCQ* (April 1992); see also KOHC interviews re: *Sisters of Nazareth* (69 hours/1900s-1970); Jos. B. Cole, *Great American Foundresses* (1968); P.J. Manion and A.P. Ware, *Naming Our Truth: Stories of Loretto Women* (1995); see also contemporary Sisters of Charity Nuns, Lucy Friebert and Miriam Corcoran, as well as sisters at *Mount St. Joseph Archives*; and oral interviews and records of the Ursuline Sisters Community at Maple Mount, KY; see articles about Maple Mount Ursuline Sister Dianna Ortiz who was abducted and terrorized while working as a missionary in Guatemala, 1996.

Stephenson

Photographs and materials furnished by Stehenson. Tape conducted of a speech given by Stephenson and alumnae of New Opportunity School, Oct. 8, 1997, including Crystal, at Morehead State University; interview with Kim McGuire conducted at New Opportunity School in Berea July 26, 1996. See Jane Stephenson, *Courageous Paths: Stories of Nine Appalachian Women* (1995); Sidney Saylor Farr, *Appalachian Women: Annotated Bibliography* (1981); Appalshop's WMMT-FM, *Tell it on the Mountain: Appalachian Women Writers*, produced by Maxine Kenny; Wendy Ewald, "Five Appalachian Women," *Journal of KY Studies* (1986) and Ewald, *Appalachian Women: Three Generation*s, Appalshop Video Productions(1981). Required reading for women who enroll in New Opportunity School includes: Wilma Dykeman,*Tall Woman* (1962); Gurney Norman, *Kinfolks* (1977); Lee Smith, *Fair & Tender Ladies* (1988).

Tafel

Photographs and materials furnished by Joanne Oldham. All quotes are from *Aus Mein Leben* (Out of My Life) by Pauline Autenreith Tafel, copyright 1907, translated from the German by Ruth Tafel, edited by Ruth Tafel, copyright 1992. See Ursula Hegi, *Tearing the Silence: On Being German in America* (1997).

Taylor

Photos and materials credited and used with permission. *The Caroline Burnham Taylor Papers* are located in the Kentucky Libraries Special Collections of Western Kentucky University Library. The Kentucky Museum at WKU has a number of Taylor's drawings and some of her designs. See also Ann Casey Glover, Louisville dress designer (some clothing is at The Filson Club).

Tevis

1 Rachel Varble, *Julia Ann* (1939)

2 Julia Tevis, *Sixty Years in a Schoolroom* (1878), 461.

3 Ibid., 306.

4 Ibid., 307.

See also Science *Hill Female Academy Papers,1825-1975*, which includes correspondence and records of Julia Tevis, Clara Martin Poynter, Juliet and Harriet Poynter, The Filson Club; *Science Hill School for Girls* (7 hours c. 1900-40),KOHC. See also *Amelia Bourne Diary*, at Woodburn Female College, The Filson Club; *Patty Smith Hill Papers* (1868-1946) include early information on her development of progressive kindergarten, Filson Club; *Mary Louise Fitch Papers*, Indiana Historical Society, in which she discusses Georgetown Female Collegiate Institute (1846-48); Margaret Voorhies Haggin (1869-1965), who endowed Margaret Hall School in Versailles; *Margaret Hall School Records* are located at Convent of St. Helena Archives, Vails Gate, N.Y.; *Potter College for Young Ladies Records*, Bowling Green, WKUL.

Thompson

Photographs of Thompson and her book used with permission of The Filson Club. Photograph of the doll used is with permission of Farmington Historic House. See "Miss Dinnie Thompson," KHC presentation by Erma J. Bush. See also Dixie Hibbs, "Anna: The Woman Who Bought Her Husband Twice," *Nelson Co. Historical Society Pioneer* (summer 1991); for information on KY Slaves sent to Liberia under auspices of American Colonization Society, see collection of *Letters of Rachel Edington(1857-1863)*, WKUL; see also Larry Ceplair, "Mattie Griffith Browne: KY Abolitionist," *FCQ* (April 1994); *Life and Adventures of Henry Bibb: American Slave* (1850),WKUL, an autobiography that includes description of slave experiences of his wife, Malinda; J. Winston Coleman, Jr., *Slavery Times in Kentucky* (1940); Federal Writers' Project for Works Progress Administration,*Slave Narratives-*, vol. 15, includes KY(1936-38); Ida M. K. C. Roberts, *Rising Above It All: A Tribute to Rowan Slaves of Federal Hill* (1994); Randolph Runyon, *Delia Webster and the Underground Railroad* (1996); see also John Korty,*The Autobiography of Miss Jane Pittman,* video(1974); Deborah Gray White, *Aren't I a Woman? Female Slaves in the Plantation South* (1985); Marion B. Lucas, *A History of Blacks in Kentucky* (1992); Mary E. Lyons, *Letters from Slave Girl: Harriet Jacobs* (1992); Patricia Morton, ed., *Discovering The Women in Slavery* (1996).

Tinsley

Photographs furnished by Tinsley. Interview conducted with Tinsley at her office, Van Hoose Center, May 28, 1997, Louisville. See back issues of *Louisville Defender* and *Courier-Journal*, c. 1950-1972. See also Melba Pattillo Beals, *Warriors Don't Cry* (1994); Cynthia Stokes Brown, ed., *Ready From Within: Septima Clark and Civil Rights Movement*; collected and edited by Candie and Guy Carawan, *Sing for the Freedom, Songs of Civil Rights Movement of1960s*; Lorene Cary, *Black Ice* (1991); David Garrow, *Montgomery Bus Boycott & Women Who Struggled: Memoir of Jo Ann Robinson* (1984); Robert A. Goldwin, *Why Black Women & Jews are not Mentioned in Constitution*(1989); Gayle Hardy, *American Women Civil Rights Activists: Bibliography, 1825-1992* (1993); Bill Harley, *I'm Gonna Let it Shine: Gathering of Voices for Freedom*, CD and cassette(1996); Kay Mills, *This Little Light of Mine: Fannie Lou Hammer* (1993); Elizabeth Peterson, *Freedom Road: Three African-American Women Who Made A Difference* (1996); Helen Rochman, *Against Borders* (1993); Jacqueline Anne Rouse and Woods, *Women in Civil Rights Movement: 1941-65* (1990); Karen Patricia Smith,ed., *African-American Voices in Young Adult Literature* (1995); Melissa Walker, *Down from the Mountaintop: Black Women's Novels in Civil Rights, 1966-89* (1991); see *Anytown* program for young people, National Conference Christians and Jews (Call 502- 574-5520).

Turner

1   Manuel Strong, "The Light Burns Late In The..." *The Courier-Journal* , Sept. 27, 1959.

2 R. G. Dunlap, "Foot soldiers recall a war of frustration," *The Courier-Journal* , June 1, 1981.

3 Anne Lewis, director. *Hard Times in the Country: The Schools*, Headwaters Video, a division of Appalshop Film & Video, Whitesburg, KY. (1988).

4. Ibid.

5 John Ed Pearce, *Divide and Dissent: Kentucky Politics 1930-1963* (1987),126-7.

6 Strong.

See also the Cora Wilson Stewart Memorial one-room schoolhouse which is open to the public and located next to the Morehead State University Library; see Granny Richardson Springs School at EKU; see Appalshop videos: Dianna Ott, *Kingdom Come School* (last 1-room school in KY) and Frances Morton,*The Big Lever: Party Politics in Leslie Co.*; see also history of Mallie Bledsole, Republican school superintendent; John Fox, *The Little Shepherd of Kingdom Come* (1911); Ellis Ford Hartford, *The Little White Schoolhouse* (1977); Jesse Stuart, *Thread That Runs So True* (1949).

Underwood

Photograph and excerpts of letters used with permission of WKU Libraries. *The Underwood Collection* is housed in the Special Collections of Western Kentucky University Libraries. It includes 363 letters, family and business correspondence and genealogical materials. See also "A Defining Moment in Quest for Freedom: African Americans in Civil War," traveling exhibit sponsored in part by KY African American Heritage Commission; for further research on women during Civil War in Kentucky, see Henrietta Hunt Morgan(1805-1891), Susan Lucy Barry Taylor(1807-1881), Margaret Wickliffe Preston(b. 1819), Mary Todd Lincoln (b.1818), Ann Poague McGinty (b.1815); Randall Capps, *The Rowan Story* (1976) which includes a chapter on Rebecca Rowan's struggles during and after Civil War; Glenn Clift, ed., *Private War of Lizzie Hardin: KY Confederate Girl's Diary of Civil War* (1963); *Gibson-Humphreys Family Papers (1847-97)*, UKL, includes correspondence between women and reflects early interest in women's equal rights; Maureen Morehead and Pat Carr, *Our Brothers' War* (1993); Mary E. Wharton and Ellen Williams, eds., *Peach Leather and Rebel Gray: Diary/ and Letters of a Confederate Wife* (1986).

Wheeler

All photographs and materials used with permission of Paducah Public LIbrary. *The Mary Wheeler Collection* is located at the Paducah Public Library. It includes extensive files of letters, correspondence, scrapbooks, photographs, and books. See Mary Wheeler, *Kentucky Mountain Folk Songs* (1937), *Roustabout Songs* (1939), and *Steamboatin' Days* (1944); see also Bonnie Cave Bradley, "Mary Wheeler: Collector of Kentucky Folksongs," *The Kentucky Review* (1982); Evelyn Jones, unpublished paper presented to Paducah Music Club (28 Feb. 1979); Ophelia Lowe, "Personality Profile," *Kentucky News of Paducah* (23 July 1975); see also *Gladys Jameson Papers*, folk music professor and music collector, c.1916, Berea College; Josephine McGill who transcribed songs in her *Folk Songs of KY Mountains*, 1917. Berea College Sound Archives has an extensive collection of recordings and oral histories for KY music.

Whitehead

Photograph credited and used with permission; others furnished by Whitehead. Taped interview with Whitehead conducted at her home in Benton, March 11, 1997. See PBS Frontline program videotape,*Who's Killing Calvert City?*; Whitehead is taped in the *Local Governance Project*, UKL Oral History; see also *KY Conservationists Oral History Project*, conducted by Louise Chawla for KOHC; see also Anne Lewis,*Yellow Creek*, Appalshop Video(1984); Wendell Berry, *Another Turn of the Crank* (1995); George Constantz, *Hollows, Peepers, Highlanders: Appalachian Mountain Ecology* (1994); Michael Gerrard, *Whose Backyard..Nuclear Waste Siting* (1994); Nancy Grant, *TVA and Black Americans* (1990); Carolyn Lynn, *KY Wildlife Viewing Guide* (1994); Daniel Mazmanian, *Beyond Superfailure* (1992); Lachelle Norris-Hall, *Pollution Industries in the South and Appalachia: Economy, Environment, Politics* (1990); Fred Setterber,*Toxic Nation* (1993); Stephen Woodley, *Ecological Integrity and Management of Ecosystems* (1993), Gayle Woodside, *Hazardous Materials and Waste Management* (1993); see oral histories at Murray State University, *Remembering Land Between Lakes before TVA*; see also Mary Allen, Union Underwear and Sierra Club; Renee Butterworth (Louisville), environment; Sara Lynn Cunningham (Louisville), Paddlewheel Alliance; Joan Robinette (Dayhoit), water contamination; Patti Wallace (Louisa), broadform deed legislation/solid waste disposal issues; Mary Wharton (Lexington), conservator of Floracliff.

Whitley

Site visits to Whitley Historic House, Crab Orchard, KY and interview with the director conducted June 17, 1997 and July 27, 1997. *Whitley Collection* includes interesting files and photographs. Photograph of rifle and photographs of all versions of the house used with permission of KY State Dept. of Parks and Historic Sites. See excellent description and photographs in Mills Lane, *Architecture of the Old South: Kentucky and Tennessee* (1993); and Clay Lancaster, *Antebellum Architecture of Kentucky* (1991); see other pioneer women: Susanna Hart Shelby(1761-1833), Rebecca Bryant Boone (1739-1813), Mary H. C. Breckinridge (1768-1858), Mary Ingles (1776); see J. H. Battle, et al, *Kentucky* (1885); Harry M. Caudill, *Dark Hills to Westward: Saga of Jennie Wiley* (1969); Lewis Collins, *History of Kentucky* (1878); Jack Clowes, "Colorful History Surrounds Wm. Whitley Family," *Tri-State*, Nov.8, 1969; (retold by) Margaret H. Francis, "A Daughter of Kentucky," *Kentucky Progress Magazine* (c.1930); Louise Phelps Kellogg, ed., *A Kentucky Pioneer Tells Her Story of Early Boonesborough and Harrodsburg*, FCHQ (1929); *Narration of Capture and Providential Escape of Misses Francis and Almira Hall, 1833*, microfiche, KLA; Mary Pineau, *Pioneer People of David, KY from 1767* (1977); George W. Ranck, *Boonesborough: Its Founding...*(1901); Otis Rice, *Frontier Kentucky*(1993); Elizabeth Madox Roberts,*The Great Meadow* (1930); Carolyn L. Siegel, *Jemima* (Boone, 1986); Roberta Ingles Steele and Andrew Lewis Ingles, eds., *Escape from Indian Captivity: Story of Mary Draper Ingles... as told by John Ingles, Sr.* (1969); Helen Irvin, 1-30. See also The Anne McGinty Cabin, which has been reconstructed at Old Ft. Harrod. It is believed that she brought first spinning wheel to KY. Archaeologists have begun digging for artifacts at the original site of Fort Logan, near Stanford, one of the first three pioneer settlements. Keep up with the dig by checking their Web site: http://www.LogansFort.org

Williams

Photo of Williams credited to Nyoka Hawkins. Others furnished by Williams, used with permission. "Ugliness in Peach Tree Hollow Do-Nothing Legislature..." editorial, Sunday, April 26, 1992, *Lexington Herald-Leader*, used with permission. Taped interview conducted at Williams' home in Peach Hollow, April 3, 1997. See Anne Lewis, *Evelyn Williams* (1995) for Appalshop Video Productions; and Lewis, *On Our Own Land* (1988); see also Kathleen Blee, *Women of the Klan..20s* (1991); Harry Caudill, *Night Comes to the Cumberlands* (1963); Carol Giesen, *Coal Miners' Wives* (1995); Marat Moore, "Coal Mining Women" (Sandra Bailey),*Southern Exposure* (winter 1981); H.D. Shapiro, *Appalachia On Our Mind, 1870-1990* (1978); Karen J. Warren,ed., *Ecological Feminist Philosophies* (1996); Laurie Westra and Wenz, *Faces of Environmental Racism* (1995); Margaret Ripley Wolfe, "Reflections of An Appalachian Historian: Personal Odyssey," *Register* (autumn 1985); see activities of Kentuckians for the Commonwealth; see also Mary Allen and Sierra Club re: Union Underwear Corp.; "Widow" Ollie Combs(Knott Co.), strip mining; Lois Scott oral history tapes at UKL.

Woosley

Editor gratefully acknowledges permission to use Woosley's book and photographs, as granted by the Rev. Mary Ann Koffenberger. See John Boles, *The Great Revival, 1787-1805* (1972) and Boles, *Religion in Antebellum Kentucky* (1976).

Yandell

Photographs are credited and used with permission. *The Enid Yandell Papers* (1875-1980) at The Filson Club contain her last will and testament and several hundred letters, the majority of which are from her mother to Yandell. See Yandell sculptures of Daniel Boone and Hogan's Fountain in Cherokee Park, Louisville; see Yandell pieces at J.B. Speed Art Museum, Louisville; see Nancy Baird, "Enid Yandell: Kentucky Sculptor, *Filson Club Quarterly* (January, 1988); Desiree Caldwell, *Enid Yandell and the Branstock School*, catalog from exhibit at Art Museum of Rhode Island School of Design, 1982; Caldwell, "Brief Account of Life and Works of Enid Yandell" (Master of Fine Arts Thesis, Brown University,1978); Stephanie Wilding Darst, "Art's Bachelor Maid: The Sculpture of Enid Yandell" (Master of Fine Arts Thesis, University of Louisville, 1993); "A Southern Girl at the World's Fair," *The Confederate Veteran*, 1893.

Index

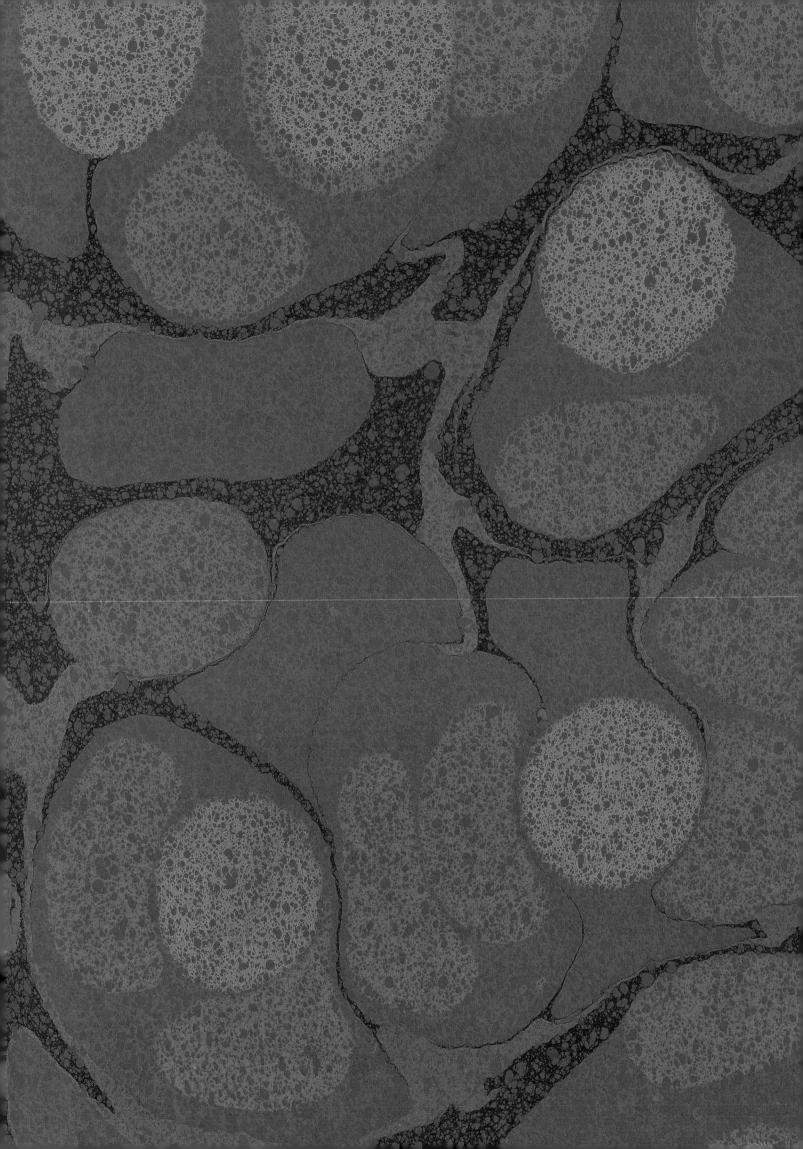